In appreciation two
quarters of Constructive
coexistence!

Basanna

Feb. 26. 1970.

DESIGN FOR DECISION

IRWIN D. J. BROSS /

DESIGN FOR
DECISION

THE FREE PRESS, *New York*

COLLIER-MACMILLAN LIMITED, *London*

First Free Press Paperback Edition 1965

printing number
3   4   5   6   7   8   9   10

ACKNOWLEDGMENTS

The sense in this book is largely due to the fortunate accident that I studied under Professor William Gemmell Cochran at the Institute of Statistics (North Carolina State College) and subsequently worked with Professor Cochran at the Johns Hopkins University (School of Public Health and Hygiene) ; the nonsense in this book is my own.

I am also grateful to my friends who read the first draft of this book and who contributed valuable suggestions and criticisms.

I wish to express my thanks to the Office of Naval Research for its support during the time that the author was at The Johns Hopkins University. The ONR has played an important role in the development of Statistical Decision by its sponsorship of much of the technical work on the topic.

IRWIN D. J. BROSS

New York City

CONTENTS

INTRODUCTION

What This Book Is About

You and I (and everyone else) are imbedded in a complex of events which, for lack of a better word, I will call the real world. Sometimes we find the situation to our liking; at other times the real world becomes a rather unpleasant place. We try to improve our lot by taking various actions which we think will avoid pain or lead to pleasure. Occasionally we are faced with a choice of actions, and it is not at once obvious which action will lead to a real world that will be more congenial in the future.

The process of selecting one action from a number of alternative courses of action is what I shall mean by *decision*.

This book does not deal with specific decisions. I do not propose to tell you what to drink or whom to marry. Instead I am going to discuss how to make decisions.

At this point you might very well snort indignantly and demand to know why a college professor thinks he can tell *you* how to make decisions. Let me hastily add that all I shall try to do is to describe and explain a recently developed method for making decisions (not *my* invention at all but the work of other—and much cleverer—men) which has been called *Statistical Decision*.

The word *statistical* may call forth unpleasant associations in the minds of many readers. It may recall the ponderous volumes of nose counts issued by government agencies, or the dreary reams of quotations published by corporations, or even (though I hope not) the absurd claims of advertising agencies.

Some readers may therefore be surprised to learn that the subject of statistics extends beyond the collection and tabulation of data; there is more to it than the calculation of averages and correlation coefficients. A statistician today may be called upon for advice on the design of a hybrid-corn yield test, the improvement of techniques for chemical analysis, the evaluation of a new wonder drug, or the purchase of baled wool.

Once upon a time, it is true, a statistician was a man with some ability at arithmetic and a knowledge of a handful of tricks of the trade. But things have changed in the last fifty years; the isolated tricks of the trade were found to be parts of a much broader structure which is called *Theoretical Statistics*. Not only did this theory lead to a better understanding of the original tricks, but it also led to the discovery of more powerful new techniques.

These new devices were found to be valuable in many and varied applications. In the period from 1920 to 1940 statistical methods quietly revolutionized many fields of science (especially the life sciences) ; moreover, they were applied beyond the academic boundaries—in agriculture, industry, and commerce.

What then took place constituted a sort of chain reaction. The new applications, especially those connected with the inspection and testing of products, led to new theories, and statistics grew so fast that there was no place in the original theory in which to fit the new discoveries. In the late 1930's the growing pains became acute, and there were a number of very heated controversies.

Just before and during World War II a new concept began to emerge—the concept of *Statistical Decision*. Not only was this new concept comprehensive enough to include all that is currently covered in the subject of statistics, but in addition it involved ideas from other subjects such as the theory of games, cost accounting, information theory, logic, economics, and almost anything else you care to name.

Consequently, the name Statistical Decision is something of

a misnomer. Many people other than statisticians have grappled with the problem of decision and have contributed important ideas. The statisticians arrived on the scene rather late (and more or less accidentally). They translated the existing ideas into statistical terms, added some ideas of their own, and then assembled all of these concepts into an integrated mechanism for making decisions. This decision machine has already been applied to such diverse purposes as military strategy and betting on horses,[1] and its use in these fields is only the beginning.

I cannot blame you if, at this point, you scratch your head and murmur, "All this looks suspiciously like the old ballyhoo. If Statistical Decision is such a world-shaking affair why haven't I felt some of the tremors?" You may not have heard of the statistical "revolution" that I mentioned earlier, and, to digress a bit, let me explain *why* you may not have heard of these matters. The main reason is that publications on the subject are written only for fellow specialists (and even these worthies have trouble understanding them). It may take twenty years before these ideas reach other *scientists* in a comprehensible form and even longer before they are taught to students. Specific techniques (in cookbook form) may be transmitted more rapidly, but the *ideas* diffuse very slowly.

A few scientists, it is true, have tried to write for the public. But while the public has eagerly accepted the television sets, wonder drugs, and bigger strawberries that scientific research has produced, they have been profoundly uninterested in the fundamental ideas, the *Scientific Method,* that have made this research fruitful. People must have the very *latest* electronic gadget, but they cling tenaciously to ideas and methods of thinking that were obsolete three hundred years ago.

This delay in the transmission of *ideas* is, I believe, one of the factors which has led our civilization to its present crisis. Moreover, the already dangerous situation is steadily getting worse

---

[1] Sprowls, Clay, "Statistical decisions by the method of minimum risk: An application," *Journal American Statistical Association,* Vol. 45, No. 250, June 1950.

because it is increasingly difficult to translate the language of science—a symbolic one—into everyday English.

In this book I have tried to make such a translation, but my task has led me into a curious paradox. Statistical Decision can be viewed as a complex machine. Into this machine is fed information from the real world, and out of this machine comes a recommendation for action in the real world. But the basic mechanism of the machine itself is this: The real world problem is translated into a symbolic language, the problem is *solved* in symbolic form, and finally the answer is translated back into the real world decision.

Not only is the symbolic language an integral part of the machine, but it is the use of this language that enables Statistical Decision to avoid the muddled thinking and verbal confusion of other processes of decision! It is therefore impossible to omit all mention of the symbolic language, but in the body of the text *there will be no mathematics beyond high school algebra.*

Since I am writing this book in everyday language, the reader must not expect to find blueprints which will enable him to construct his own Decision-Maker. Such blueprints can only be given in the symbolic language. I will give references to publications which *do* give the blueprints, however, and I hope that some readers will be stimulated enough to go ahead on their own.

All that I will try to do is to describe the Decision-Maker and to explain some of the principles on which it operates. For these purposes the decision-making machine will be taken apart so that the functioning of the pieces can be studied separately. Then it will be reassembled, and its operation in some fairly simple situations will be described.

Some readers may be primarily interested in the applications. Routine decisions occur in various phases of administration (purchasing and selling, control of manufacturing, assembly, and inspection processes, etc.), and Decision-Makers have already demonstrated their utility in these applications. Similar routine decisions also occur in applied research and testing programs and in the day-to-day operation of commercial and governmental agencies.

Readers who have already had experience with statistical applications may find that Statistical Decision provides a vantage point from which it is possible to see all the scattered techniques in their proper perspective. It then becomes much easier to understand when a given methodology should, or should not, be used and what interpretation can be given to the results.

Some readers may be intrigued by the ideas of Statistical Decision because they represent a new advance toward the solution of a basic human problem. The principles have a wide scope; they apply to the choice of a foreign policy or to the private decisions that we all must make. They are, if you like, philosophical principles, a way of looking at the world in which we live, a guide to action in that world.

CHAPTER 1

HISTORY OF DECISION

Natural History

Man is a decision-making animal. This trait sets him apart from his friends and relations in the animal world. It is probably responsible for his domination of this planet, but it also may be responsible for many of his gray hairs, ulcers, and neuroses. The following outline of history, from Ooze to Oak Ridge, is intended only to indicate how Statistical Decision is related to other decision mechanisms. A real history of decision would be worth doing—but it would take more than the next dozen pages!

To a limited extent all living organisms encounter the problem of decision. Even a one-celled organism has to act; it assimilates particles in its immediate environment, and these particles may either be nutritious or poisonous. The biological composition of the organism and the laws of chemistry and physics determine whether a given particle is assimilated or not. Hence the decision is made *automatically* by a biological mechanism.

As the organisms become more complex and acquire eyes and legs and a nervous system, the animal may face more complicated decisions. For example, it may have to decide whether to attack another animal or run away from it. However, the biological equipment of the animal is good enough to enable him to make his decisions without assistance from mathematicians and philosophers.

Scientists have studied the decision processes of various animals by making them solve puzzles or run through mazes. A typical maze consists of a pathway with several forks, and the animal must decide which direction to try. If the animal follows the right routine—say LEFT, RIGHT, LEFT, LEFT—it is rewarded by some food. Any other choice will lead it into blind alleys which may sometimes produce a penalty such as an electric shock.

The biological equipment of the animal includes a built-in Decision-Maker which enables the animal to solve the maze. The first few times the animal runs "at random" or "purposelessly" and succeeds by trial and error. After enough trials, however, the animal learns to run through the maze without making mistakes. A second mechanism for decision has then come into play—memory.

Although the biological Decision-Makers seem adequate for animals under natural conditions (or even for a maze), ingenious human beings have devised situations which will result in a breakdown of this natural equipment. One such method is to let a guinea pig learn a procedure for getting food and then to double-cross the poor creature by putting a glass plate or an electrically charged strip of metal in its path. In this way, experimenters have succeeded in making a guinea pig (which is naturally the most inoffensive of animals) become a vicious, aggressive little beast. The consequent behavior of the guinea pig resembles that of a neurotic human; it cannot make up its mind, it will approach the food and then turn away at the last moment (even though the barrier has been removed), and it will repeat this indecision again and again.

In all fairness to the guinea pig it should be added that it took years of intensive experimentation to learn how to make this animal misbehave as badly as a human being. The biological Decision-Makers of our evolutionary cousins are remarkably well built!

In the insect world potentials for very complex forms of behavior, such as nest-building and web-spinning, are built into the genetic material of the animal. Our own closest relatives, the other mammals, seem to lack some of these elaborate instinctive Decision-Makers, and humans are even worse off in this respect.

In the world of mammals, most behavior seems to be learned by the young either from parental behavior or by trial and error. These systems have a great advantage and a considerable disadvantage at the same time. The advantage lies in the greater flexibility of the Decision-Maker. The mammals have the opportunity to develop new and better responses to various situations. Consequently, they can adapt much more rapidly to new environments than organisms with completely built-in and therefore unchangeable responses. The disadvantage lies in the necessity of transmitting the successful new responses to the progeny, who otherwise are practically helpless. Many of the mammals have overcome this disadvantage through the mechanism of the family. In dogs and cats, for example, the parents teach the young animals the secrets of survival. Human scientists have interfered with this process by removing the young animals from the mother. A kitten thus isolated from its heritage will share its cage with mice or birds and will not harm them (a mode of behavior which would not be practical under natural conditions).

The success of the mammalian way of life indicates that the advantages of the more flexible Decision-Makers outweighed the disadvantages. Moreover, within the hierarchy of mammals the trend was to replace the biological Decision-Maker by rudimentary cultural Decision-Makers. By the time human beings arrived on the scene, the biological Decision-Maker was nearly gone—only vestiges remained. In fact, man is a decision-making animal because of a biological deficiency!

Culture

Because of an inadequate biological Decision-Maker, the education of the young is, necessarily, a major occupation of the human animal. Perhaps as a consequence, man developed a new method for transmitting behavior patterns—language. Another result of the very long training period required to develop the human Decision-Maker was the emergence of more or less permanent social groups. This development, in turn, combined with the tremendous flexibility of the human Decision-Maker, has produced the remarkable variety of cultures that exist to this day.

The advantage of cultural patterns as opposed to a simple parent-child transmission lies in the pooling of experience that is obtained. Instead of the responses being limited to the experience of the individual or of his family, the cultural pattern combines the experience of hundreds of individuals. In this way the young get advice on appropriate actions to take in a great variety of situations.

On the other hand, the experience may not all be concordant, and contradictory instructions may put a severe strain on the Decision-Maker. If a young man receives one set of rules concerning sexual behavior from his companions and virtually the opposite set of instructions from priests or elders, he then may not know what to do. He may begin to exhibit neurotic symptoms like those of the guinea pig.

If success is measured in terms of population density, the cultural Decision-Makers were, on the whole, a big success. The flexibility of response enabled man to improve his hunting methods and to discover agriculture. The cultures preserved the discoveries and transmitted them to successive generations. Cities and relatively stable societies became possible and this in turn paved the way for the growth of civilizations.

The decision problems presented by civilizations became more complex, however, and neither the biological nor the simpler cultural Decision-Makers were adequate to handle them. The increasing degree of specialization which civilizations made possible provided a solution. A class of specialists arose whose job was making decisions.

The emergence of such a group represented a simple solution to the problem. The process of making decisions was becoming a greater and greater chore. If the decisions could be received from someone else, however, the individual could be freed from this chore. It is not surprising that such an idea had a great deal of appeal and was adopted by nearly all the early civilizations. Nor has the idea lost its early appeal; businessmen (as well as Socialists) have adopted the pyramid of organization that is implied by this solution.

The principle of referring decisions to a special class of Decision-Makers possesses many potential advantages. The specialists so created may indeed make better decisions because they can receive special training and gain experience in making decisions. Moreover, by making decisions for a group, they may be able to coordinate actions to obtain solutions which would be impossible for the individual. For example, they may be able to solve the drinking water problem for a large group of citizens by having a dam constructed—a course of action which would not be possible for an individual.

There is another subtle advantage possessed by the professional Decision-Maker—he thinks about the problems of *other* individuals. It is generally easier to make a decision when someone else must bear the consequences.

The disadvantages of this solution to the decision problem need no elaboration here. All of us have had experience with benevolent bureaucracies and ruthless tyrannies.

The individual is concerned, and rightly so, with the repercussions of decisions on himself, and he evaluates the consequences of a decision in terms of his own pleasure and pain. If he allows someone else to make his decisions and things turn out very badly, he will then lose confidence in the professional Decision-Maker. He may now wish to make his own decisions, and in this event the professional Decision-Makers may employ their superior resources to enforce their decisions. If the dissatisfaction is sufficiently widespread and well organized, the decision-making pyramid may be shattered by revolt.

Most recorded history is a chronicle of the specialized Decision-Makers—kings, generals, and priests. Judging by the record, these professionals botched their job miserably. It is hardly surprising that a distrust of professionals eventually developed into a creed. This creed exalted individual decision and insisted that it was the privilege, responsibility, and right of each individual to make his own decisions. But freedom in itself does not solve the problem. Even with a free choice the individual may select a course of action which will lead to disastrous personal consequences. Thus it becomes even more important for the individual to learn the principles underlying successful decision as they have been slowly and painfully developed over the centuries.

Devils

With the evolution of more elaborate cultural devices to replace the inadequate biological decision mechanisms and the appearance of classes of professional Decision-Makers, some systematization of the process was necessary to prevent chaos. One of the greatest dangers was the presence of contradictions within a given system because, as we have seen, this complication has often led to the breakdown of the Decision-Maker.

Since the number of situations requiring decision was very large, even in simple cultures, and since this number was multiplied manyfold with the advent of cities and civilizations, it became increasingly difficult to specify in detail the appropriate course of action for every situation.

As a result of this multiplicity of situations, a tremendous strain was placed on the individual and even on the collective memory. In the primitive cultures that are the joy of the anthropologists, the number of ritual responses that a well-trained medicine man must know may number in the thousands. Learning these rituals is a feat requiring much more perseverance and memory than the rituals required of graduate students in a modern college. Moreover, it is vitally important that the ritual responses be remembered *exactly* since any deviation will ruin the entire performance and can lead to negative or even dangerous consequences. This last provision is necessary since the development of multiple responses can lead to disaster insofar as the Decision-Maker is concerned.

The task was considerably eased with the invention of written language. The storage of symbols on stone, wood, or papyrus was much easier than their storage in the human memory. But while the invention of writing greatly simplified the process of transmitting accumulated past experience to future generations, it did not solve the problem altogether. There remained, moreover, the possibility of contradictions arising within the system among the various ritual responses.

To meet this pressing need for simplicity, the intellectual decision systems came into vogue. Instead of dealing with a large number of specific responses, certain broad principles were developed which would enable a decision to be made in a large number of different situations. Although we are inclined to sneer at the systems of magic which were developed, they represented a tremendous step forward.

In order to take this step, the medicine man (like the scientists today) had to construct an abstract picture, or model, of the real world. It is hardly surprising that man created the pictures in his own image and that he attributed to the objects and phenomena of the real world desires, passions, and motives corresponding to his own. These worlds of anthropomorphic devils and gods greatly simplified decision. Desirable consequences could be obtained either by insuring the cooperation of the gods and devils or by taking magical protective measures. Since these deities controlled the course of future events, it was only logical to take them into consideration if this model of the real world was accepted.

This anthropomorphic model of the real world cannot be branded as either right or wrong. A model must be judged by the results of directed action taken in accordance with the model. We now believe that incantations and witchcraft are not effective actions to take to insure desirable consequences such as good health, and we have various public health statistics to back up this contention.

Not all the rituals were ineffective, however. The Jewish dietary laws are generally in accordance with public health practices that would be applied by scientists in a warm country, such as Jerusalem, if no refrigeration were available. Similarly the practice of boiling drinking water performed as a ritual by some South American Indian tribes in order to drive out the devils would have the approval of a modern medical scientist, although he would have some fancier names for the "devils" that are being exorcised.

The Devil theory of the real world has the advantage of being simple, comprehensive, and easily understood, and it continues to be a very popular theory in the modern world. To be sure the names of the devils have been modified; they are now labeled "alcohol," "Communists," "Capitalists," or given a different political, racial, or geographical label.

Starting from a Devil theory, the professional Decision-Makers wove elaborate, and sometimes beautiful, models of the real world. From this intellectual portraiture of the real world, elaborate codes of behavior were constructed, and even in non-codified situations a decision could be made on the basis of certain principles. Certain possible lines of action could be ruled out as likely to incur the wrath or disfavor of the deities who controlled events, and therefore such actions must lead to unpleasant consequences for the individual. On the other hand, different lines of action would please the gods or frustrate the devils, and a most effective action could be chosen on that basis.

While the layman might become acquainted with parts of the intellectual superstructure, a real understanding and appreciation required long and difficult training. Hence, on really complex decisions, it was necessary to consult the professional Decision-Maker (or at least to obtain his approval for a contemplated action).

The trade of Decision-Maker admits one serious handicap—if disastrous consequences befall an officially approved decision, the layman is likely to blame the specialist whom he has consulted. Part of the professional's equipment must therefore include a code of excuses which will remove the onus of failure. Some very ingenious alibis were fabricated, and sometimes they were built into the theoretical superstructure. Doubletalk, ambiguous advice, and mysticism have been found to be very useful for this purpose, but the most ingenious way out was to insist that misfortunes were temporary or even desirable and that "prosperity was just around the corner" and only required some additional rituals—the completion of a five-year plan— or perhaps the final misfortune of death which would open the gates to a really superior reward and happiness.

Although such excuses generally placated the populace, and especially the "educated men," there were men who had enough common sense not to be fooled by these excuses. They judged the Decision-Makers by the results, and the results did not please them. They became skeptics. Mere skepticism was not a solution to the problem, however; it was still necessary to find a successful scheme for making decisions.

Reason

Spoken language facilitated the communication of experience from individual to individual. Written language was even more efficient in making accessible the experience of men of other times and even of other civilizations.

But language had other uses, and it was not long before man was playing tricks with it. It was developed into a lethal weapon to vilify and confound enemies. It was forged into a powerful yoke to control groups of men. It was even useful for amusement, and the construction of riddles and paradoxes became the sport of nimble minds.

In ancient Greece a new class of specialists arose, the Sophists, and words were their stock in trade. The Sophists became adept at manipulating words, at argument, and at persuasion. They fashioned verbal snares and caught such a large crop of fools that Sophism became a synonym for trickery. But they also learned some of the idiosyncrasies of language and evolved a set of rules for playing verbal games.

Their set of rules, systematized by Aristotle, was *logic*. The proper employment of these rules was called *reasoning*. The sport became a serious game and finally a cult which is still alive. Indeed, many people today feel that Reason is the highest accomplishment and main distinction of the human animal.

In evaluating the importance of Reason as a mechanism for making decisions, it is necessary to distinguish at the outset between the process of arriving at a choice of action and the process of convincing others that this is indeed the appropriate action to take. Although the latter process is essential for situations that require cooperative or joint action, the primary interest of this book is in the first process.

As a method of persuasion Reason is, even today, the most important procedure. As a mechanism for arriving at a decision, however, Reason is subject to several weaknesses which will be discussed in more detail in Chapter 3.

Nonetheless, Reason and Logic represent a substantial advance beyond the Devil theory. Both points of view regard the phenomena or events of the real world as the products of *causes,* but whereas the earlier theory considered the causes to be devils, the proponents of Reason felt the causes were material or natural.

Another contribution of Reason was the concept of *consistency*. The assertion of two statements which contradicted each other was prohibited by the rules of the verbal game. The proudest achievement of Reason was the creation of Euclidean geometry which served as a model for clear, precise thinking for two thousand years. The principles of deductive logic, the rules for going from one set of statements (axioms) to another set of statements (theorems) in a *consistent* manner, are an important part of Statistical Decision.

Unfortunately, the proponents of Reason confused *consistency* with *truth*. Truth involves the real world; a theorem of geometry is true if it is a perfect description of the state of affairs in the real world. Consistency is a logical question that does *not* involve the real world. This distinction was not

realized until the discovery of several *consistent* geometries
which led to theorems *contradicting* those of Euclidean geometry. For example, in one of the newer geometries the sum
of the angles in a triangle is *less than* 180 degrees. Modern
physicists are still arguing the question of which of these several
geometries is *true* (i.e., describes the world in which we live).

The fact that Reason is divorced from the real world was not
realized until comparatively recently (and many people today
are not aware of this gap). A necessary ingredient for successful decision was missing, and the record shows it. No one could
build dams or design boats using the physics of Aristotle; no
one could predict the weather from the meteorology of Aristotle. In terms of actual results, the science of the Greeks which
was based on Reason was on a par with the science based on the
Devil theory.

The concepts of Reason failed to diffuse. The mass of the
population retained the older devil theories. Only a small cult
kept the idea of Reason alive, but they proved to be poor cus-
todians. The original ideas were not advanced; instead much
nonsense was allowed to dilute them. At last the basic ideas were
virtually lost, and about all that remained was the tradition.

For over a thousand years devil theories held undisputed
sway. Then a series of discoveries, inventions, and explorations
made these ancient ideas topple. The circumnavigation of the
world, for example, was an unanswerable challenge to the idea
that the earth was flat. An action had accomplished what
reasoned arguments had failed to do. As men learned to doubt
again, the beautiful theoretical structures of devil theories
crumpled into nothingness and recently rediscovered ideas of
Reason were enthusiastically seized upon in order to fill the
resulting void.

The first wild enthusiasm for Reason subsided only slowly;
the American Constitution is a stirring hymn to Reason. The
most violent reaction to Reason has come in this century and
old devil theories (in modern costumes) have pressed forward.

The same era that witnessed the rediscovery of Reason also

saw the birth of the successor to Reason—Science. The new techniques introduced by the scientists closed the gap between Reason and the real world by means of an *inductive* logic, a procedure for going from observations to statements. The new techniques of experimentation, measurement, and a symbolic language very quickly demonstrated their power in a convincing manner—they produced results.

Some readers may be surprised that I list Science as a mechanism for making decisions. By *Science* I am referring here not to subject matter, such as physics or chemistry, but rather to the principles used in research. Perhaps I should therefore use the phrase *Scientific Method* instead. Statistical Decision is based on Scientific Method, so I will not discuss the techniques in detail at this point. These principles will be dealt with at greater length in the body of the book.

Summary

The decision problem is as old as life itself, for a biological mechanism for decision was a necessity for survival. The human animal evolved itself out of a biological mechanism and substituted a cultural mechanism. This cultural process was so successful that human civilizations developed, but these civilizations led to decision problems which were too complex for the cultural mechanism. The civilizations therefore produced classes of specialists whose business was making decisions. These specialists devised intellectual mechanisms for decision. The first mechanism was the Devil theory, the next was Reason, and the latest is Science. Statistical Decision is an intellectual mechanism based on the Scientific Method.

CHAPTER 2

/ NATURE OF DECISION

The Problem

Statistical Decision is intimately associated with Science. The knowledge and methods of various scientific fields such as physics, chemistry, and biology often provide the data on which the decision is to be based. Scientific equipment, such as punched-card machines and electronic computers, is occasionally used in the actual process of Statistical Decision. But these are superficial connections; the relationship goes much deeper than this.

Science and Statistical Decision "speak the same language," both in a literal and figurative sense. The early work in statistics borrowed heavily from the symbolic language (and even the shop talk) of various fields of science, especially physics. This debt is being repaid with interest, for current theories in physics use a good deal of the specialized symbolic language developed by statisticians. The association, however, goes beyond the technical notation of the symbolic language. Science and Statistical Decision share a common outlook, a way of looking at the curious and complex phenomena which comprise the real world.

Statistical Decision attempts to deal with the problem of action in the real world, but there are many ways of looking at the real world. In order to attack the problem—in order even to *state* the problem—it is necessary to make some assumptions about the real world. The attitude toward the real world taken by Statistical Decision is the one accepted by modern Science. It is perfectly possible to devise a theory of decision based on a different attitude—say one of the devil theories—but the reader must consult some other book if this is what he wants!

Decision requires the selection of a course of action. This may be stated a little more precisely as follows:

(1) There are two or more alternative courses of action possible (which may be symbolized by A_1, A_2, . . . etc.). Only one of these lines of action can be taken.

This last sentence is a restriction which does not limit the practical problem in any way. Any combination of actions can be considered as a single action. Consequently any list of actions can be *restated* so as to make the restriction apply. It is convenient to agree at the outset to work with lists which meet this restriction so as to avoid some ambiguities. Such a list is often called a list of *mutually exclusive* actions.

(2) The process of decision will select, from these alternative actions, a single course of action which will actually be carried out.

This innocent statement will, I think, be readily accepted by nearly all readers. But it actually involves a controversial point that has been argued for hundreds of years: Can man actually choose his actions? (This is the old question of free will versus predestination.) In the climate of this century the statement seems quite reasonable.

Perhaps the best way to determine additional specifications for the problem of decision is to consider a simple example. Suppose that I am sitting in my easy chair at six o'clock tonight and that I am trying to make up my mind as to what method of transportation I will use to get to the office tomorrow. Preliminary considerations of practicality have reduced my choice to one of two possible lines of action:

A_1: Drive my car.
A_2: Take the bus.

There is a very simple way to make the decision: Flip a coin. What is the objection to this process? The question is not very

easy to answer. Broadly speaking, the objection is that there is
no assurance that a decision made in this way will be satisfactory. But such an objection requires that a satisfactory decision be carefully specified. Evidently the degree to which a
decision is satisfactory depends on what happens when the line
of action selected by the decision process is actually carried out.
If this outcome or result of the decision process is agreeable to
me, then the decision may be adjudged satisfactory.

Such an attitude in turn requires that I specify just what outcomes will or will not be agreeable to me. In other words, when
I am trying to make up my mind whether to drive or take the
bus various purposes actuate my decision. I choose a line of action which I believe (or hope) will fulfill these purposes.

(3) The selection of a course of action is to be made so as
to accomplish some designated purpose.

Generally speaking the purpose will be to choose an action
which will lead to a desirable situation in the real world in the
future. Without this condition the decision problem would be
trivial. There are all sorts of mechanisms which could be used
for making a purposeless choice. For example, the possible
courses of action could be numbered and the choice made by
drawing a number from a hat.

Even a simple problem like the car vs. bus example may involve a number of different (and sometimes conflicting) purposes. I may be primarily concerned with saving money, or perhaps the saving of time is more important. To make the matter
easier, let me specify that my purpose is to enjoy a specific situation in the real world tomorrow night at six o'clock, to be
sitting comfortably in my easy chair at that time.

Note that time is an ingredient in the decision problem. First
of all there is the present time, tonight at six o'clock, the time
at which my decision is to be made. Let me denote the situation
that exists in the real world by the symbol X so that I will not
have to keep repeating the phrase "the situation at the time of
decision."

Then there is the time of reckoning, six o'clock tomorrow night. Whether or not the decision was satisfactory will depend on what situation exists in the real world at this future time (which I will denote by Y). Therefore the decision itself must be regarded as part of a larger process which takes place over a period of time. In this process the decision leads to action which in turn leads to some outcome. This process can be represented by the little diagram given below:

Fig. 2.01

Thus if I drive my car I will set into motion a chain of events which will lead to some outcome tomorrow night. On the other hand, if I decide to take the bus I will actuate a different chain of events which may lead to a different outcome. To make my decision I must anticipate the future. Decision is *predictive*.

Presumably the outcome depends on which action I take (or otherwise the decision does not really matter). For the decision to be consequential, therefore, I must consider that different actions will lead to different outcomes. This can be expressed symbolically by means of the notation $Y \mid A_1$. (Read: The outcome if action A_1 is taken.)

To make my decision I must *trace down the consequences of each of the alternative lines of action,* I must consider alternative futures. This involves imagination (foresight) because in reality only one course of action will be taken and only one outcome will occur. The alternative futures can be represented diagrammatically by:

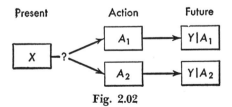

Fig. 2.02

The diagram for the car vs. bus problem might look like:

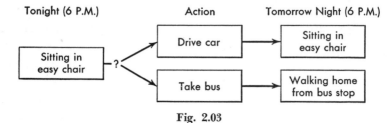

Fig. 2.03

If, as I have stated, my purpose is to be sitting comfortably in my easy chair at 6 P.M. tomorrow night, then the above diagram permits me to make my decision. Evidently I will only be able to accomplish my purpose if I drive my car.

In order to construct Figure 2.03 I must have some way of knowing what will be the outcomes for each of the actions. The outcomes that I have written down were obtained from past experience. Thus I must consider not only the present and the future but also the *past*. The past contributes the information or *data* upon which the decision can be based.

Fig. 2.04

The process of decision as I have presented it for the car vs. bus problem is greatly oversimplified, yet it contains the three basic steps toward decision:

(1) The outcomes for each action are predicted.
(2) The outcomes are evaluated in terms of some scale of desirability.
(3) A *criterion* for decision, based on the purposes, is then used to make the actual selection.

The prediction in step (1) was based on my past experience with cars and busses. The evaluation in step (2) was based on whether or not the outcome accomplished my stated purpose. The comparison in step (3) was based on the criterion: Select the line of action which accomplishes the stated purpose.

These three steps are given a more precise formulation in the process of Statistical Decision. They are translated from this rather vague verbal language into the precise symbolic language. The translation will be described later.

This detailed analysis is, of course, unnecessary for the over-simplified car vs. bus problem of Figure 2.03. However, any decision problem in the real world, including the example, has a much more complex structure than Figure 2.03. For example, I have listed a single outcome for each action but to do this is unrealistic. If I drive my car, I might be sitting home in my easy chair at 6 P.M. tomorrow, but I also might be sitting in a hospital bed with my leg in a plaster cast. While it is true that there will be only one actual outcome if I drive, at the time of decision I can conceive of a large number of possible outcomes that might happen. Moreover, I have stated a very restricted purpose. I might specify a broader purpose: I want to have a general feeling of well-being at 6 P.M. tomorrow night.

In the latter case I might be in a much happier frame of mind if I were walking home jingling in my pocket the extra cash that I had saved on the bus than if I were sitting in my easy chair figuring out how much it would cost me to fix the dent that someone had just put in my fender. Thus my purposes might conflict. Consequently an outcome might have both desirable and undesirable aspects. A measure of the desirability of the outcome would try to weigh the pleasant against the unpleasant.

Finally, when the problem is given a more realistic statement the criterion for decision is not easy to state. The rule for striking a balance, for comparing the actions, must be able to deal with many outcomes and cross-purposes.

Alternative Futures

The simple structure of Figure 2.02 is an inadequate picture for most decision problems. Instead of a single outcome as-

sociated with each action one can conceive of a number of possibilities (as in Figure 2.05).

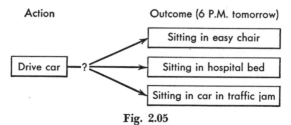

Fig. 2.05

The notion of alternative futures is a useful *conceptual device* but only that. There is just one future in the real world and much as we might like to turn back the clock to some earlier time and try a different line of action, this possibility is denied to us. The closest that we can come to doing this is when situations recur that resemble some past situation. We can then profit by past mistakes to choose a more appropriate course of action. It is such repeatable events that have suggested the concept of alternative futures.

Instead of the symbol Y the symbols Y_1, Y_2, . . . etc. may be used to represent specific outcomes. Thus Y_1 might stand for sitting in an easy chair tomorrow night at six and $Y_1 \mid A_1$ for the occurrence of this outcome *if* action one, driving the car, is taken. The concept of alternative futures leads to a structure such as Figure 2.06.

Any one of the possible routes in Figure 2.06 (such as the one indicated by the heavy arrow) may represent the actual course of events. Such a route is like a chain with a number of different links. It is appropriate to call such a sequence of events an *event chain*. The concept of an event chain is very useful in many applications.

Such chains are familiar in everyday experience. The simplest event chain would be one (like Figure 2.02) which did not keep branching off. Each event would lead to a single event and so on down the line. Such a chain is often called a *strict causal chain*. When I push the starting button in my car, for example, a series of events happen which follow a definite sequence that terminates in the purring of the motor. I might say that pushing the button "caused" the current to flow through the starting motor and this current "caused" the motor to rotate and so on. This is the origin of the name *causal chain*.

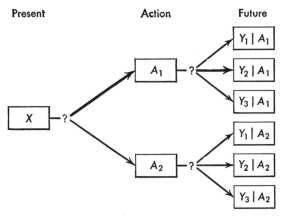

Fig. 2.06

This terminology is fine so long as I use the phrase "A causes B" as an abbreviation for the phrase "when event A occurs then event B will follow." Trouble starts when more than this is read into the word "cause." Because of the metaphysical connotations, many scientists steer clear of the word "cause" even though it is a convenient abbreviation.

Some everyday decisions involve sequences of events that are *almost* strict causal chains. Thus if I act *as though* the motor will *always* start when I push the button, it will probably do me no harm. In such cases the predictive part of the decision problem is easy, and the structure of the process is adequately represented by Figure 2.02. In most cases of practical decision the problem is not so simple, and the branching process of Figure 2.06 is more realistic.

In the strict causal chain the prediction is "certain," but when alternative futures are admitted it is no longer "certain" which outcome will occur. This condition of uncertainty makes many people quite uncomfortable. They sometimes argue that there can be no guide to action if the situation is uncertain. This argument is absurd because all actions in the real world are shrouded in uncertainty. The question is merely one of learning to live with uncertainty. Statistical Decision is designed to accomplish this purpose.

For reasons which will be explained later, chains of events such as those in Figure 2.06 are called *probability event chains*. One of the requirements for an understanding of Statistical Decision is to learn to think in terms of *probability event chains* instead of the simpler and more familiar *strict causal chains*.

These concepts belong to the part of Statistical Decision that I will call the *Prediction System*.

Conflicting Values

In addition to alternative futures a realistic formulation of the structure of decision includes the notion of conflicting values. This difficulty arises when the *purpose* of the decision is stated broadly. A broad statement may mean that a given outcome will have both desirable and undesirable aspects and an *evaluation* of the desirability of the outcome must take these conflicting values into account.

The problem of measuring desirability has been sadly neglected by science. It is, admittedly, a nasty topic to tackle, but it is a job that will have to be done. The main work so far has centered around monetary values, the measurement of desirability in terms of *dollars and cents.*

In the choice of car vs. bus, a number of cash values enter into the picture. The costs of each method of transportation must be considered. Moreover, some of the outcomes may involve additional costs (such as hospital costs).

The actual dollar and cents outlay does not, however, cover all of the values in the problem. There is the saving of time to be considered. Now desirability measured in minutes cannot be compared easily with desirability measured in dollars. It may be possible to convert time to a monetary scale. For example, I may value my time at so-and-so much per hour.

Other values such as convenience or peace of mind may not be easily converted to a monetary scale. One way to make the conversion would be by an introspective questioning: Would I prefer to stand up on the bus all the way home or to pay out a dime, a quarter, a half dollar, etc.? In this way I can try to establish the cash value of the inconvenience of standing up in a crowded bus.

When the values are converted to a dollar and cents scale (or other common scale) the conflict of values can be resolved by a little bookkeeping. The costs associated with a given outcome are subtracted from the gains and the result is the dollar and cents value of the outcome.

Many of the problems where Statistical Decision has been used have employed this monetary scale for values. However, it does not follow that such a monetary scale is completely satisfactory, but rather that the development of alternative scales has lagged. This part of the decision problem will be called the *Value System*.

When an action has only a single outcome, the desirability of the outcome may also be regarded as the desirability of the action. When several outcomes are associated with an action, however, this transfer of desirability is not so easy. One way to meet the problem is to determine a sort of *average* desirability of the outcomes associated with a given action. The result may then be regarded as the desirability of the action.

Then the rule or *criterion* may be set up: Choose the action with the highest desirability. This rule leads to the selection of one course of action to follow. The comparative part of the decision problem will be called the *Decision Criterion*.

Thus the process of decision may be regarded as a machine for making decisions. Such a machine may be called a Decision-Maker.

Components

When an engineer wants to design a complicated piece of equipment he often begins by making a *block diagram*. In a radio, for example, radio waves are converted into sound waves by a rather complicated process. This process can be broken down into smaller steps as indicated in Figure 2.07.

Block Diagram: Radio

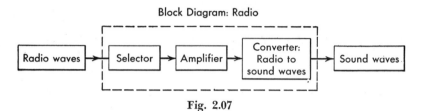

Fig. 2.07

The radio engineer would attach more technical labels to his boxes, but the block diagram would look very much like the one I have pictured.

The use of a block diagram has two advantages. First, it provides a clear picture of the process as a whole. Second, it enables the engineer to concentrate on the design of one component at a time. The discussion in this chapter enables us to construct a similar block diagram for a Decision-Maker.

Feeding into the Decision-Maker will be data. This information is used in two ways. In the first place it goes into the *Predicting System*. From the Predicting System we obtain a list of possible outcomes for each action and also a probability associated with each outcome. The information also feeds into the *Value System* which in turn provides a second quantity associated with each outcome, the desirability.

At this point we have

(1) A list of actions.
(2) A list of outcomes for each action.
(3) A probability associated with each outcome.
(4) A desirability associated with each outcome.

We then apply a *Decision Criterion* and obtain, with the aid of this criterion, a recommended course of action.

Thus at one end we feed data into the Decision-Maker and at the other end a recommended course of action comes out (as shown in figure 2.08).

Block Diagram: Decision-Maker

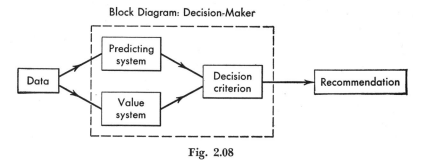

Fig. 2.08

The Pragmatic Principle

At this point I want to discuss very briefly what might be called the philosophical foundations of the problem of decision as I have outlined it. This outline presupposes a way of looking at the real world, an outlook which, while in accord with modern science, is not entirely in accord with the attitude that prevails outside the laboratories.

First I want to state what I consider to be the basic tenet not only of science but of common sense. There are many ways of putting it, perhaps the simplest being the proverb: The proof of the pudding is in the eating. In other words, to my way of thinking, the court of final appeal is not brilliant verbal argument, high-sounding abstract principles, or even precise logic or mathematics—*it is the results in the real world*. Not all cases have to be carried all the way to the final court, but in event of disagreement, the real world has the last word.

Therefore in judging any system—Devil theory, Reason, or Science—the test is: Does it work? John Dewey has put it this way: "The true purpose of knowledge resides in the consequences of directed action." [1] Statistical Decision is this pragmatic attitude phrased in the language of science.

The pragmatic principle cannot really be justified since it amounts to a standard for justification. There is, however, one argument that I wish to present because it is generally overlooked. The pragmatic principle, and (so far as I know) only

[1] Dewey, John, *The Quest for Certainty*, G. P. Putnam's Sons, New York, 1939.

this principle, can provide all of us with a protection against specialists. This protection is desperately needed because as our civilization becomes more and more complex, it is increasingly necessary to seek the advice of specialists to make decisions that will affect large numbers of people. You and I cannot comprehend the technical aspects of these specialties, but we *can* tell whether or not the consequences of the decisions are to our liking.

To accept any other standard—in particular, to accept abstract standards which can only be interpreted by the specialists —is to surrender to *domination* by specialists. This domination has been disastrous in the past and is just as dangerous today.

If we insist that the claims of the specialists be judged by the pragmatic principle, we can, without a technical knowledge of the field of advice, select our advisors and thereby provide a guard against unscrupulous charletans who exploit the principle that what the people cannot understand, they must accept on faith. It also provides a protection against the even more dangerous "honest fanatics," individuals who insist that they are right *because they have a special access to truth.*

I like the pragmatic principle because it seems to me that it is compatible with the values of democracy and individualism. It stands as a bulwark against tyranny, intellectual and otherwise.

Some care must be taken, however, in the interpretation of this first principle. The real world referred to is the world of sensation, the world of sight, sound, smell, taste, and touch that provides us with experience. This is the real world of modern science.

The principle presupposes that the individual has a value scale, that he can distinguish sensations as agreeable or unpleasant. Moreover, the individual has memory and can compare time segments of experience. It is such a time segment of experience that I have called a "situation in the real world." The pragmatic principle requires the individual to compare one group of situations with another group.

If the experience of the individual is insufficient, he can draw upon the experience of others in order to assess the performance of an intellectual or theoretical system. The use of the principle assumes that what has been successful in the past will continue to be successful in the future. This assumption, while in no sense a guarantee, can be justified by the pragmatic principle.

These remarks emphasize that *values* are intrinsic in the pragmatic principle. The "eating of the pudding" is a value appraisal and there is no way of dodging altogether the ticklish problem of values. It is true that many eminent philosophers, such as Bertrand Russell, have denied that Science has anything to do with *values*. This apparent contradiction results, I feel, from ambiguities in the word "value." There are specialized *value systems* that are widely used in Science (see Chapter 5), but some philosophers would quarrel with my use of the word "value" in this connection.

An immediate consequence of the pragmatic principle is that we must abandon *absolutes*. Thus a statement can no longer be regarded as *strictly* true or false; a situation is not *simply* good or bad, and an action is not *absolutely* right or wrong. Instead we must think on a *relative* scale.

There is no real loss when we go from absolutes to a relative scale, for the absolutes persist as endpoints of the scale. In fact, we gain because our thinking is freed from a verbal straight jacket. We do not even need to forsake the use of such handy words as "true" or "good"—we need only to understand that the words are used relatively, or in other words that the phrase "for practical purposes" is automatically added whenever the words are used.

For example, the theoretical system called Euclidean geometry (high school geometry) is widely used in construction, surveying, and astronomy. As a system, Euclidean geometry passes the pragmatic test with flying colors, the consequences of its use having been generally favorable. We can therefore say that Euclidean geometry is true—but this truth is not absolute.

In fact there are some astronomical situations where the use of Euclidean geometry does not lead to adequate predictions.

This same relativity also applies to good and bad or right and wrong. If a woman falls down in the street and the only two actions open are kicking her or letting her alone, then the latter may be the right action. On the other hand, if additional actions (such as assisting her) are possible, then letting her alone might be wrong.

The use of absolutes is similar to the use of a thermometer with only two intervals on the scale. We would not get very far in discussing temperature if the only two reports that could be made were hot or cold. In order to deal with the phenomenon in a scientific manner it is necessary to set up a graduated scale (as physics does). This is often hard to do (it took centuries to evolve our present temperature scales), but it must be done. Statistical Decision involves two such graduated scales, a value scale and a scale for measuring uncertainty (probability).

Summary

A Decision-Maker is considered to be a machine. Into the machine flows information; out of the machine comes a recommended course of action. The mechanism consists of three basic components. The Prediction System deals with alternative futures. The Value System handles the various conflicting purposes. The Criterion integrates the other two components and selects an appropriate action. It is emphasized that the pragmatic principle is basic for the construction and comparison of Decision-Makers.

CHAPTER 3

/ PREDICTION

Prediction Techniques

The component of the Decision-Maker that has led to the name Statistical Decision is the part I have called the Prediction System. This component has received the most attention and we know a good deal more about how to set up the Prediction System than we do about the other parts of the Decision-Maker.

One reason for this somewhat lop-sided development is that few topics have tempted and tormented mankind more than the question: How can man foresee the future? For thousands of years man has searched for the answer—the secret that would endow its possessor with riches, fame, and possibly happiness. Many seers have come forth with the proclamation that the secret was theirs, that their eyes could see beyond today and into tomorrow. Some have generously offered to share their secret, for a small fee, with their fellow men. These claims have never stood up when judged by the pragmatic principle.

Yet man has never abandoned his efforts to read the future— too much depends on it. He has, however, become more modest in his demands. Since he cannot peek into the future, he will settle for shrewd guesses. The more modest question: How can man predict the future? has at least a partial answer. The answer: By studying the past.

Even in the mysterious and erratic world in which we live, there are some threads of continuity. There is chaos and confusion all about, but also some system and stability. Our progress in the real world is like driving along a road that is shrouded in a heavy fog; there are no sharp, clear details, but only vague outlines. By looking very hard through the swirling, random fog shadows we can distinguish enough of the more permanent road shadows to enable us to go ahead successfully if we go slowly and use caution.

Similarly, the first step toward prediction is the search for stable characteristics—those characteristics which persist over a period of time. In fact the simplest procedure for prediction is a method often called *Persistence Prediction.*

Persistence Prediction means nothing more than the prediction that there will be no change. If one wishes to predict the weather tomorrow by this method, one simply describes the weather today. Sometimes this device works out surprisingly well.

In weather forecasting, for example, Persistence Prediction is hard to beat. The modern meteorologist uses the data from hundreds of weather stations, combined with a complicated air-mass theory, in order to arrive at weather forecasts. But in one hundred predictions the scientific weatherman will (on the average) be right in only about ten more cases than a weatherman who used Persistence Prediction. This is not because modern methods are bad, but because persistence methods are good (they give the correct prediction about three quarters of the time so that there is not too much room for improvement).

A fan who used Persistence Prediction would do just as well as the sports experts in predicting the outcome of the National and American League pennant races. This is especially true in the American League over the last few years! Some sports writers seem to have noticed this fact and follow the policy of sticking with the champion.

The method has its limitations, of course. It only works in relatively stable or slowly changing situations. It is often of little practical value because, as in the stock market, the money is to be made by predicting *changes.* Nevertheless, Persistence Prediction is the basis of a number of successful predicting systems including those used by insurance companies. Insurance life tables rely on the fact that death rates, while not actually constant, change rather slowly.

A second scheme for forecasting is *Trajectory Prediction*. This scheme assumes that, although there is change, the extent of change is stable. If noon temperatures were recorded on successive days as 75, 76, and 77 degrees then the Trajectory Prediction for the next day would be 78 degrees. In making this prediction we have assumed that the rise of one degree per day will continue. This method may give fairly good predictions for the next time-interval, but it can also lead to ridiculous long-range forecasts. If we used the assumption of a one-degree rise per day to predict the temperature a year ahead, we would obviously be in hot water.

Trajectory methods are used in artillery fire control, some weather forecasting, short-range stock market prediction, and in estimating the size of human populations. The word "trend" is often used instead of trajectory.

Cyclic Prediction is based on the principle that history repeats itself. The method had some notable early successes: the first effective long-range predictions made by man employed this device to foretell eclipses and other astronomical events.

In Cyclic Prediction, it is assumed that cycles or patterns of events are stable. The method has been used in predicting the return of comets, the occurrence of sunspots, insect plagues, high and low agricultural yield, weather, stock prices, and even (by Spengler) the course of our civilization.

The early successes of Cyclic Prediction stirred great hopes in the breast of man that here, at last, was the long sought-for secret of prophesy. Even today some investigators, notably in the stock market, are still striving—but without much luck—to realize this ancient promise. Astrology, a perversion of the method, still survives on the strength of this old prestige.

In going from Persistence Prediction to Cyclic Prediction, there is a utilization of more and more data. The former needs only the most recent occurrence of the event, while in the latter the available historical information is used—in fact, the stand-ard alibi for the failure of Cyclic Prediction is that the record does not go back far enough.

Associative Prediction differs from the foregoing in that it uses the data from one type of event to predict a second type. Conditioned response is an example of Associative Prediction. Pavlov made dogs salivate by ringing a bell. To accomplish this, he rang a bell just before feeding and repeated the pat-tern over a period of time. The association of the two different types of events, ringing of the bell and feeding, is very similar to a causal event chain. In both cases the stable element that is the basis of prediction is the stability of a *relationship* between two events.

In politics, economics, and everyday life, Associative Predic-tion is the favorite method. Commodity market speculators feel that they must stay abreast of national and international events in order to judge the movements of the market. Even the gen-eral public is aware of the violent gyrations of prices imme-diately after war scares or peace scares.

A relationship between events is often expressed by the word "cause." People say that a large national debt "causes" inflation, that overproduction "causes" unemployment, that armament races "cause" war. In everyday life overeating "causes" indiges-tion, nasty remarks "causes" hard feelings, and extravagance "causes" ruin.

In all of these examples one type of event, the cause, generally precedes the second type of event, the effect. From the point of view of Pavlov's dogs the bell "caused" the feeding. As long as the word "cause" is used in this sense, it serves a useful descrip-tive purpose.

If we stick to the simple meaning of the word "cause," our quest for causes will not go off on wild goose chases. All that we really want to do is to identify the bell that comes before feeding.

This is not always easy to do because Associative Prediction greatly enlarges the area that must be searched for clues. If we want to predict the price of a stock, we cannot focus our attention solely on the previous history of the stock; we may have to examine events of many different kinds. Our "bell" may be an event that takes place ten thousand miles away—a political speech by a foreign leader or the report of some new scientific discovery. Of the many events that we might study, only a few will have any discernible association with the events we wish to forecast.

A serious weakness of Associative Prediction is that unless a great deal of care is exercised in the selection of the "bell," the whole process may degenerate into nonsense. Fortune-tellers use Associative Prediction, their "bells" being such events as the fall of cards or the configurations of tea leaves. They have never demonstrated that the events they use in exposing the future are *relevant* to the events predicted.

Analogue Prediction sets up a correspondence between two sets of events. One of the sets is simple, or at least familiar, and consequently predictions can be made for this set of events. The analogues of these predictions are then made for the second set.

If modern nations with atom bombs are analogous to small boys playing with sticks of dynamite (as has often been suggested) then the fate of the nations can be predicted by analogy with the fate of the boys.

Analogy is one of the most potent gimmicks in an author's arsenal, especially if he is dealing with strange or difficult topics. Not only will an apt analogy make a reader feel that he understands what the author is saying, but it also may convince the reader that the author knows what he is talking about. However, verbal analogies have a dangerous tendency to blow up in the user's face, especially when they are carried too far. Because of the great overuse of analogy, argument by analogy is no longer in good standing with logicians.

Nevertheless, when properly used, analogy may be a powerful tool for prediction. This is especially true if a *mathematical* analogy (or model) can be constructed. By mathematical arguments, the performance of this model can be predicted. Events in the real world may then be forecast by analogy.

The use of scale-model airplanes in wind tunnels to predict the performance of full-sized aircraft and the use of experimental animals to test drugs destined for human consumption are two examples of Analogue Prediction in the field of science.

This list of techniques for prediction is not intended to be exhaustive. Many special techniques have been developed to meet the many different prediction problems that arise.

There is one method of prediction that deserves mention here because it (and it alone) is 100 per cent successful. This is the technique of *Hindsight Prediction,* the prediction of an event after it has already occurred. Radio commentators, newspaper columnists, economic authorities, and politicians use this I-told-you-so method with excellent results. All that is necessary to apply the method are the ability to make ambiguous (or even contradictory) remarks and a talent for selective amnesia. Examples of Hindsight Prediction abound in the writings of historians and philosophers.

Numbers Versus Words

When we are faced with a specific forecasting problem, we may have to study the subject intensively in order to see what prediction techniques are applicable. After making a choice, we must then decide what information or data will be needed for the operation of this technique. Next this data must be collected. Sometimes the information may be obtained from available records, but often existing records are inadequate for the purpose, and it may be necessary to go out and make our own observations. The prediction techniques can be tested on this data and perhaps modified in the light of the additional experience. If we are clever or lucky, we may wind up with forecasts that will be sufficiently accurate for our particular purposes. This whole process, from data to forecast, will be called a Predicting System.

Sooner or later in this process we are bound to run into the problem of error. Few things are so disheartening, embarrassing, and (alas) inevitable as a "busted" forecast. What can be done about this problem?

The first step that can be taken is to face up to the problem, to meet it honestly. This means admitting, to others and to ourselves, that the Predicting System is fallible. This means abandoning face-saving alibis and acknowledging that incorrect predictions are not accidents but are as much a part of the Predicting System as the correct predictions themselves.

The second step is to abandon all-or-none prediction. If any one of several outcomes may occur the possibilities should be explicitly stated. Whenever possible a list or range of outcomes should be given.

Some device for stating the chance of occurrence of each outcome is now necessary. One such device is that used on a racing sheet where the chance of each horse is described verbally. Thus a horse may be a "favorite," a "contender," a "longshot," or "just out for the exercise."

A more conventional verbal *scale* would be to employ such words as "likely" or "unlikely" and perhaps modify them with adverbs such as "very." In this way the Predicting System becomes a device for *classifying* the possible outcomes.

How can we tell whether the scheme is doing a good job of classification? This question can be answered by examining the *record* of the Predicting System. First, let us consider those events which were classed as "very likely." Suppose that this classification was used in a hundred cases and in ninety of these cases, the event actually occurred. This would indicate that the classification "very likely" was justified. On the other hand if only ten of the hundred cases actually occurred, we would not have much confidence that the scheme was properly classifying the events.

In the same way the other categories could be examined, and in this fashion the Predicting System could be evaluated.

The verbal scale, though a step in the right direction, is not very satisfactory. The word "likely" is not precise; it may mean different things to different people. Some might feel that if events classed as "likely" actually occurred more than half of the time the classification was all right; others might feel that an event should happen oftener than this to deserve the classification "likely."

The vagueness of words has been misused by prophets so often that qualifying words such as "likely" are sometimes scorned as weasel words. Professional gazers into crystal balls soon become adept at putting verbal loopholes into their predictions: "Podunk has a terrific team and should win easily but Oshkosh U. might spring a surprise."

It has long been recognized that words are inadequate tools for really precise description, that disagreements over definitions are likely to arise, and that manipulation of words is subject to a variety of pitfalls that are hard to avoid. I will not labor the point—the semanticists have made a profession of it.

While it is easy to criticize language as a tool, it is a much more difficult matter to suggest a substitute means of communication. It took mankind several thousand years to come up with a workable replacement.

The introduction of this new tool coincides with the birth of modern science. Galileo transformed physics by substituting numerical measurements for verbal descriptions and mathematical derivations for verbal arguments. Since then, one field of science after another has made the slow and painful transition from words to numbers. Some scientists regard this step as the distinction between scientific and unscientific study. Said Lord Kelvin:

When you cannot measure what you are speaking about, when you cannot express it in numbers, your knowledge is of a meager and unsatisfactory kind; it may be the beginning of knowledge, but you have scarcely in your thoughts advanced to the stage of a *science,* whatever the matter may be.

The third step that we shall take in dealing with the problem of uncertainty is to go from a verbal scale (such as likely—

unlikely) to a numerical one. In taking this step we shall be in accord with scientific tradition. Moreover, it is a step that often leads to important results.

How can a verbal scale be replaced by a numerical one? First of all, the Prediction System must be modified so that it associates a number instead of a word with each outcome. It is customary to use for this purpose either a common or a decimal fraction, i.e., a number between zero and one. This number is to be regarded as a measure of the chance that a particular outcome will actually occur.

The Predicting System is still engaged in classifying the outcomes, but now the classification is a numerical one. Once again we want to know how good a job of classification is being performed.

A predicting system which leads to probabilities will be called a Probability Prediction System (or PPS for short). As was indicated in the block diagram (Figure 2.08) of Chapter 2, such a system is an integral feature of the process of Statistical Decision. In fact, it is essentially this particular component that distinguishes Statistical Decision from the other theories of decision that exist at present.

Because the concept of probability plays such a key role both in the theory and practice of Statistical Decision, I want to pause at this point and tell you a little about the history and nature of probability.

History of Probability

It was realized even in the earlier civilizations that uncertainty, chance, or a degree of chaos is a characteristic feature of the real world, or at least of human knowledge about the real world. Not only did humans learn to survive in an uncertain world but, curiously enough, they found it entertaining to introduce deliberately additional uncertainty in the form of gambling games.

Some of the cleverer individuals, in the idle segment of the population which engaged in dice or cards, found that a little research into the nature of uncertainty offered the prospect of considerable profit. This research was favored by the fact that the instrument producing the uncertainty, say a pair of dice, was a fairly simple one and furthermore it was easy to do experimentation.

The theory of probability was born about 1654 in these frivolous surroundings when a French nobleman and gambler asked a mathematician, Pascal, for advice on the proper odds in a dice game.

For some fifty years mathematicians amused themselves, and possibly the gamblers, by working out "fair" odds in various games of chance. By 1713, some mathematicians, such as James Bernoulli, had become convinced that the theory of probability was capable of providing advice on more important subjects than dice or card games and that the concepts could be useful in a much wider field of human affairs.

One such application was to the problems of life insurance and annuities. In 1662, Captain Graunt constructed a life table from the London death registers. By 1693, Halley (after whom the comet was named) had constructed a table and used it in the calculation of annuities. Out of these researches the subject of actuarial science developed. For more than a century actuarial studies represented the main, and perhaps the only, fruitful application of probability theory to human affairs.

In the eighteenth century most of the great mathematicians toyed with various aspects of the theory of probability. But while the theory became very fancy, little practical use was made of it. Nevertheless the conviction grew that the theory could be very useful in business and everyday life. Laplace, writing in 1814, was so enthusiastic that he produced a glowing essay for popular consumption.

Apart from the work of Gauss, which was useful in astronomy and surveying, there was little that occurred in the nineteenth century to justify the high hopes that probability theory would be useful in everyday affairs. It was not until K. Pearson and R. A. Fisher, working mainly in the present century, that the applications of the concept of probability to real life situations exerted a major influence on science and even on agriculture and commerce. The stimulus for these developments came largely from the biological sciences.

Why did it take three hundred years for the concept to develop? This is not an easy question to answer, but at least part of the answer lies in a curious attitude that has prevailed (especially among mathematicians). The theory of probability was growing in an era that acknowledged the triumph of Reason. Reason, and Reason alone, could solve all human problems with little more than a passing reference to the real world.

At the theoretical level, it was true that an elaborate mathematical superstructure could be created entirely in terms of abstract symbols. However, when it came to applications and it was necessary to replace the abstract symbols by numbers, these numbers could only be found by going into the real world and collecting data (such as death certificates).

This process brought the mathematicians into bruising contact with the real world. Their enthusiasm quickly faded when faced with a tedious and prosaic job of gathering data. Many of the people who possessed the necessary theoretical background threw up their hands and retired to their ivory towers. Here they focused their attention on problems, mathematically interesting but without practical meaning, which did nothing to advance the subject.

The moral of this history of probability (and this same sad story holds for many other subjects) is that academic sterility is an ever-present danger. It can only be avoided by maintaining close contact with the real world—unpleasant as this contact may be at times.

Interpretation of Probability

When we turn to the interpretation of these numerical quantities that are called probabilities it is necessary to be especially wary of Academitis (a disease characterized by hairsplitting and, eventually, rigor mortis). There are at least four major

schools of thought on the subject and each of these schools is
subdivided into branches. The literature of the subject gives
the impression that there are great differences of opinion concerning probabilities, but this is not really the case.

Nearly everyone agrees on (1) the actual numerical value of
the probabilities in the simpler problems, (2) the rules for
manipulating probabilities, and (3) the broad principles for
acting in the face of specific probabilities. In short, there is a
remarkable unanimity of opinion with respect to practical applications of the concept of probability. The area of disagreement is mainly one of outlook and philosophy.

While some of the arguments markedly resemble the question
"How many angels can dance on the head of a pin?"—a popular
topic in medieval academic circles—there are other points
which have been raised that have practical importance. These
questions, although philosophical in character, have a direct
bearing on the problem of decision.

To pin matters down, let us consider a simple instance in
which nearly all the experts can agree that the probability has
a specific numerical value and further that this value is ½.
Let us say that you and I have agreed to flip a coin to see who
pays for the cokes. If the coin comes up heads I will pay, and
if it comes up tails you will do the honors. We have examined
the coin carefully and have found it to be a newly minted and
balanced nickel. We are also agreed on the rules of the game,
that the coin must spin repeatedly in midair on the toss, and
that such eventualities as landing on edge, etc. will not be
counted. What is the probability that heads will appear?

Nearly all of the experts would agree on the value ½. However, if we asked why they chose this particular value, we would
immediately start a hot argument. This would demonstrate
that the probability is associated both with the event (as specified above) and with the Probability Predicting System (i.e.,
the expert).

Various attempts have been made to tie the interpretation
of the probability either to the event or to the Predicting Sys-

tem and to disregard the other association. The objective school concentrates on the event, while the personal school concentrates on the Predicting System (mainly regarded as the predictions of a hypothetical person).

From the objective point of view the probability $\frac{1}{2}$ comes about as follows: Imagine that a very large number of tosses is made with the nickel and that a count is kept of the proportion of heads. Then presumably, after a sufficiently long time, we would discover that the proportion of heads is very nearly equal to $\frac{1}{2}$. Thus this probability refers to what would happen in a hypothetical experiment which consisted of tossing the coin a large number of times. Specifically the number $\frac{1}{2}$ is the *relative frequency* with which heads would appear in this hypothetical series.

If the question arose as to whether this number $\frac{1}{2}$ was appropriate, it could be answered by performing an actual experiment which would correspond to the *hypothetical* experiment. Thus if the empirical frequency of heads was quite different from $\frac{1}{2}$, it would indicate that the original choice was not appropriate.

This viewpoint is, I think, rather easy to follow and it is justifiably a popular one. It does involve difficulties, however, when an attempt is made to apply it to practical problems. Most practical situations, unlike the coin flip, are not easily *repeatable*. Even if an attempt were made to carry out an actual experiment along the lines of the hypothetical one, it would not be possible to do so. Thus if the probability is used in reference to the yield on a corn field, any *actual* repetition of the experiment would have to take place under different weather conditions and so on. Hence as soon as one leaves gambling game situations it is difficult to *verify* whether a numerical probability is appropriate or not.

Difficulties in the interpretation of probabilities when the events are not repeatable have led some to take the personal point of view. From this standpoint the number $\frac{1}{2}$ is a measure of the individual's confidence or degree of belief in the outcome heads. The number, therefore, might be expected to be different depending on how the individual analyzed the situation (i.e., depending on the PPS that was used). However, some holders of the personal point of view do not regard this multiplicity of numbers as satisfactory and take the position that only one probability predicting system can be right and the probability is the number produced by *this* system.

In the coin example, it would be argued, the coin has two sides and they are equally likely to occur. Hence the probability of heads must be equal to the probability of tails. Now one of these two events *must* occur, so the probability of heads plus the probability of tails must add up to one. Consequently the only number that can be assigned for the probability is the number $\frac{1}{2}$.

If it is asked, "Why should the two sides be regarded as equally likely?" the reply would be, "Since we have no reason to think that one or the other side is more likely, the two sides should be considered equally likely." This justification has been given the title *the principle of insufficient reason.*

I regard this principle as rather silly. If any of the proponents of this principle took the trouble to try it out in practice, say as a guide to betting on horse races, they would either give up the principle or lose all their money!

However, rather than detail wherein both the objective and personal viewpoints break down, I want to go on to give a sort of synthesis of these ideas that has emerged in modern statistics. From the objective view we shall borrow the concept of probability as a relative frequency and from the personal view we will borrow the notion that probabilities depend on the Probability Predicting System.

Let us begin by regarding the probability simply as a number produced by a PPS, in line with the personal point of view. Now consider once again the question, "Is the number $\frac{1}{2}$ appropriate for the problem of tossing a coin?" Suppose we answer: "The number $\frac{1}{2}$ comes from a PPS. Therefore whether it is or is not appropriate depends on whether the PPS is a good one or not." This gets us into various complexities (i.e., we must go ahead and specify what we mean by a "good" PPS). But the problems that are encountered, while difficult, are not hopeless. Accepting the pragmatic principle, we must consider a PPS good if it works; that is, if the probabilities generated by the system lead to desirable consequences when used to make decisions.

While the ultimate judgment will depend on these consequences, we can try to set up for a PPS standards which are more directly applicable. When we do it is with the understanding that a system which meets these auxiliary standards is not, *ipso facto*, a "good" system. However, if these standards are met there is a better chance that the system *will* work in practice.

One widely accepted auxiliary standard is "validity." Suppose the PPS (that leads to the probability ½ in the coin toss case) has been used in the past. In previous instances it has assigned to a number of events the probability ½, and the outcomes of *these* events are known. Then if the *relative frequency* of occurrence of these past events (as calculated from our records) is nearly ½ the PPS would be called valid. It would then be plausible to feel that the PPS will continue to be valid in the future.

More generally, if we were to consider cases in which the PPS gave some other numerical value of the probability, which I will represent symbolically by p, then if the system is valid it should be true that

(3.01)

$$p = \frac{\text{Number of cases in which event occurred}}{\text{Total number of cases where the probability assigned was } p}.$$

Notice that the validity of the system can be checked even though the events involved are *not* repeatable. For example, one event might be a scientific experiment, another might be a horse race, and a third might be a stock market forecast. If the same PPS were used in all cases and if, in all cases, the probability assigned were $\frac{1}{2}$, then (with a long enough series) the validity of the PPS could be studied despite the fact that none of the events predicted was repeatable.

The interpretation of the probability in terms of the predicting system is now fairly easy. If I obtained the probability $\frac{1}{2}$ from a PPS which I have reason to believe is a "good" one, or more specifically is a "valid" one, it means that the event "tossing heads" belongs in the class of events which actually occurs about half the time.

This interpretation leads more or less directly to advice on action. It indicates that it would be foolish of me to toss coins with you if I had to pay you two dollars when tails appeared, while you had to pay me only one dollar when heads appeared. For if we agreed to play ten times, I could expect to win five times and collect five dollars, but you would be expected to win five times and receive ten dollars. I could expect to lose five dollars in the game, so it would be bad business for me to take you on.

Sharpness

While validity is a desirable property of a probability predicting system, the fact that a system has this property does not automatically insure that it will be a useful system in practice. A second important auxiliary requirement of a PPS is that it be "sharp."

A system will be called "sharp" if it exercises discrimination and does not put events in the same numerical category if it is worthwhile to classify them further. Suppose, for example, that we want to bet on a series of horse races and, for the sake of simplicity, there happen to be six entries in each of the races. When we visit the track we look at the horses in each race and, since we know very little about horse flesh, they all look pretty much the same to us. We therefore can see no particular reason for preferring one horse to another. If we apply the principle of insufficient reason we conclude that each of the entries is equally likely to win. Consequently we assign to each horse the probability ⅙.

This is a very naive system, for it is well known to devotees of the sport of kings that every horse does *not* have the same chance to win. Nevertheless, the system is completely *valid*.

To see this, notice that *some* horse must win each race. So the numerator in equation *(3.01)* (the number of cases where the event occurs) is simply the number of races in which we use the system. The denominator, the total number of cases, will be the number of races multiplied by six (the number of horses in each race). The number of races appears both in the numerator and denominator and therefore cancels. Consequently we are left with the fraction ⅙ which is exactly the assigned probability.

However, any individual who chose to risk his money on the basis of this completely *valid* system based on the principle of insufficient reason would lose his shirt in very little time. He would lose to a PPS which, while perhaps not completely valid, was a good deal sharper.

This competitive PPS would discriminate more closely between the events (i.e., horses). It would not lump the horses into a single class but would separate the better horses from the poorer horses and assign larger probabilities to the better horses and smaller probabilities to the poorer horses. Since the methods of doing this are complicated, let me go back to a dice game example where the nature of this discriminatory process is easier to see.

In the game two dice are rolled and the spots which appear on the top faces are added together to obtain the "point." Eleven points are possible since any number of spots between two and twelve may occur. The game is played according to rules which are designed to prevent control of the dice.

Now a very innocent person might think that the eleven possible outcomes are equally likely: in other words, that the probability associated with each point is 1/11. This system is also completely *valid,* but it is a very impractical one to try in actual play. In order to develop a sharper PPS the various outcomes must be separated into more and less likely categories. The standard system for assigning probabilities in this game gives the following table:

Standard Table of Probabilities in Dice Game

POINT (*Outcome*)	PROBABILITY	POINT (*Outcome*)
2	1/36	12
3	2/36	11
4	3/36	10
5	4/36	9
6	5/36	8
7	6/36	7

Thus instead of lumping all of the outcomes into a single class with probability $\frac{1}{11}$, this system distinguishes six different classes. The standard table has been found to be the sharpest system that can be constructed. It would presumably be *possible* to have eleven different classes, instead of only six, but it has been found that this further discrimination accomplishes no practical purpose.

From the above table it is possible to devise a large number of valid systems which will be intermediate in sharpness between the "equally likely" case and the "tabular" case. For example, the outcomes 2, 3, 4, 10, 11, and 12 could be put into a single class with probability $\frac{2}{36}$ for *each* outcome in the class.

This explains how different predicting systems, even if they are valid ones, may assign different probabilities to the same outcome or event. It may also serve to clarify a point that I made earlier that the probability should be interpreted in terms of the PPS rather than in terms of the event.

Now the tabular probabilities are sharper than the equally likely ones. How is this an advantage? Why will the sharper system be more practical?

Part of the answer lies in the fact that, in general, it is easier to take action when the probabilities are close to zero or one, that is, when the event is "sure" to occur (or the event will "surely" not occur). It will be noted that the probability of getting the point two (snake-eyes) has gone from $\frac{3}{33} = \frac{1}{11}$ in the equally likely PPS to only $\frac{1}{36}$ in the sharper PPS. If we have a choice of one point on which to bet (the payoff being the same for all points), we would obviously be foolish to select either two or twelve.

A more complete answer involves the idea of *competition* between systems. Consider what would happen if Mr. A (who believes in the equally likely system) were to agree to play against Mr. B (who is aware of the tabular system). Mr. B proposes the following game: Each player will wager one dollar. Mr. A will win if 2, 3, 4, 10, 11, or 12 comes up. Mr. B will win on the other five numbers.

Using the equally likely system, Mr. A figures his chances as follows: Of the eleven possible cases he will win in six and his adversary in only five. In a hundred and ten plays he can therefore expect to win $60.00, lose $50.00, and come out with a modest but worthwhile profit of $10.00. Consequently Mr. A's decision, based on the equally likely system, is to accept this foolish offer on the part of Mr. B.

On the other hand, Mr. B, who is the sharper, calculates his chances by adding up the probabilities which appear in the table for the cases 5, 6, 7, 8, and 9. This gives:

$$\frac{4 + 5 + 6 + 5 + 4}{36} = \frac{24}{36} = \frac{2}{3}.$$

In a hundred and eleven plays he therefore would expect to win $74.00 and to lose only $37.00 which would mean a tidy profit of $37.00. This looks to Mr. B like an excellent business proposition.

If Mr. A is foolish enough to gamble, he will learn (unless he is remarkably lucky or stupid) that it is not enough for a PPS to be valid, that for a PPS to be practical it must also be sharp.

This example illustrates how a PPS can be made the basis for decisions in a fairly common situation which might be called *competitive decision*. Rivalry of PPS's occurs in many everyday affairs and particularly in horse racing, football pools, the stock market, and business decisions.

The people who bet on races are using predicting systems of various kinds. Some are *form* bettors and base their decisions on the records of time trials and previous races. Others bet on the jockey, while still others play hunches or dreams. These different predicting systems lead to different opinions concerning the outcome of each race. Those bettors with enough confidence and cash may pit their systems against a sort of *consensus* system represented by the parimutuel machines.

In actual track wagering it is not enough for the individual's PPS to be merely better than the concensus, because the track and state take out a sizeable cut for operating expenses, profits, and taxes. Consequently in order to win consistently, the individual's PPS must be much better than the parimutuel PPS. This does not seem to happen very often; "horse-players die broke."

It is not very easy to give a clear-cut definition of sharpness in complex situations like horse racing. Perhaps the closest that we can come to a mathematical formulation is one similar to the quantity *information* in the technical sense defined by Shannon [1] in the promising new work on information theory.

This theory is a bit too difficult to describe briefly and I will only add that with the aid of the mathematical yardstick, "information," it is possible to make quantitative comparisons between PPS's insofar as sharpness is concerned.

Let me remind you that even if a system is *both* valid and sharp it still may not be useful in a given situation. However, these criteria are useful in rejecting PPS's since, if a PPS is neither valid *nor* sharp, it is very unlikely that it will have any practical value.

[1] Shannon, C., *Mathematical Theory of Communication*, University of Illinois, Urbana, 1949.

Summary

Although several techniques have demonstrated utility for practical prediction, no methods are known which provide completely accurate forecasting. However, progress can be made by facing up to the problem of uncertainty, by attempting to measure the degree of uncertainty in a quantitative fashion. The theory of probability provides a method of measuring uncertainty. Application of this theory leads to predicting systems which associate a probability with each possible outcome, and this probability can be used to make decisions. Two desirable characteristics of such a probability predicting system are validity and sharpness. A PPS which is deficient in these respects may lead to decisions that have unfortunate consequences.

CHAPTER 4

/ PROBABILITY

The Direct System

Although the last chapter pointed up the need for a probability predicting system and went on to discuss the desirable characteristics that we would want such a system to have, it did not go into the practical question: How do you construct such a PPS? While it is not going to be possible in this book to give a thorough answer to this question (in fact, human knowledge has not reached a stage where such an answer could be given) it will be possible to have a look at some of the simpler systems.

Any one of the prediction techniques used in science utilizes the past as the guide to the future. All of us are in the habit of dealing with impending situations by searching through the past for similar situations and then using these to make our decision. By and large this is our most useful habit and most prediction systems are essentially *codifications* of this habit.

As I look out of my window the sky is heavily overcast. The question in my mind is: "Will it rain in the next hour?" Let me call the present situation X and the outcome Y. Then what I do is search my memory for past situations which resemble X and try to recall whether or not it rained in those cases. Now my memory is rather unreliable, so that I might try to extend this collection of past experience. I could ask my friends, or a meteorologist if one were handy, or perhaps see what was available on the subject in the stored experience of books or periodicals.

In this way I could try to gather together information about a large number of past situations that resembled X and also the past outcomes. Suppose only two outcomes are possible: *Y*, it will rain in the next hour, and *Y'*, it will not rain in the next hour. Then if I have quite a large number of past situations which I feel resemble *X* it is likely that I will encounter conflicting precedents—both outcomes may have occurred. Clearly I must find some method of resolving this conflict. One plausible way to do this would be to count the cases in which the outcome was "rain within the hour" and divide this number by the total number of cases in my experience. This calculation would give the proportion of cases in which the eventual outcome was rain.

If I now called this proportion the probability of rain I would have a probability predicting system! This method I will call the Direct System. Despite its simplicity, it is the basis for all other systems and is, in this simple form, of great practical importance.

Let me therefore list the steps involved in using the Direct System:

(1) Collect a series of situations which are similar to the situation to be predicted. Each situation in the series will be called a *case*.

(2) List the outcomes which have occurred for each case.

(3) Count the number of occurrences of each type of outcome and also the number of cases.

(4) Calculate the probabilities by the rule:

$$\text{Probability of outcome} = \frac{\text{Number of occurrences of outcome}}{\text{Total number of cases}}.$$

The information that goes into the Direct System is not always obtained by searching past records. It is characteristic of science that instead of searching the past, an experiment may be set up to obtain the information. It is not very feasible to set up such an experiment in the case of weather, but suppose instead that I wanted to predict what would happen tomorrow if I use a particular nickel in flipping for cokes.

It is now possible, and indeed quite easy, for me to run an

experiment today in which I flip this coin, say, 100 times. When I perform the experiment I find that heads appears 56 times.

Then, applying the Direct System:

$$\text{Probability of heads} = \frac{\text{Number of occurrences of heads}}{\text{Total number of flips}}$$
$$= \frac{56}{100} = 0.56.$$

In exactly the same way I would find the probability of tails is $44/100 = 0.44$. The probability of heads plus the probability of tails adds up to 1.00 as must always happen regardless of the particular experimental results since

Number of flips = Number of heads + Number of tails.

If both sides of this equation are divided by the number of flips then the left-hand side of the equation is equal to one and the right-hand side of the equation is equal to the sum of two quantities, one of which is the probability of heads and the other the probability of tails. This same reasoning extends to the case in which there are more than two outcomes possible providing that one and only one outcome can occur in a given case.

The probability of heads which I have obtained by the coin-tossing experiment is not equal to $\frac{1}{2}$, the number that was previously mentioned as the probability of heads. This fact is a further demonstration that the probability depends on the **PPS** used and in particular on the body of data utilized by the **PPS**. If instead of 100 tosses, I had made 1000 flips, then a still different value would be obtained. Broadly speaking, the larger the experience, the more reliable are the values obtained by the Direct System. Since there is a voluminous literature of coin-tossing experiments (some of which involved hundreds of thousands of tosses), there is a great deal of experience with the subject. The probability of heads as calculated by the Direct System using this vast experience is practically $\frac{1}{2}$.

This raises the questions: Is all this past experience on other coins in other lands and years really applicable at all? Do these previous experiments provide situations that are really similar to the situation that I am trying to predict? These questions expose a very serious difficulty that arises in the practical application of the Direct System. It is often very hard to decide whether a past situation is close enough to the situation X so that it should be included in the calculations.

Repeatability

The coin-flipping situation is an example of what I have previously called a gambling game problem. Although such exercises are very popular because of their simplicity, it must be understood that they represent a very special problem of rather limited utility in practical applications.

The distinguishing characteristic of such situations as flipping a coin is that the events are repeatable. This concept of repeatable events is of great importance in many of the mathematical theories that deal with probability so a closer examination of it is worth while.

I have not been very specific about the situation to be predicted which I have called flipping a coin. If I wanted to go into detail in describing this situation, I would have to say (1) what person was doing the tossing, (2) what coin was being used in the toss, (3) when and where the flip was to be performed, and so on. If the event to be forecast were described in this much detail, the question arises: Are the coin flips in the preliminary experiment actually similar to the one to be predicted?

Even if the same person and coin were involved in the preliminary experiment and in the event to be predicted, the experiment may very well be performed at a different place and necessarily at a different time. Atmospheric conditions, humidity, magnetic fields, the position of the moon, and many other conditions will be different during the experiment from what they will be in the situation to be predicted.

An impatient reader will feel that these remarks are irrelevant, that the moon does not affect the flipping of the coin, and I will agree at once. Experience has shown that one flip of a nickel resembles another and hence that the cases in the coin-tossing experiment are similar to the situation to be predicted.

What I want to emphasize is that this characteristic is more or less peculiar to gambling game problems. The fact that the coin flips are indistinguishable is the basis for the name repeatable events.

In other words, the experiment on coin flipping has been performed by different people with different coins in different places and even in different centuries, but the results are such that in almost all of the various experiments the application of the Direct System leads to probabilities close to $\frac{1}{2}$ or 0.5. Still another way of saying this same thing is to say: The probabilities associated with coin flipping are *stable*. This stability is partly due to the fact that the rules of the game are set up to try to insure it.

Since the gambling game situations have been extensively studied for over three hundred years, a great deal has been learned about the performance of the Direct System. On the whole the Direct System is a good one. It has been found that it becomes progressively better as the size of the experiment is increased.

This statement requires some qualifications. If a large number of individuals perform the experiment of flipping a nickel a hundred times and then each individual applies the Direct System to obtain a probability of heads, the numbers obtained will not all be the same. If these numbers are examined, it will be found that they tend to be closer to $\frac{1}{2}$ than to either 0 or 1.

If these numbers are plotted on a graph, the points will be clustered about $\frac{1}{2}$, but some of the points will be wide of the mark.

If a 1000-flip experiment were used instead of a 100-flip one, and if the probabilities were obtained by the Direct System, the corresponding graph would also show a clustering around

½ and some scatter. The difference would be that in the larger experiment, there would be less scatter and the points would be more closely grouped about the central value.

Occasionally a 1000-flip experiment will lead to a probability that will be further from the mark than a 100-flip experiment but the opposite will be true much more often. On the whole, the larger experiment will lead to more nearly valid probabilities.

Sharpness was the second characteristic of a predicting system that was discussed in the previous chapter. In the case of coins and other gambling game problems, the Direct System is sharp. The repeatability of the events implies the futility of further discrimination between outcomes.

Baseball

Let us turn now to a situation which will resemble more closely the sort of problem that will be encountered in practical predictions. Let the X situation be: The New York Yankees will play a baseball game with the Boston Red Sox at Fenway Park.

More than two outcomes are possible since the game may result in a tie or it may be rained out; however, for simplicity let the outcomes be limited to Y, the Yankees win, and Y', the Red Sox win. (Baseball partisans may substitute other teams in this example if the two teams chosen here stir up unpleasant emotional reactions.)

The first thing that must be done is to collect a series of situations which are similar to the situation to be predicted. But this poses a problem—what situations, if any, are similar to the one to be predicted.

One possibility would be to consider all games played between these two teams so far this season. The Direct System would then give

$$\text{Probability of Yanks winning} = \frac{\text{Games won against Red Sox}}{\text{Games played against Red Sox}}.$$

It may be noted that quantities such as the above are widely used in reporting baseball results. They are generally called *percentages* rather than probabilities.

Baseball fans would be likely to object to the above method on the grounds that home games differ from road games. In other words, all of the games played between the two teams should not be regarded as similar; the games played in Yankee Stadium should be omitted from the series and only those played in Fenway Park should be used.

Still other baseball fans would want to know who were the starting pitchers and what other players were on the starting lineup. It might also be objected that, if this were a late season game, the results of the games played at the start of the season should not be included because the Red Sox have a reputation for improving over the season.

Note that if these objections are considered in judging what is a situation similar to situation X, the effect is to whittle away at the original series, to throw out cases which could be used to obtain the probabilities by the Direct System. First, those games played at Yankee Stadium would have to be omitted, then early season games would have to be dropped, and, in fact, if all of the objections are to be met, the series would get shorter and shorter until eventually it would disappear altogether! No games previously played could be regarded as similar to the one to be predicted.

Research workers who have gone to great lengths to collect data frequently encounter this shrinkage of experience. A doctor may begin with a series of three hundred cases but after eliminating cases for one reason or another, he may find he is left with only fifty cases on which to base his article.

Now as the series gets longer the *validity* of the predicting system improves; similarly as the series gets shorter and shorter, the validity deteriorates. If the definition of a similar situation is made too strict so that only a few cases can be found, the use of the Direct System will lead to unreliable probabilities.

On the other hand, if the definition of a similar situation is made too loose the series may be longer, the validity may be improved, but there will be a corresponding loss of sharpness. Thus if a Direct System using all the games between the two teams is in competition with a Direct System using only those games at Fenway Park, the latter may very well come out ahead even though its validity is not so good.

This problem of validity versus sharpness is one of the major headaches in setting up a predicting system based on the Direct System.

The same problem is encountered in most applications of probability which lie outside the province of gambling games —for example, in calculation of the risks in insurance. An applicant for insurance may be a fifty-two-year-old man. Elaborate life tables by age and sex are available, but should these be used? Suppose that this applicant is a butcher. Presumably the probabilities should be calculated from experience with fifty-two-year-old butchers. Insurance companies have actually constructed tables for different occupations. It may also be known that this applicant lives in Massachusetts, and there is evidently no limit to the further details that might be added. Each additional condition will reduce the number of cases that can be used to determine the probabilities by the Direct System. At some point a line must be drawn.

The place to draw this line is where the advantage of increasing the sharpness is offset by the decreasing validity, but the actual determination of this point is no easy matter. A partial answer is discussed later under the heading Relevance.

Another method of getting around this limitation of the Direct System is to devise more involved probability predicting systems.

I want to emphasize one point very strongly. The distinction between the baseball problem and the coin situation is one of degree rather than *kind*. In the real world, there is no such thing as a completely *repeatable* event. Any real coin is subject to wear and hence successive flips are not similar in an absolute sense. Gambling games do represent the nearest thing that we have to repeatable events. Some experiments in physics which are rigidly controlled are also very nearly repeatable events. The repeatability is considerably less in the biological sciences and still less in the social sciences. There has been much argument as to whether or not the complex situations encountered in the study of history can be regarded as repeatable even in a loose sense.

Most practical decisions involve prediction in situations in which the problem of what constitutes a similar situation is at least as difficult as in the baseball example.

To summarize:

(1) The Direct System may be applied very easily to repeatable events.

(2) In this case the longer the series, the greater the validity of the Direct System.

(3) The Direct System is sharp insofar as repeatable events are concerned.

(4) When the events are not repeatable, the Direct System begins to run into difficulties, and its use necessitates that a balance be struck between validity and sharpness.

(5) To deal with nonrepeatability more elaborate predicting systems may be needed.

The Randomization System

Much of the discussion of probability in the older textbooks on the subject concerns games of chance: coin flipping, dice throwing, and card playing. In such games a device or mechanism is deliberately introduced to provide a random or chance factor. The use of such a device is called *randomization,* and this process has many practical applications outside of the province of gambling. When this process is used, it is possible to construct probability predicting systems by what I will call the Randomization System.

The basic principle of the Randomization System is to construct a set of possible outcomes, all of which have the *same* probability. A balanced die, for example, has six faces and the corresponding six outcomes have the same probability. Suppose that I win if a 5 or 6 appears and lose if a 1, 2, 3, or 4 appears. The probability of an event, such as winning, is calculated by:

Probability of event
$$= \frac{\text{Number of possible outcomes where the event occurs}}{\text{Total number of possible outcomes}}.$$

To calculate my chances of winning on a cast of the die I note that there are six possible outcomes and that I will win if either of two of these outcomes should occur. Hence

$$\text{Probability of winning} = 2/6 = 1/3.$$

Notice that it was not necessary to collect data or to perform an experiment to arrive at this number; it was only necessary to know how a die is constructed. To apply this Randomization System to the coin-toss problem we need only know that the coin has two faces, one of them heads, and we arrive at the result that the probability of heads is $\frac{1}{2}$.

At first sight this looks like a much quicker and easier way to set up a PPS than the Direct System. A closer look, however, shows that the Randomization System implements rather than supplants the Direct System. If we want to apply our Randomization System to the real world, then its success or failure will depend on the particular randomization device that is used in the real world. We can take great care in the manufacture of this device (such as a coin), but when we want to test the device and see if the probabilities are, in fact, equal, then we are back to the Direct System. After a randomization device is thoroughly tested we may confidently use the Randomization System, and its use may be very successful. Sometimes the user may forget the part played by the Direct System.

Mathematicians seem to be especially prone to amnesia of this type; in fact, they may even forget that a randomization device is involved. This leads to the unhappy use of the Randomization System as the *definition* of probability, a usage which was nearly universal in textbooks on probability until the past decade. The definition of probability in terms of equally probable outcomes is patently circular, but in spite of this (or, perhaps, because of this) this definition was popular with mathematics teachers.

The Randomization System is used in practical problems, such as sampling, with considerable success. This success, say in the calculation of the odds quoted by gambling houses, has been regarded by some innocents as a verification of the principle of insufficient reason. Actually, of course, there is a very good and sufficient reason for the equal probability of the outcomes on the roulette wheel in a legitimate casino; if the owner does not keep his equipment in balance then smart customers can "break the bank."

A very great effort is devoted by legal gambling establishments, such as those in Nevada, to insure that the real world roulette wheel comes very close to an ideal randomizing device. The wheels are continually tested and adjusted. The equal probabilities do not come from *ignorance* but from the use of the Direct System to insure that the randomization device leads to equally probable outcomes.

I might add—and this will be news only to the *very* innocent —that illegitimate gambling houses sometimes have an equally good and sufficient reason to rig their equipment and, in such cases, the numbers on a roulette wheel and the faces of a die are *not* equally probable.

Advanced Systems

Over the centuries a tremendous amount of experience has been accumulated, organized, and analyzed. Frequently it is possible to boil this experience down into a few general rules— a process at which the scientists have become expert. Hence, in facing problems of prediction, we are not operating in a vacuum. There are many things that we may know which might assist us in making predictions. For example, we have the laws of physics and chemistry which we can use in an engineering situation. This body of information can appropriately be called *advanced knowledge.*

It would be wasteful not to take advantage of advanced knowledge when it applies to our prediction problems. It may enable us to avoid much of the experimentation or historical research which would be needed to apply the Direct System.

The more advanced systems for prediction are technically complex and require the construction of a mathematical model. I will therefore not attempt to describe these systems in this chapter, but will postpone the discussion until the chapter on measurement.

Symbolic Language

One of the major advantages of numbers over words is that numbers are much easier to manipulate. Contributing to this advantage is the fact that the *rules* for manipulation can be given precisely and completely. Consequently it is not only easier to perform the manipulation but also to check the procedure.

The rules for manipulating probabilities can be reduced to a few simple axioms, and more elaborate rules for more complex problems may then be derived from this original set of rules. This method of stating rules avoids the danger of conflicting instructions. I shall present these axioms without justification other than the remark that they have worked very well for many years. It is rather curious that although there are many different viewpoints on the topic of probability, all of the approaches that I have seen eventually lead to this same set of rules. The justifications differ, and experts differ on whether the justifications are valid, but the end result is the same three axioms.

Since there are only three rules, and since these rules are fundamental to an understanding of probability, I hope that the reader will forgive me if the discussion becomes a little technical at this point. I think it will be worth your while, if you are new to this subject, to reread this section several times so as to master the ideas introduced here.

Before I introduce the rules themselves it is necessary to set up a shorthand method of expressing probabilities since verbal descriptions are very cumbersome. This shorthand is, of course, the symbolic language which I have frequently mentioned before. However, if you think of it simply as a shorthand device, a convenient abbreviation, it should occasion little difficulty.

One obvious thing to do is to abbreviate the word "probability" all the way down to the initial letter P. Now we will usually want to refer to the probability *of* some event so we need a replacement for the word "of." Suppose that the event itself is Y; then we can use a parenthesis to symbolize the word "of" and write $P(Y)$ for "the probability of Y." This device is regularly used in mathematics.

We have already seen that the probability of an event depends on the event and also on the predicting system, and we need to bring this concept into our notation. I have used the term predicting system to cover the entire process of determining a numerical probability, that is, it includes the details of the situation to be predicted, the method of prediction, and the data used in prediction. Let me now draft the symbol X to stand for the whole kit and kaboodle involved in the prediction system.

The information represented by X is *given* in advance, and hence, when I refer to the probability of Y, it is understood that this is the probability of Y *if* this information X is given. I have already introduced a vertical line to represent the word "if" when I used $Y \mid A_1$ to represent the outcome Y *if* action one is taken. In the same way I can write $P(Y \mid X)$ to represent the probability of Y if the prediction system X is used to obtain the numerical value. Notice that $P(Y \mid X)$ represents some numerical quantity. If X is fully specified then the probability of Y, according to this PPS, can be calculated numerically. One word of caution: Do not confuse the vertical line which will be used for "if" with the slanted line which will sometimes be used to signify a ratio.

Strictly speaking we should always carry along this X in our notation, but quite often the PPS involved is specified in detail and it is common to omit the X when extensive symbolic manipulations are involved. In this event the X is understood to be in the formula, but is not actually written down because it does not ordinarily enter into the manipulations and hence is excess baggage in the formulas. Therefore when dropping the X will cause no confusion, I will omit this symbol from the notation and write $P(Y)$ instead of $P(Y \mid X)$.

I have emphasized this point because you will frequently find that the X is omitted in much of the technical work on probability. Even though it may be dropped for convenience, the X is still there in spirit; otherwise the symbol is meaningless because, as we have seen, the numerical value for the probability of Y depends on the predicting system. Neglect of this detail has led some experts astray.

Let us go on to consider three little words which are the key to the logical structure of our language. As soon as we want to talk about *combinations* of events these words must be pressed into service. These words are "and," "or," and "not."

Suppose that a penny and a nickel are flipped and that the outcomes are designated

Y Heads on the penny.
Y' Tails on the penny (or not-heads on the penny).
Z Heads on the nickel.
Z' Tails on the nickel.

If we want to talk about the outcome of this double toss we use the words "and," "or," and "not." For example, we would deal with such combinations as:

Both the penny and the nickel turned up heads	Y and Z.
One of the two coins (or both) showed tails	Y' or Z'.
The coins were not both heads	not $(Y$ and $Z)$.

We run into difficulties immediately with ambiguities in ordinary language. The word "or" has two meanings in English ("or" and "and/or"). In technical probability discussions the word "or" is used in the sense of "and/or" (see the example above). When the other meaning is intended a restatement is made. For example, to describe the outcome when one of the coins showed tails but *not* both coins we could say:

$$Y' \text{ or } Z' \text{ and not } (Y' \text{ and } Z').$$

Although this sort of thing may look like academic hair-splitting it is not trivial. It is very important to know just what combination of events we are talking about. In everyday language this is sometimes made clear by context or additional comment, but in symbolic language the ambiguity must be eliminated at the outset.

The notation used by statisticians is to employ a comma for the word "and." Thus Y,Z represents "Y and Z." This comes from standard mathematical notation. The logicians use a somewhat different symbolism which provides an analogy to ordinary arithmetic. I will use the words "and," "or," and "not" at first so as to avoid introducing extra notation. Later on I will use the comma notation for "and," but I will not need symbols for "or" and "not."

Rules for Manipulation

Now that we have our shorthand, we can go on to the three rules for manipulation. The first of these rules consists of three sub-rules which have the practical effect of specifying the *scale* which will be used for measuring uncertainty. It would be possible to set up a different scale; the use of odds represents such a scale. However, the word "probability" is used in its technical sense to refer to numerical quantities that are common or decimal fractions; i.e., to quantities between 0 and 1 such as $\frac{1}{2}$ or 0.5.

If the predicting system assigns a probability to an event that is very near to *one* then (if the PPS is a good one) we would act as if the event were going to occur. Although in practice we would not be able to make useful predictions that are going to materialize 100 per cent of the time, we can construct a trivial case in which we can predict that an event will occur, and we will always be right! Suppose that I am predicting the weather and I set up two predictions: "It will rain tomorrow" and "It will not rain tomorrow." Then I can safely predict: "It will rain tomorrow" *or* "it will not rain tomorrow." This prediction isn't of much practical use, but it can be used to set the *upper limit* of the scale:

(*4.01*)   **Rule Ia:** $P(Y \text{ or not-}Y \mid X) = 1.$

The probability of Y or not-Y is equal to 1.

In a similar manner there is a compound event that I can feel confident will *not* materialize, and it can be used to set the *lower limit* of the scale. If I predict: "It will rain tomorrow" *and* "It will not rain tomorrow," then no matter what happens *this* forecast will be "busted."

(*4.02*)   **Rule Ib:** $P(Y \text{ and not-}Y \mid X) = 0.$

The probability of Y and not-Y is equal to zero.

Finally we will want to insure that all the numerical probabilities will lie between these limits. It is enough, for this purpose, to specify that the probability is zero or positive; the rule that it cannot be greater than one can then be derived.

(*4.03*)   **Rule Ic:** $P(Y \mid X) \geq 0.$

The probability of Y is zero or greater than zero.

This first rule for manipulation, while useful in theoretical manipulations, is unimportant in practical work. But now we come to the two "bread-and-butter" rules of probability which are continually used by the statistician.

Let me take a simple decision situation involving two events. I look outside and notice that it is cloudy. Should I take my rubbers? I really don't mind getting my feet wet—the thing that bothers me is the possibility that I will catch a cold if I get my feet wet. Consequently I must deal with two events: Y, getting feet wet, and Z, catching cold. Assuming that I do not take my rubbers, how can I determine my chances of catching cold?

To answer this question I must consider the compound event,

Y and *Z,* getting my feet wet *and* catching cold. For simplicity let me assume that if it rains I will get my feet wet, but that this will not otherwise happen. Hence the probability that I will get my feet wet is the same as the probability that it will rain, and this probability might be determined by some predicting system *X.* This gives me some quantity $P(Y \mid X)$.

There is another probability that is of interest here—the probability that *if* I get my feet wet, I will catch a cold. This is a new kind of probability and is called a *conditional* probability because it depends on the "if." Presumably there is some predicting system that might enable me to obtain this conditional probability. Let this system be X'. I can write $P(Z \mid Y,X')$ to represent the probability that I will catch cold *if* I get my feet wet. Notice that the vertical line is used as before to stand for the word "if" and that it applies to both terms after it; i.e., *if* I get my feet wet, *and if* I use predicting system X'.

The compound probability, that I will get my feet wet *and* I will catch cold, would be written $P(Y \text{ and } Z \mid X,X')$. This notation clearly distinguishes between $P(Z \mid Y,X')$ and $P(Y \text{ and } Z \mid X,X')$ but unfortunately the English language is rather ambiguous here. The phrase "the probability that I get my feet wet and subsequently catch cold" might be used in either case.

This particular ambiguity is a very dangerous one and has led to serious mistakes on the part of research workers and, occasionally, experts.

The three probabilities, $P(Y \mid X)$, $P(Z \mid Y,X')$, and $P(Y \text{ and } Z \mid X,X')$, are directly related. Consequently, if we know any two of them we can calculate the third. This relation is the second rule for probabilities and is called the *multiplication rule:*

(4.04) **Rule II:** $P(Z \text{ and } Y \mid X,X') = P(Z \mid Y,X') P(Y \mid X)$.

It says that the probability of *Z and Y* is equal to the probability of *Z if Y* occurs *times* the probability of *Y.* An alternative notation which I will now use is to write $P(Z,Y)$ for $P(Z \text{ and } Y)$.

If we think in terms of the frequency interpretation of probability then this rule is nearly obvious.

$$P(Y) = \frac{\text{Number of cases where } Y \text{ occurs}}{\text{Total number of cases}}.$$

$$P(Z \mid Y) = \frac{\text{Number of cases where } Z \text{ occurs (Given } Y \text{ occurs)}}{\text{Number of cases where } Y \text{ occurs}}.$$

$$P(Z,Y) = \frac{\text{Number of cases where both } Z \text{ and } Y \text{ occur}}{\text{Total number of cases}}.$$

If these ratios are substituted in equation (4.04) then it will be noted that "the number of cases where Y occurs" appears in both the numerator and denominator of the right-hand side of equation (4.04) and therefore can be cancelled out. When this is done the right-hand side and the left-hand side of the equation are evidently the same.

In order to use equation (4.04) in the "catching cold" example let us suppose that $P(Y) = 0.5$ (there is a fifty-fifty chance that it will rain) and $P(Z \mid Y) = 0.2$ (there is one chance in five that I will catch cold if my feet get wet). Then by equation (4.04)

$$P(Z,Y) = P(Z \mid Y) P(Y) = (0.2)(0.5) = 0.10$$

so that there is one chance in ten that I will catch cold from the rain if I do not wear my rubbers.

The multiplication rule has a very important special case, the case of *independence*. The event Z is independent of the event Y if the conditional probability of Z (if the first event is known to have outcome Y) is just the same as the probability of Z when the outcome of the first event is not known. If I flip a penny and a nickel, and I learn the outcome of the penny this does not help me to predict the outcome of the nickel. In fact I feel that the flip of the penny has no effect at all on the flip of the nickel, and the two events are therefore independent.

In terms of the shorthand I have said that

$$(4.05) \qquad\qquad P(Z \mid Y,X') = P(Z \mid X')$$

and substituting this in equation (4.04) gives the multiplication rule for *independent* events.

(4.06) $P(Z,Y \mid X,X') = P(Z \mid X')P(Y \mid X).$

For the tossing of two coins the standard predicting system gives

$$P(Z \mid X') = 0.5 \qquad P(Y \mid X) = 0.5$$

so equation (4.06) tells us that

$$P(Z,Y) = P(Z)P(Y) = (0.5)(0.5) = 0.25$$

and there is one chance in four that both coins will come up heads.

It should be clearly understood that equation (4.06) may only be used if the events are independent. In the "catching cold" example we would not expect that $P(Z \mid Y,X') = P(Z \mid X')$, that is, I would feel that the chances of catching cold were greater if I get my feet wet. In some extreme cases $P(Z \mid Y,X')$ may be near to one although $P(Z \mid X')$ is near zero. The chance that a given person will die in the next minute will ordinarily be near zero, but if there is the additional information that the person has just jumped from the top of a sixteen-story building then the conditional probability would be nearly one.

An important use of conditional probabilities in a decision problem is the comparison of probabilities of events if different actions are taken. Thus I have assumed that if I do not wear rubbers the probability that it will rain is the same as the probability that I will get my feet wet. If I do wear rubbers then I will not get my feet wet.

P (I will get wet feet | it rains, I do not wear rubbers) $= 1.$
P (I will get wet feet | it rains, I do wear rubbers) $= 0.$

The probabilities of various outcomes may be markedly influenced by the action that is taken (in this case wearing rubbers). The alteration of these conditional probabilities is really the motive for taking action.

The multiplication rule deals with compound events in which the two events are joined by the word "and." The next rule, the *addition rule,* deals with compound events in which the two events are joined by the word "or" (used in the sense of "and/or"). I will omit the X's for simplicity. The addition rule is:

(4.07) **Rule III:** $P(Y \text{ or } Z) = P(Y) + P(Z) - P(Y,Z).$

The probability of Y *or* Z occurring is equal to the probability of Y plus the probability of Z minus the probability of Y *and Z.*

This rule can answer such questions as: If I cut a well-shuffled pack of cards, what is the probability that I cut an ace (Y) *or* a spade (Z)?

The standard prediction system gives us the probabilities on the right-hand side of equation (4.07). Since there are 4 aces in 52 cards the probability of an ace, $P(Y)$, is 4/52. Since there are 13 spades and 52 cards the probability of a spade, $P(Z)$, is 13/52.

The probability that the card will be an ace *and* a spade can be found from equation (4.06) since these are independent events (i.e., if we know the suit of a card this tells us nothing about whether it is an ace or not):

$$P(Y,Z) = P(Y) P(Z) = (4/52)(13/52) = 1/52.$$

Hence:

$$P(Y \text{ or } Z) = 4/52 + 13/52 - 1/52 = 16/52.$$

This same result may be found directly by counting the number of cards in the deck which are aces *or* spades. There are 13 spades and 4 aces but the ace of spades is counted in both categories; hence there are 16 cards which are aces *or* spades and therefore $P(Y \text{ or } Z) = 16/52$. This argument indicates why $P(Y,Z)$ is subtracted.

The addition rule also has an important special case. When $P(Y,Z) = 0$ then the events are called *mutually exclusive.* On one single roll of dice, for example, any two points are mutually exclusive (i.e., they cannot *both* occur). When

(4.08) $$P(Y,Z) = 0$$

then equation (4.07) simplifies the addition rule for mutually exclusive events:

(4.09) $$P(Y \text{ or } Z) = P(Y) + P(Z).$$

In Chapter 3 (page 51) Mr. B. calculated the chances of getting one of the points 5, 6, 7, 8, or 9 by adding up the probabilities in the standard table (page 50). In taking this step he was using equation (4.09).

There are many other rules for manipulating probabilities, but they can be derived from the three that I have given. In other words if the rules are regarded as axioms (like those in geometry), many other rules can be deduced (like geometrical theorems). There are a few qualifications that I would have to append to this statement for it to hold strictly, but I will not bother you with these technicalities.

Now that you have seen the three basic rules I think that you will agree with me that the symbolic structure of probability theory is, fundamentally, remarkably *simple*.

I would like to illustrate the derivation of other rules by an example of the process for the following useful rule:

$$P(\text{not-}Y) = 1 - P(Y).$$

First substitute not-Y for Z in Rule III to obtain

$$P(Y \text{ or not-}Y) = P(Y) + P(\text{not-}Y) - P(Y \text{ and not-}Y).$$

But by Rule Ia

$$P(Y \text{ or not-}Y) = 1$$

and by Rule Ib

$$P(Y \text{ and not-}Y) = 0$$

so that substituting back in our first formula we obtain

$$1 = P(Y) + P(\text{not-}Y) - 0$$

and rearranging this result gives the rule we wished to prove.

I have a great temptation at this point to rattle off a few more demonstrations, but I shall resist the urge. I would like to emphasize, however, that once you overcome unpleasant associations acquired in high school you will find that mathematics is a delightful game and also a very *easy* sport. At first it looks formidable because the rules are precisely stated in symbolic language—but it is this precise formulation that makes manipulation so simple. Mathematicians are simply highbrow [and sometimes very high-powered] solitaire players. It is much more difficult to be a good farmer than a good mathematician because the farmer must deal with so many vague and complex problems.

Probability Event Chains

In many practical applications prediction involves chains of events rather than single events. Often the probabilities at each link in the chain may be found by the Direct System. The rules for manipulation may then be used to find other probabilities associated with the chain.

An example of such an event chain is the decision to purchase a bunch of grapes after sampling one of the grapes of the bunch. Although this is an everyday method of reaching a decision, it contains the basic ideas that have been developed into the subjects of *inspection sampling* and *quality control*. Let us examine the logical process involved in this purchase of a bunch of grapes.

First of all, note that the bunch itself can be regarded as a sample of the grapes on the fruit stand. The chain of events starts with the selection of one particular bunch of grapes as a candidate for purchase. The next event in this chain is the selection of a grape from this bunch. This grape is tested by a "taste-test." If the grape is good, the bunch is purchased; otherwise the bunch is rejected.

The justification for this process is not a simple matter. Why should the fact that the grape is good cause us to conclude that the bunch from which it is taken will be good? Past experience plays a role in this logical process. Experience tells us that all the grapes on a bunch are more or less at the same stage of ripeness. The grapes on a single bunch have had more or less the same environment so that they may be expected to be similar. There is always the possibility that the grape chosen for the sample is unrepresentative, but it is acknowledged that purchasing always involves some risks. The sampling is designed to reduce rather than eliminate the risk.

If several bunches are sampled and all of the sampled grapes are sour, the purchase of grapes is likely to be postponed. Here past experience has also entered—it is known that a consignment of grapes tends to be fairly uniform.

The same general principles apply to the purchase of a consignment of machine parts. If the manufacturer has his processes in control nearly all of the parts will have the right dimensions. On the other hand, if the processes get out of control there will be a number of defective parts. Consequently, the quality of consignments tends to be relatively uniform *within* a consignment. On the other hand, there will be quality differences *between* consignments.

This phenomenon is a common one in the real world and has been given the name of the *principle of local homogeneity*. I emphasize this point because it is sometimes believed that the sampling process itself is the justification for inferences from samples. This is not the case; the inference also depends on past experience.

In order to clarify the principles involved in prediction from samples, I want to set up a card game which will have an interpretation in terms of purchasing decisions. The card model is used because the probabilities can be readily determined by the Randomization System, whereas in practical problems these probabilities would have to be determined from actual data.

In this game the cards in the deck have a definite order (as in the case of a new deck) and run in sequence from king down to ace. The king of clubs is the top card and the suits are in sequence clubs, diamonds, hearts, and spades, so that the bottom card is the ace of spades. If you have trouble visualizing all this, try it out with a deck of cards.

The deck may now be interpreted as a manufacturing process: the black cards represent good machine parts while the red cards will be considered to be defective parts. Thus during the sequence of clubs the process is in control and is turning out only good parts. After the ace of clubs, the process goes out of control (turns out only bad parts) through diamonds and hearts and then goes back into control for the sequence of spades. The deck of cards is a model of an extreme production process which produces all good for a while and then all bad.

The deck is now cut repeatedly. This does not change the *order* of the cards. The purpose of this repeated cutting of the deck is to insure that the color of the top card is unknown. A shipment of three cards is taken off the top of the deck and placed face down on the table. These three cards correspond to a shipment of parts or to the bunch of grapes.

These three cards are mixed up, and one sample card is picked at random. This card represents the sample of the shipment which is to be inspected. On the basis of this card a decision is to be made as to whether or not to accept the shipment.

The symbols introduced in the last section will now be interpreted in terms of this model:

X Initial knowledge about the deck and rules of the game.
Y Situation in the three-card shipment.
Z Situation in the one-card sample.

The specific outcomes will be indicated by a subscript on Y and Z. The subscript will be a number—the number of red cards (defectives) in the situation. Thus:

Z_0 No red card in the sample
Z_1 One red card in the sample

There are four possible outcomes in the shipment (going from no red cards to all red cards) so that in general we may use the symbol Y_k where k takes the values 0, 1, 2, and 3.

Y_0 No red card in shipment
Y_1 One red card in shipment
Y_2 Two red cards in shipment
Y_3 Three red cards in shipment

The card model is a two-link chain. The first link goes from the deck to the drawing of the shipment. The second link goes from the shipment to the drawing of the sample. Since the situation X is common to all of the probabilities, I will consider it as understood in the notation and will not write it down each time.

The probabilities in the first link, such as $P(Y_0)$ and $P(Y_1)$, are easily calculated. The repeated cuts on the deck render it equally likely that any card may be at the top of the deck when the shipment is drawn. If any club between the king and the three (and including the three) is the top card in the pack (after cutting) then all 3 cards in the shipment will be black. If any spade is cut this will also be true. Consequently there is a total of 11 plus 13 or 24 cases where the shipment will be black and Y_0 will occur. Similarly if the top card is any diamond or is a heart down to the three then the shipment will be all defective (red). There are 24 cases where Y_3 will occur. If the two of hearts or the ace of clubs is the top card then Y_2 will occur (2 cases). If the ace of hearts or the two of clubs is on top then there will be one red card in the shipment and Y_1 will occur (2 cases). Hence:

$$P(Y_0) = 24/52. \; P(Y_1) = 2/52. \; P(Y_2) = 2/52. \; P(Y_3) = 24/52.$$

The probabilities for the next link are also easy to calculate. For example, if Y_2 occurs then there are two red cards in the shipment. The probability that the sample is a red card *if Y_2* occurs, $P(Z_1 \mid Y_2)$, is therefore 2/3. These conditional probabilities are listed in tabular form below.

Once the link probabilities are known it is possible to combine these to obtain other probabilities which may be of interest. For example, it may be important to determine the proba-

If the Shipment Is:	Probability That the Sample Is a Black Card (Z_0)	Probability That the Sample Is a Red Card (Z_1)
Y_0	1	0
Y_1	2/3	1/3
Y_2	1/3	2/3
Y_3	0	1

bility of getting a red card in the sample rather than the *conditional* probabilities of getting a red card *if* the shipment is known. It may happen that the composition of the shipment is not known and in this case the conditional probabilities could not be used directly.

To find $P(Z_1)$ a clever dodge is used. By Rule II (4.04):

$$(4.10)\ P(Z_1, Y_0 \text{ or } Y_1 \text{ or } Y_2 \text{ or } Y_3) =$$
$$P(Y_0 \text{ or } Y_1 \text{ or } Y_2 \text{ or } Y_3 \mid Z_1)\, P(Z_1).$$

But $P(Y_0 \text{ or } Y_1 \text{ or } Y_2 \text{ or } Y_3 \mid Z_1) = 1$ by an extension of Rule Ia (4.01) so that $P(Z_1)$ can be found by evaluating the left-hand side of equation (4.10).

This is not hard to do. The Y's represent *mutually exclusive* outcomes, so, by an extension of Rule III (4.09),

$$(4.11)\quad P(Z_1, Y_0 \text{ or } Y_1 \text{ or } Y_2 \text{ or } Y_3) = P(Z_1, Y_0) + P(Z_1, Y_1)$$
$$+ P(Z_1, Y_2) + P(Z_1, Y_3).$$

To avoid having to write out all the terms in the sum on the right-hand side let me introduce another symbol (the last new symbol for a while). All the terms in the sum have the form $P(Z_1, Y_k)$ where k takes on the values 0, 1, 2, and 3. So let me introduce a symbol meaning "the sum of terms where k takes successive values." The right-hand side of equation (4.11) can then be written:

$$\Sigma\, P(Z_1, Y_k) \qquad (k = 0, 1, 2, 3).$$

The new symbol is the Greek capital letter S which stands for *sum*. It is one of the handiest notational gadgets in mathematics. If you remember that this letter, *sigma*, stands for *sum* you will have no difficulty reading formulas which use this symbol.

Combining equations (4.10), (4.11), and this new notation gives

(4.12) $P(Z_1) = \Sigma\, P(Z_1, Y_k)$ $(k = 0, 1, 2, 3)$.

One more step and the job is all finished. Going back to Rule II (4.04) once more

$$P(Z_1, Y_k) = P(Z_1 \mid Y_k)\, P(Y_k).$$

When this is substituted in equation (4.12) the very important *rule of reduction* is obtained:

(4.13) $P(Z_1) = \Sigma\, P(Z_1 \mid Y_k)\, P(Y_k)$ $(k = 0, 1, 2, 3)$.

Note that $P(Z_1)$ is now expressed in terms of the link probabilities that have already been determined. Consequently $P(Z_1)$ can be calculated as follows:

$$
\begin{aligned}
P(Z_1 \mid Y_0)\, P(Y_0) &= \quad (0)\,(24/52) = \quad 0 \\
P(Z_1 \mid Y_1)\, P(Y_1) &= (1/3)\,(2/52) = \quad 2/156 \\
P(Z_1 \mid Y_2)\, P(Y_2) &= (2/3)\,(2/52) = \quad 4/156 \\
P(Z_1 \mid Y_3)\, P(Y_3) &= \quad (1)\,(24/52) = 72/156 \\
\hline
\Sigma\, P(Z_1 \mid Y_k)\, P(Y_k) &= \qquad\qquad\qquad\quad 78/156 = 1/2
\end{aligned}
$$

I have deliberately chosen this example so that there is an easy way to get to the same result. Notice that going through the steps of drawing the shipment and then picking the sample is equivalent, so far as the sample is concerned, to simply cutting the cards. The probability of cutting a red card is 1/2, the same result as was obtained by using the link probabilities. This is only an artificial example, of course. In most practical situations there is no short cut, and the rule of reduction is the only method.

The rule of reduction can often be used to break down a complex predicting problem into a number of separate links. These individual link probabilities are generally easier to determine than multi-link probabilities so that this is a useful procedure in many fields of research.

The simple rule of reduction can be extended to chains having many links, and the study of such complex probability event chains is an important part of the theory of probability.

Bayes Rule

The technicalities of the last section were presented in order to set the stage for a concept basic to Statistical Decision and action for samples: Bayes rule. The reader may have noticed that so far we have been going *forward* along the event chain; that is to say, we went from X to Y to Z. The probabilities so far discussed are sometimes called "forward probabilities" for this reason.

But in order to use the results of a sample to make decisions, it is necessary to go in the other direction. In practice we know what has happened in the sample (we know Z), but we do not know the nature of the shipment (Y). Consequently, we want to go from Z to Y. Probabilities that go backwards along the event chain are often called "inverse probabilities." There is no essential difference between forward and inverse probabilities other than the direction along the event chain.

Suppose that it is known that the sample is a black card. What is desired is the probability of the various Y's when this additional information is known. These probabilities may be found very easily by an application of Rule II (4.04).

Equation (4.04) gives:

$$P(Z,Y) = P(Z \mid Y) P(Y)$$

and

$$P(Y,Z) = P(Y \mid Z) P(Z)$$

but the probability of Z *and* Y is the same as the probability of Y *and* Z, hence

$$P(Z \mid Y) P(Y) = P(Y \mid Z) P(Z).$$

Solving for $P(Y \mid Z)$ gives Bayes rule:

(4.14)
$$P(Y \mid Z) = \frac{P(Z \mid Y) P(Y)}{P(Z)}.$$

All of the probabilities on the right-hand side of the expression are known. Both $P(Z \mid Y)$ and $P(Y)$ are link probabilities. The rule of reduction (4.13) gives $P(Z)$.

For example: If the sample card is black (Z_0), then the probability that all of the cards in the shipment are black (Y_0) is

$$P(Y_0 \mid Z_0) = \frac{P(Z_0 \mid Y_0) P(Y_0)}{P(Z_0)} = \frac{1(24/52)}{(1/2)} = \frac{48}{52}.$$

Note that whereas the probability of Y_0 *before* the sample was taken, $P(Y_0)$, is only 24/52, the probability of Y_0 *after* the sample has been examined and the card was found to be black, $P(Y_0 \mid Z_0)$, is much higher. The additional information has had a great effect on the probabilities.

The practical consequence is this. If the shipments are automatically accepted, then half of the parts purchased will be defective. If the shipments are sampled and if the shipments giving a bad sample are rejected, then only a little less than 10 per cent of the parts purchased will be defective. The use of a sample to make the decision has greatly improved the quality of the shipments that are purchased.

Note that the information in the sample is not enough; this gives only the quantities like $P(Z_0 \mid Y_0)$. It is also necessary to have additional experience or knowledge of the production process. This additional knowledge is used to evaluate the quantities like $P(Y_0)$ in Bayes rule. If the deck of cards is thoroughly *shuffled* instead of being *ordered* as in the model, the sampling procedure will be ineffective. The reader can verify this for himself. Some readers may also amuse themselves by constructing variations of the game by increasing the size of the shipment or by choosing a more realistic order for the cards so as to stimulate a manufacturing process which when out of control produces 20 per cent or 50 per cent defectives rather than all defectives as in the model I have used.

I want to return now to Bayes rule itself, for it is a keystone in the structure of Statistical Decision. It was first used by an English clergyman, Thomas Bayes, in a paper that was published in 1763. Since it was published by friends after the death of Bayes, there have been some suggestions that Bayes himself was not convinced that the application he made of the rule was proper. There is no theorem in mathematics that has had a more controversial history.

Let me emphasize that this controversy has not questioned the rule (4.14) itself. The objections concern the quantities like $P(Y_0)$ which are sometimes called a priori probabilities. In problems in which these probabilities are unknown, Bayes rule cannot be used. However, many clever people, including Pierre Simon Laplace, refused to accept this limitation. They went ahead and put in arbitrary values for the a priori probabilities. Since these values were not obtained by experience, the name a priori (i.e., prior to experience) was used. Naturally this led to contradictions when someone else chose a different arbitrary value to use, and the whole process fell into disrepute.

In the course of the long controversy, which became violent at times, the participants took more and more extreme positions. The proponents of a priori probabilities advanced justifications which bordered on the ridiculous. Their adversaries sometimes retorted that not only were these a priori probabilities absurd but, further, that quantities such as $P(Y_0)$ were meaningless, i.e., could *never* be evaluated in any practical situation. The position that the a priori probabilities are meaningless in practical problems was upheld by R. A. Fisher, the greatest statistician of all, and because of Fisher's reputation, acquired widespread currency. Some readers may have encountered this point of view in books on statistics.

The development of Statistical Decision has led to a better understanding of Bayes rule. It was found that the methods proposed by R. A. Fisher to replace Bayes rule also make assumptions about the quantities such as $P(Y_0)$ although these assumptions are concealed in the theoretical developments! This is also true for the work of Neyman and Pearson. Hence the substitutes for Bayes rule actually represent special cases [1] of

[1] This point will be discussed more fully in Chapter 13.

the rule. Consequently Bayes rule has been restored to its central position in the theory of probability.

Summary

All methods of determining numerical probabilities are ultimately based on the simple Direct System. There are, however, other useful methods such as the Randomization System and Advanced Systems. Once determined, the probabilities are manipulated (either numerically or algebraically) by rules which stem from three simple axioms. One derived rule, Bayes rule, is singled out for discussion because of its central role in decision. The curious history of Bayes rule is briefly related.

/

CHAPTER 5

VALUES

Values and Science

In the two previous chapters the Prediction System has been discussed. Now I want to consider the second component in the decision-maker—the Value System. Like the Prediction System, the Value System also assigns a number to each possible outcome but this second number measures the desirability of the outcome rather than the chance that the outcome will occur. We shall be concerned here with Values only in this limited sense.

Even in this restricted sense, however, the problem of Values is a very difficult one. Insofar as the Prediction System is concerned there is substantial agreement among experts on the broad principles. Furthermore, the theory of probability provides powerful and well-tested tools for the construction of predicting systems in fairly simple situations. Even then, as I have emphasized before, the actual job of constructing a predicting system is no easy matter.

When we turn to the Value System the situation is much worse. There is very little agreement among experts on general procedures—in fact, there is not even agreement as to what constitutes an expert in *this* field. There is no comparable theoretical development or theory of desirabilities to assist in the actual construction process.

In the field of Values the transition from words to numbers has been accomplished only in a very limited area. What little research on the subject of Values is currently in progress is largely at the verbal stage. As is characteristic of subjects in this stage of development, there is a great tendency for discussions of Value to flounder around and finally drown in a sea of platitudes. While I shall try to avoid this tendency in my discussion, I must confess that I find it more difficult to write this chapter than any of the others.

Yet the statement of the problem of decision which I formulated earlier makes it impossible for me to dodge the question of Value. If, as I have insisted, the decision is to be based on the consequences of the possible actions, then these consequences must be evaluated and hence a Value System must be incorporated in the Decision-Maker.

Actual decisions, of course, do involve a Value System—ordinarily an intuitive one. We avoid actions because of the potentially unpleasant consequences; we obey traffic signals in order to avoid accidents. Similarly we take other actions because we regard the consequences as good; we order ice cream because of the anticipated pleasure which we will experience when we eat it. All of us have this intuitive Value System which allows us to consider a given turn of events as good, bad, or indifferent.

Not only do we distinguish good and bad but further we acknowledge degrees of goodness and badness. In practice we no more use the two-point scale good or bad for desirabilities than we use the corresponding two-point scale true or false for probabilities. As in the case of probabilities, there seems to be a continuous scale for values. In verbal terms we indicate this scale by such phrases as "very bad" or "extremely good."

Various attempts have been made to convert this intuitive scale to a quantitative one. The Utilitarians, such as J. S. Mill, have discussed the pain-pleasure scale and have suggested that numerical measurements would be nice to have. Unfortunately most such discussions carry the suggestion only to this stage, and no attempt is made to construct a procedure for measurement of desirabilities.

A majority of scholars have insisted that Values cannot be measured numerically. The only effective rebuttal to this argument is to present a quantitative system which deals with Values. Since no such system exists at present (except for very special situations), the only answer that can be made is that many of the quantities which we now regard as being measured fairly well were formerly considered to be unmeasurable. Just a century ago it would have seemed absurd to claim that the intelligence of a person could be stated as a number. Today numerical measures of intelligence are commonplace and—what is more important—are used to make practical decisions in the employment of personnel.

Nevertheless, it is true that there has been almost no scientific exploration of the field of Values and that what progress has been made in the numerical measurement of desirabilities has taken place outside of the present boundaries of science. Why is this the case? The subject of Values is, today, mainly in the hands of the speculative philosophers and they have posted big "No Trespass" signs on this domain. However, this is not much of an explanation because the scientists have been poaching on the preserves of the speculative philosophers for three hundred years. In some cases—psychology for example—the battle over property rights is still going on.

Another reason for reluctance on the part of scientists to deal with Values might be that the subject is intrinsically subjective and liable to violent and destructive controversies. Scientists who have dabbled with such borderline fields as human sexual conduct have sometimes found out in very painful fashions that "scientific immunity" does not apply in such subjects. While this might frighten some investigators, there are other scientists (contrary to popular opinions) who are not pale, timid characters, and who are not unwilling to get into a no-holds-barred battle with influential segments of the general public. In fact, there are some scientists who will go out of their way to get into a good rough-and-tumble fight.

I would attribute the absence of scientific inquiry to a mental attitude which has dominated science, an attitude largely fostered and preserved by the Continental and British scientists and scientific philosophers. This viewpoint stems from pre-scientific academic traditions plus the somewhat snobbish premise that scientists are an intellectual aristocracy.

I am referring to the often stated attitude that the role of the scientist is that of Seeker After Truth. This in itself is not too misleading a statement providing Truth is interpreted pragmatically. What I dislike is the implicit Value System which can be constructed from this interpretation of the role of a scientist. In this Value System there is an identification of truth and desirability—what is true is automatically desirable, what is false is automatically undesirable—and the further extension that no other values are of any concern to a scientist.

It is this dogma that I believe is responsible for the remarkable doctrine of Scientific Optimism: Science automatically improves the well-being of the people. This particular doctrine, shaky for some time, has now been shattered altogether by the atomic bomb. The destruction of this unwarranted doctrine is one of the more constructive things that the fission of uranium has accomplished. It has demonstrated that the simple Value System which associates truth and desirability, while useful in many scientific researches, is not an adequate value system even for Science.

I hope, therefore, that the long period of neglect of Values by scientists is coming to an end. Certainly the A-bomb has caused even physicists (harried by parental responsibility) to take a closer look at values. Some leaped at once to the traditional philosophical value systems, others searched this work but were disappointed because the traditional specialists in Values were still using the approach, even the outmoded tools, that Aristotle had once applied to physics. Moreover, the traditional value systems were in direct conflict with what little had been learned by anthropologists and sociologists.

But this is enough discussion of research that has *not* been done—let us now take a look at what has been accomplished in the measurement of values. This will take us outside of the current boundaries of science and into the marketplace, the world of business and everyday affairs—a realm which I am afraid is distasteful to academic scientists-philosophers. But it is the unscientific folks in the workaday world who have provided the principal value scale currently available for use in a decision system. In short, let us get down to dollars and cents.

Dollars and Cents

There is a large class of events for which I would be willing to specify the desirabilities numerically. For example, I could quote a number which would seem to be the appropriate desirability for such events as receiving a new suit or title to a new Chevrolet. The numerical value I would choose would be the *market value* of the item.

Because market values are so much a part and parcel of our everyday life, we may be inclined to overlook the remarkable features of this particular Value System. In the first place it assigns a numerical value to a very wide range of commodities and services. There is not much in common between a new car and a bushel of apples, but both are evaluated on the same scale; that is, in terms of dollars and cents. This in itself is a noteworthy accomplishment.

But even more surprising is the widespread acceptance of this Value System by people in all conditions of life and various backgrounds. To be sure there are some disagreements—one person may think the market price of a cup of coffee is too high and another person might feel it is too low. These disagreements reveal differences between the market values and individual value systems, but by and large there is rather good general agreement that market values are the appropriate values. In view of the diversity of backgrounds and tastes of individuals and the tendency for differences in value systems to produce emotional reactions, this widespread acceptance of market values gives us some hope that it is possible to construct other value systems which will also be acceptable to a majority of the people.

The process which leads to the numerical market values

seems to be a very complex one. Broadly speaking it resembles
the parimutuel betting arrangements which, I have already
mentioned, constitute a sort of consensus Predicting System.
Market values represent a consensus Value System except when
monopoly conditions exist. The monopoly may be set up by the
sellers, the buyers, or sometimes by the government. When
prices are fixed by a monopoly then the market value is no
longer a real consensus but instead is merely the Value System
of the monopoly. It is not surprising that the whole market
system tends to break down under monopoly conditions. A conflict of value systems may ensue which may lead to black mar-
kets, complete disorganization, or even to the collapse of gov-
ernments or cultures.

So far I have been discussing market values of goods or commodities, but very early in human history it became necessary
to extend market values to more abstract quantities such as
labor and services. The market value of labor or services was
fixed in pre-industrial times by a process of individual bargaining rather similar to the processes already used to fix the value
of goods. With the advent of the Industrial Revolution, however, the employer had to hire large numbers of workers. This
resulted in a monopoly on the part of the employers and the
individual worker had to accept the Value System of the employer. The period of unrest and even violence continued until
countermonopolies on the part of labor were formed. The
unions eventually became powerful enough to force a genuine
bargaining procedure and today the market value of labor is
often determined through the agency of this collective bargaining. Values obtained in this way are more nearly consensus
values and hence seem to be more widely acceptable.

Modern corporations have found it necessary to extend the
market value idea to quantities which are even more intangible
and complex than human labor. Thus it is not unusual for large
corporations to spend money on such abstractions as good will
or employee loyalty. An academic philosopher might very well
insist that such values could not be translated into numbers. It

is rather curious that this translation of abstract values should have been attempted by people whose outlook is completely practical.

The extension of market values to abstract quantities employed methodologies already developed for more prosaic values. The techniques of cost accounting, time-and-motion studies, and other commercially developed procedures have been used in these attempts to assess, in dollars and cents, various intangible quantities which have seemed relevant to business management.

Some readers, perhaps, may be appalled by the thought of treating loyalty, good will, or human effort as a matter for bookkeeping. They may find that it goes against their grain to put a price tag on such things. Other readers might disapprove of such efforts because these intangibles do not, in their opinion, have any real monetary value. I confess some sympathy for both viewpoints and I would not insist that because dollars and cents seem to be an appropriate scale for some events this scale necessarily is the only one that can be used or is appropriate for all events.

Nevertheless I feel that the principles of cost analysis merit more consideration from the academic world than they have so far received. The dollar-and-cents scale, whatever its deficiencies, is the basis for the Value Systems which are used in many of the current applications of Statistical Decision. This state of affairs may change when and if other useful scales are developed, but I believe the monetary scale will prove useful even in situations outside of commerce and industry.

Utility

Although the most useful quantitative Value System has come from the world of everyday affairs, the academic world has considered some theoretical Value Systems which may some day prove to be valuable. Since most of this work is in the province of economics, psychology, and sociology, and since I know very little about these fields, I will attempt to touch only on a few topics that seem to me to be relevant to the construction of a Value System.

The contribution of the economists lies in the conception of an alternative value scale to the dollar-and-cents scale—the Utility scale (Utility has a specialized meaning here). The process of constructing this scale is similar to the process which determines market values. The resemblance is not surprising since the concept Utility grew out of attempts to explain market values. However, the Utility scale is an *individual's* value scale rather than a consensus.

Suppose that I were interested in exploring the intuitive Value System of a child and I knew that the child liked gumdrops. If I wished to determine the relative value of some other confection—chocolate kisses—I might try the following experiment. First I offer the child a choice of a chocolate kiss or a gumdrop. If he took the chocolate I would next offer a choice between a kiss and two gumdrops. He might again choose the kiss. By increasing the number of gumdrops a point would presumably be reached at which the child might make either choice, a sort of balance point. This point is generally called the *indifference point* since the individual is *indifferent* as to whether he is given the kiss or the gumdrops. If I added still more gumdrops to my offer the child might generally take the gumdrops.

If the indifference point were five gumdrops, then I might say that a kiss was worth five gumdrops, or, in different words, the Utility of both offers was equal. Other delicacies could be measured on the gumdrop scale, so presumably I could obtain a fairly complete picture of the Value System of the child in this way. Let me hasten to add, however, that while such an experiment is easy to visualize, it would be a good deal harder to carry out. Any reader with some experience with children would have no trouble pointing out reasons why the experiment might break down!

In principle, at least, this procedure could be extended to study the intuitive Value System of any individual and to measure the Utility of goods or services on some single scale (which might be gumdrops or dollars or something else).

An introspective application of this principle is sometimes helpful in assigning desirabilities to outcomes. Thus if I wished to determine some desirability for the event "getting home late because of traffic delays or long waits for a bus" (as in the car vs. bus example), I might proceed as follows. I would ask myself whether I would be willing to pay a dime to get home early, whether I would be willing to pay a quarter, etc. While the numerical values obtained introspectively might not be very precise, the principle does provide a procedure whereby the magnitude of the desirability can be determined.

The economists have been especially interested in the question of the Utility of money itself. Although this question has been much debated for many generations, the *first* attempt to conduct an *actual* experiment, one which would correspond to the conceptual experiment described above, was done in 1950!

The experiment is discussed by Mosteller and Nogee in a paper in the *Journal of Political Economy*.[1] If you are at all interested in the problem of Values, I warmly recommend that you read this paper. It is a fascinating piece of intellectual pioneering.

The experimental procedure used was too complicated to describe here, but it involved a group of students and another group of national guardsmen who were paid to gamble! The subjects were given a series of offers (in which both probabilities and payoffs were systematically varied), and they had the option of taking or refusing the bet. A dice game was then used to determine the outcome, and the game was played for "keeps"—the subjects kept the money which they won and paid in the money which they lost.

From the information on which offers were accepted and which were refused, Utility curves were constructed for the different subjects. If the Utility of money were simply equal to

[1] Mosteller, F., and Nogee, P., "An experimental measure of Utility," *Journal of Political Economy*, Vol. 41, No. 5, October 1951.

the *amount* of money, then the Utility curves should have been straight lines such as the solid curve in Figure 5.01.

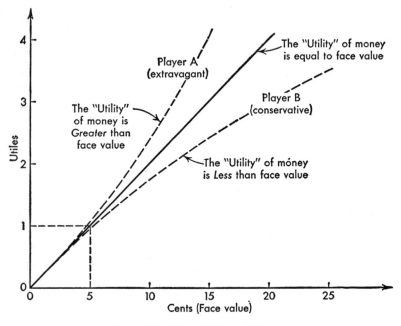

Fig. 5.01   The Utility of Money

Some individuals had curves which deviated from the straight line in manner A and others in manner B. If a person had a curve which resembled B it meant that he acted as though money had a *diminishing* Utility. In other words, a dollar has somewhat less than twenty times the Utility of a nickel. Classical economic theory would lead one to expect this sort of curve of decreasing Utility. It is interesting to note that the Harvard students behaved in accordance with conventional theory while the national guardsmen sometimes seemed to act in just the opposite manner.

Let me emphasize that Utility has so far been employed as a handy *conceptual* tool only. The process for the determination of Utilities as *numbers* needs much more development.

Preference

Still other value scales which are at least worth noticing have been suggested. The psychologists have done some work in investigating values and in constructing scales. The procedures devised for measuring public opinion and individual attitudes may turn out to be applicable to the construction of value systems. Unfortunately the psychologists have tended to focus their attention on verbal responses such as questionnaires. The procedures that have evolved for analysis of these verbal responses are a bit too complex, statistically and otherwise, for me to describe here.

Recently there has been a vigorous effort devoted to the construction of preference scales. The impetus for this research has come mainly from the world of business, especially from corporations in the food processing field. The motive behind such studies is quite different, however, from the motive behind the surveys which have resulted in absurd advertising claims. The purpose of consumer preference studies was to adjust the product to the public rather than, as in the advertising studies, to adjust the public to the product.

The general process of setting up preference scales is fairly straightforward. For example, a company may wish to see what the public likes in strawberry ice cream. Do they like to have large pieces of strawberry? Do they want very creamy mixtures? Do they prefer dark pink or light pink color?

To answer such questions a number of different batches of ice cream would be made up, some with plenty of strawberries, others with extra cream, and so on. A panel, or group of tasters, would then have to be carefully selected. This panel would taste the different mixtures and indicate their preferences. This latter step might be done in several ways. The individuals might be given just two samples of ice cream at a time and told to indicate which one they liked better. Or the judges might be given more than two batches and told to rank the samples in order from most desirable to least desirable. Still another method would be to give several samples and ask for numerical ratings on a one-to-five or one-to-ten scale.

There are numerous technical problems that arise in this process and there are various ways in which this experimental data may be analyzed. The final result is some sort of preference scales for the individuals on the panel and also single consensus scales. I want to emphasize that tastes are rather intangible and that it is encouraging that even crude quantitative measurements have been developed. These measurements have been used as a basis for administrative decisions by various corporations. The current vogue for taste and other preference testing seems to indicate that some measure of success has been attained in measuring taste.

Relatively recently the academic world has begun to pay more attention to preference scales and value systems in general. An important step in this direction was taken by Morgenstern and von Neumann [2] in their book *Theory of Games and Economic Behavior*. In this book the concept of mathematical expectation, which will be discussed in the next chapter, was used to suggest a process for converting a preference scale to a Utility scale. In this work the concept of probability enters in a new role; essentially it serves as a mathematical trick (i.e., to convert discrete problems into continuous ones). Mosteller and Nogee utilized this device in their experiment on the measurement of Utility.

These academic efforts represent a start, at least, toward building up a theory of value systems comparable to the theory of predicting systems. Unfortunately, the work has been dominated by what is called the axiomatic approach. In this approach the mathematician sits back in his easy chair and conjures up a number of statements which, from the armchair at least, look like plausible descriptions of the real world. Naturally the mathematician selects statements which can be readily formulated and manipulated mathematically.

---

[2] Morgenstern, O., and von Neumann, J., *Theory of Games and Economic Behavior*, Second Edition, Princeton University Press, Princeton, 1947.

The rest of the story is all mathematical. The end results, or theorems, are sometimes interpreted in terms of the real world and naive people may regard these results as "proved," i.e., as holding in the real world. Whether the theorem is any good depends on whether the axioms that went into it are sound. Despite mathematical window-dressing, therefore, results obtained by the axiomatic method will be useful or not depending on whether the mathematician who used the method had some common sense or not. I have never encountered any strong evidence to show that the proportion of mathematicians with common sense is much higher than the proportion of non-mathematicians with common sense.

I do not want to disparage current efforts by the academic world to investigate value systems (though I would wish for firmer bonds with the real world) and I would like to present one interesting result obtained in this way by K. Arrow.[3]

Taste testing is an example of a situation in which the preference scale may not lead to a *number* associated with each alternative; instead a simple ranking (i.e., ordering) of the alternatives is obtained. There has been a long-standing argument as to whether a ranked (ordered) scale is more appropriate for a Value System than a numerical scale. This in turn brings up the following question: If a number of individuals make a taste test and *rank* their preferences, can an over-all ranking of the ice creams be made which will express the preferences of the group (in some sense)?

Arrow attempted to answer the question as follows: Suppose that some group preference scheme is constructed. What characteristics would one expect from the scheme? One such characteristic (axiom) that Arrow proposed was that if everyone in the group preferred a particular ice cream to all others, then this ice cream should top the list of the group preferences. Another such condition was that if a new ice cream mix which was ranked at the bottom by everyone in the group were added,

[3] Arrow, K., *Social Choice and Individual Values*, John Wiley & Sons, Inc., New York, 1951.

then the introduction of this additional alternative should not affect the original ordering of the group preference.

Starting with these axioms (and one other) Arrow was led by his mathematics to a very curious result. He found that the only group preference which satisfied his conditions was a dictatorial one; i.e., the only group preference was, in fact, the particular preferences of some one individual of the group. Such a group preference hardly seems to agree with our intuitive ideas that a Value System should be some sort of consensus. This would appear to indicate that an ordered scale might be less useful for a Value System than a continuous scale (like dollar and cents or Utility), and consequently we should bend our efforts to the construction of continuous scales.

I will only mention in passing that some work is in progress on the construction of special scales and value systems for specific applications. For example, in the field of public health it is desirable to evaluate in some objective fashion the effectiveness of public health programs for the control of communicable diseases, home accidents, and so on. Scales based on death or illness rates or other indices are generally used instead of dollars-and-cents scales. Military decisions are another special application, but most of the work in this field is shrouded in secrecy.

Simple Values

I want to emphasize *very* strongly that the most important barrier to a wider application of the principles and procedures of Statistical Decision lies in the fact that adequate value systems are lacking. This is especially true in the field of scientific research itself because the consequences of this research are hard to pin down. This deficiency may be removed by time and research on Value Systems, but in the meantime stop-gap procedures are necessary.

In most scientific experimentation the direct end product of a study is generally a publication, a paper that will be printed in the scientific journals. In this paper the scientist will generally state the conclusions which have followed from his labors and occasionally these conclusions are stated in the form of recommendations which, presumably, will have some effect on the actions of other scientists. Even when specific recommendations are made, however, there is often no way to predict what use will be made of them—they may be followed or ignored. Hence in scientific research the pattern which was set up earlier, recommendation-action-consequences, becomes rather hopeless to elucidate. For practical purposes in setting up a Decision-Maker, it may be necessary to regard the process as terminating with recommendation.

The methods of decision which involve tracing down the outcome are therefore not very helpful in most scientific work except as a frame of reference. The question arises: How can the concepts of Statistical Decision be applied if little is known (at the time of decision) about what will happen when the conclusions or recommendations are published?

Note that I am *not* saying that the recommendation-action-consequence chain actually terminates with the recommendation, but only that what happens next cannot be adequately predicted at the time of decision. The chain goes on, of course, in the sense that other research workers may read the paper and be inspired to attempt to duplicate the reported results and thus confirm or invalidate the conclusions. Broadly speaking, if the results are confirmed, the prestige of the scientist is enhanced, while if the work is tossed out by a "jury of his peers," the scientist may face a rather unpleasant situation. It is therefore not surprising that scientists are often primarily concerned with avoiding this second eventuality—repudiation of the conclusions. With this attitude the scientist will not want to use techniques, statistical or otherwise, which will lead him to conclusions that will be contradicted by subsequent research.

Now this places the experimental scientist in something of a dilemma. He knows that his experiments are subject to what is called *experimental error* and that while he may constantly strive to control or avoid these experimental errors it is not practically possible to eliminate them altogether. As a result of such experimental errors he may be led to make statements which will subsequently be shown to be erroneous. Most experimental scientists realize this fact. They also realize that it is impossible to make useful statements or recommendations which will always be upheld by future research.

A way out of this dilemma has been suggested by certain developments of modern statistics. The scientist can be given protection against drawing erroneous conclusions, providing he is willing to state numerically how much protection he wants and also providing he does not insist on complete protection.

A widely accepted statistical "insurance policy" is the one which provides 95 per cent protection. This set of techniques is designed to allow the scientist to draw conclusions from his data which, in spite of the experimental error in this data, will be right about 95 per cent of the time and wrong only 5 per cent of the time. To some readers acquainted with the Hollywood version of the white-coated and infallible medicine man, this may seem to be an excessive margin for error. However, especially in the biological sciences, a batting average of .950 is regarded as sufficient protection in most research.

In some applications, of course, in which the consequences are more obvious (as in situations in which an erroneous recommendation might lead to injury or death of humans) a greater degree of protection may be required.

Although this point is not obvious, these widely used statistical "insurance policies" are based on a specific value scale. Since this scale has only two points (zero and one) it is called a *simple* scale. The associated Value System is essentially one which makes the identification, which I discussed earlier in the chapter, between desirability and truth (or confirmation). To put the statement in terms of costs I might say that we agree to say that it costs us one unit to make a statement which is controverted by subsequent research, while it costs us nothing to make a statement which is later confirmed.

This Simple Value System is quite useful in applications in which the detailed tracing of consequences is impractical. The use of this simple scale essentially eliminates values from the problem and reduces the Decision-Maker to a Predicting System and a Criterion. The statistical procedures developed before the advent of Statistical Decision may be regarded as special cases of Statistical Decision in which a simple value scale is used. Looking at it the other way Statistical Decision can be considered as generalizing the earlier statistical methods so as to bring directly into the structure the information that may be available concerning costs and consequences.

Now it is not difficult to find objections to this simple scale which really assumes that all wrong statements are just as bad. Actually, of course, in terms of academic promotions or prestige some wrong statements may be inconsequential and in other cases a single wrong statement (or sometimes a right one) may be disastrous. The medical field provides many examples in which degrees of wrongness are apparent. If a child is erroneously diagnosed as undernourished, the therapy (i.e., food) is not likely to do much harm. On the other hand, an incorrectly diagnosed eye condition for which the therapy is removal of the eye is a more serious matter.

Nevertheless when the consequences are obscure or difficult to evaluate, as they very often are in practical research situations, the Simple Value System seems to be a useful first approximation. Whenever the consequences are more obvious and can be evaluated, the broader structure of Statistical Decision can be put to use.

Summary

A main obstacle to the wider application of Statistical Decision is the lack of adequate Value Systems. The study of such Value Systems has been largely neglected by the academic world and the main development of useful systems has come from the world of commerce and industry, systems based on dollars and cents. Some academic contributions, Utility and preference scales, are noted. A stop-gap procedure that can be used when more realistic Value Systems are not available is the Simple Value System which identifies desirability and truth and which has been useful in scientific research situations.

CHAPTER 6

/ **RULES FOR ACTION**

Calculated Risks

In looking for rules for action it is well to realize at the very beginning that no rules can be constructed which will lead to the most favorable results in every case. Since both prediction systems and value systems are imperfect, it follows that the rules for actions which spring from these systems must likewise be imperfect.

It is true that most authors who have laid down rules for action have not taken this view, that they regard actions as right or wrong in an absolute sense. This authoritarian attitude is popular with politicians, moralists, and editorial writers but the long, sad history of failures of the infallible has led to widespread skepticism in our times. People with the courage to look at the world about them as it is, rather than as they would like it to be, have realized that all action is attended by risk.

More and more one hears the phrase calculated risk in connection with decisions, especially at the international level. When this is used to justify a choice of action it implies that the favored action is not guaranteed to lead to a desired end, but rather that it seems more likely to do so than the alternative actions. Moreover the word "calculated" implies that this conclusion is reached by a deliberate analysis of the situation and historical precedents.

This attitude of calculated risk underlies Statistical Decision. However, Statistical Decision carries this viewpoint one stage further and translates the uncertainties and values into numbers rather than words. Hence in Statistical Decision the risks are, quite literally, *calculated*.

The preceding chapters have discussed the quantification of values and uncertainties and the determination of desirabilities and probabilities. When this has been done we have a list of possible actions, a list of possible outcomes for each action, the numerical consequences of each outcome, the probability associated with each outcome, and the costs associated with each line of action. What is needed now is some way of putting all of these numbers together in such a way that the choice of action can be determined. I have previously called such a rule a *criterion for decision*.

This rule should reflect the *purposes* of the individual who is making the decision. There are two types of decision criteria which are in widespread use at present, but there are other possible rules for actions which may be useful in the future.[1] The criteria for decision have not yet been thoroughly explored.

Some Possible Rules

The various possible rules for action may be most easily understood in terms of a specific example, so let me go back to the decision situation in which I want to choose between driving my car or taking the bus. In order to have a simple example let me make the patently unrealistic assumption that there are only a limited number of outcomes possible. I will choose the probabilities and desirabilities more or less arbitrarily so that we will have some specific numbers to play with. Suppose that the relevant information in the car vs. bus problem is summarized in the table on the following page.

The desirabilities in this table are in terms of dollars and cents and the minus signs are to remind us that these are costs.

[1] Savage, J., "The theory of Statistical Decision," *Journal American Statistical Association,* Vol. 46, No. 253, March 1951.

ACTION	DRIVE CAR			TAKE BUS	
Cost of Action	−0.75			−0.30	
Outcomes	Arrive home early and without incident	Arrive home late due to traffic delays	Accident	Arrive home early and without incident	Arrive home late due to missed connections
Probability of Outcome	0.850	0.145	0.005	0.100	0.900
Desirability of Outcome	0.00	−1.00	−50.00	0.00	−1.00

Thus, for example, the table indicates that I feel that the time and trouble involved in getting home late are equivalent to a cost of one dollar. The probabilities are *conditional* probabilities and represent the probability of the outcome *if* a given action is taken. This is evident since the probabilities for each set of outcomes add up to one.

Now how can the information in the above table be combined and manipulated in such a way as to lead to a decision? I shall list four possible answers to this question—but many others are possible.

Answer 1. Consider the most probable outcome for each action (the outcome which has the largest probability) and the desirabilities associated with these most probable outcomes. Choose the action for which the desirability of the most probable outcome is as large as possible.

For the car vs. bus example this leads to:

Action:	Drive car	Take bus
Most Probable Outcome:	Arrive home early	Arrive home late
Desirability:	−0.75	−1.30
Choice:	Drive car	

The numerical values of the above desirabilities are obtained by adding the cost of the action to the desirability of the outcome:

$$0.00 + (-0.75) = -0.75.$$
$$-1.00 + (-0.30) = -1.30.$$

The reasoning which underlies this answer is the following. Since the most probable outcome is most likely to occur, we should act as if it will occur. Then we simply compare the desirabilities of these most probable outcomes in order to make our choice.

Answer 1 emphasizes the probabilities. It would be possible to use this procedure even if the desirabilities were imperfectly known. It is unnecessary to know the desirabilities of any outcomes other than the most probable outcomes. Moreover, it is not necessary to have numerical values for the desirabilities, but only a ranking of the desirabilities of the most probable outcomes.

When one outcome has a very high probability (i.e., is almost certain to happen) this sort of rule for action is often used. Thus if it is very threatening weather I act as if it were going to rain although it is possible that it will clear up without rain.

Instead of concentrating on the probabilities, the rule for action may focus on the desirabilities. Just how this is to be done depends on whether a pessimistic or an optimistic viewpoint is presumed.

Answer 2. (Optimistic.) Choose the action which *could* lead to the *most* favorable outcome.

Action:	Drive car	Take bus
Most Favorable Outcome:	Arrive home early	Arrive home early
Desirability:	−0.75	−0.30
Choice:		Take bus

On the other hand if this Pollyanna attitude seems unsuitable, the opposite point of view also provides an answer.

Answer 3. (Pessimistic.) Consider the *least* favorable out-

come possible for each action. Of this set of least favorable outcomes one will be more favorable than others. Take the action
associated with this outcome.

Action:	Drive car	Take bus
Least Favorable Outcome:	Accident	Arrive home late
Desirability:	—50.75	—1.30
Choice:		Take bus

The reasoning behind this viewpoint emphasizes security.
Thus in following this rule we are protected against the occurrence of extremely unfavorable events (such as an accident).
The control of heavy losses is the essential purpose of this
rule, and I will refer to rules of this type as loss-control criteria.

Notice that Answers 2 and 3 do not require the evaluation
of the probabilities. Answers 2 and 3 seem to be used in practical decisions. The purchasers of numbers tickets seem to be
thinking along the lines of Answer 2. They are not concerned
with probabilities and are only interested in the fact that if
they win they will get a lot of money. On the other hand all
of us have acquaintance with confirmed pessimists who always
act as though the very worst eventuality is sure to materialize.
Many people never learn to drive because they are afraid of
having an accident.

Now let us turn to an answer which will utilize both probabilities and desirabilities in the process of decision. In this
answer we have to shift our focus of attention from what will
happen in a specific situation (i.e., tomorrow) to what will
happen in a long-run sense. Ordinarily I wouldn't want to make
a separate decision each day as to whether or not I will drive
or take the bus. If I make my decision to drive, I might very
well continue to drive to work every day for the rest of the
year. Consequently I might ask: What will happen if the choice
is presumed to guide my action over a period of time?

Suppose, for convenience, I ask: What will happen in the
next thousand days? If I drive during this time I can expect
the following balance sheet:

Outcome	Expected Occur-rences (Days)	Cost per Occurrence (Dollars per day)	Cost of Out-come (Dollars)
Arrive home early	850 days	$ 0.75	$ 637.50
Arrive home late	145 days	1.75	253.75
Accident	5 days	50.75	253.75
All	1000 days		$1145.00

In exactly the same way a balance sheet can be prepared for the case in which the bus is taken.

Outcome	Expected Occur-rences (Days)	Cost per Occurrence (Dollars per day)	Cost of Out-come (Dollars)
Arrive home early	100	$0.30	$ 30.00
Arrive home late	900	1.30	1170.00
All	1000		$1200.00

When the balance sheets are compared it is seen that the decision is a very close one. There is a slight advantage if I drive, but there would be a question as to whether this difference really meant much. In other words, we know that the probabilities and desirabilities are measurements and as such are subject to errors. Perhaps inaccuracies in our measurement system could account for this very small difference that we have found in the balances. In any case I would not go very far wrong either by driving or by taking the bus.

It might therefore be worthwhile to experiment with both methods of transportation in the hope that in this way additional information could be obtained which could be used to make a final decision later.

Now there was no very good reason for choosing 1000 days (except that it simplified the arithmetic), and I might have picked any other number. To make these different results comparable I could put all my results on a per-day basis, and in this way my answer would not depend on the choice of the number of days. This is easily accomplished by dividing my balances by

1000 so as to obtain a figure of $1.14½ as the per-day cost of driving and $1.20 as the per-day cost of taking the bus.

These results could be obtained more easily by the following rule: Multiply the probability of each outcome by the corresponding desirability and add up these products for all the outcomes. Then subtract the cost of the action.

In this case the application of the rule to the driving situation gives:

$$(0.850) \ (0.00) + (0.1450) \ (-1.00) + (0.005) \ (-50.00) -0.75$$
$$= -1.145.$$

Here I have carried along the minus signs to denote costs. I did not do this on the balance sheets because the entries were labeled "costs." The word "cost" implies a negative desirability.

The rule that is given above leads to a quantity that is called the mathematical expectation. This concept has been useful in the theory of probability for three centuries. The use of this concept of mathematical expectation enables us to formulate a fourth answer to our original question.

Answer 4. Choose the course of action which has the largest mathematical expectation.

Rules based on this principle of maximum expectation play a very important role in Statistical Decision and will be discussed more fully in subsequent chapters.

Often a decision must be made in the absence of reliable information about the probabilities. This has led to another rule for action which combines the concepts of loss control (Answer 3) with mathematical expectation.

Let us suppose that the probabilities which have been given for the car vs. bus problem are not given as numbers but as ranges. For example, suppose that the probability of having an accident if I drive my car is not given as 0.005 but as a range, 0.003 to 0.007. This says that all I can say about the probability of an accident is that it is somewhere between three chances in a thousand and seven chances in a thousand. This sort of statement might be more descriptive of my state of knowledge concerning this probability. In the same way the other probabilities involved might be given as ranges:

ACTION	OUTCOME	PROBABILITY (RANGE)
Drive Car	Arrive home early without incident	0.80 –0.90
	Arrive home late because of traffic	0.10 –0.20
	Accident	0.003–0.007
Take Bus	Arrive home early without incident	0.05 –0.15
	Arrive home late because of connections	0.85 –0.95

In this case I might want to use the following rule for action:

Answer 5. Select the action associated with the largest of the least favorable expectations.

This rule is easily applied as follows. Evidently the least favorable situation in driving is to have the probability of an accident as high as it can be (0.007) and the probability of getting home early as small as it can be (0.80). Since the probabilities must add up to one the corresponding probability of arriving home late must be 0.193. The expectation for driving may be calculated as before, using these least favorable probabilities. This gives:

$$(0.800) \ (0.00) + (0.193) \ (-1.00) + (0.007) \ (-50.00) -0.75$$
$$= -1.293.$$

Similarly for the case in which I take the bus, the least favorable probabilities are going to be 0.05 for getting home early and 0.95 for getting home late. This leads to an expectation associated with taking the bus of:

$$[(0.05) \ (0.00) + (0.95) \ (-1.00) -0.30 = -1.25.$$

A comparison of these two least favorable expectations, —1.293 and —1.25, indicates that by the principles of Answer 5 the decision still seems to be a close one, but this time there is a slight edge in favor of taking the bus.

Five answers have been presented to the original question and a number of others could be added. At this point our trouble is not that we cannot answer the question but that there are too many answers!

Selection of Rules

Some sort of choice of criteria for action must be made in order to set up a Decision-Maker. The last section gave some of the important alternative rules which have been proposed and I will confine the discussion to making a selection from the five answers given in that section. It will be noted that two of the rules advised me to drive my car and three of the rules advised me to take the bus, so unless I can decide on some one rule of action to follow, I will be no closer to making a decision than I was at the beginning. This brings up the question: What are the criteria for selecting the rules which will be used to make decisions?

I have already noted that the various rules for action reflect various attitudes that might be taken toward the real world—optimism, pessimism, and the like. So presumably we should select the rule which comes closest to expressing the outlook of the customer, the person who has come for advice on decision. While this procedure is plausible, it is not very practical. The statistician would have to find some device for measuring the customer's general outlook on life. Things are complicated enough with predicting systems and value systems without having to take this further step—although it may come about someday.

For the time being it will be simpler to concentrate on rules that might be acceptable to *most* of the customers. We might also consider a selection of criteria for decision which meet various intuitively sensible requirements. To suggest just one such requirement: The rule for action should take into consideration all of the relevant information pertaining to a given decision. This requirement would toss out Answers 1, 2, and

3 because these rules disregard the desirabilities or probabilities.

To be perfectly frank, however, I don't feel that our knowledge of Statistical Decision has reached a stage where it is possible to select any specific rule for action and say "This is *the* rule." Indeed, it is doubtful whether a single rule can be found which will have universal application. As I have indicated, Answers 4 and 5 seem to be the most promising of the current crop, but it is too early, and we have too little experience on the subject, to make any final selections.

Nevertheless, it seems worthwhile to discuss in more detail the motivation behind Answers 4 and 5, to try to discover how these two different criteria have arisen. These two answers can be regarded as covering two different situations which might be exemplified by the following two extreme cases. Case I is a situation in which great losses or gains are possible and in which the situation is unique in the sense that it is likely to occur once and only once in the lifetime of a given individual. A prospective bridegroom deals with this sort of situation when he is trying to make up his mind whether or not to marry the girl. Perhaps I ought to specify that this bridegroom is *not* a movie star.

Case II is a decision problem in which moderate losses or gains are possible and in which there is a large number of similar decisions over a period of time. Purchasing a batch of raw materials for a factory would be an instance of this *routine* decision.

In Case II common business practice is to focus attention on the *long-run* profits. The decision to purchase a batch of raw materials will, of course, lead to some profit or loss on the deal, but ordinarily the factory would not be wiped out even if a series of unfavorable purchases were made. Consequently management tends to think in terms of an annual profit-and-loss statement rather than concentrating on the outcome of a particular transaction. The annual profit-and-loss statement is closely related to the concept of mathematical expectation which is also a long-run balance. Hence the criteria which maximize the mathematical expectation correspond to the efforts of the businessman to show as large a profit on his annual statement as is possible. Answer 4 becomes very nearly a translation of the dictum, "Choose the action with the most desirable consequences," the only qualification being that "most desirable" is to be interpreted in a long-run sense.

Therefore, Answer 4 seems quite appropriate to Case II when the probabilities and desirabilities can be adequately measured. In general both a Prediction System and a Value System are easier to set up when a series of similar transactions are known from past experience. Of course, if this information is lacking then other criteria may be pressed into service as stopgap measures.

When we turn to Case I, however, the whole idea of long-run consequences may break down. Consider now a small business with $10,000 capital. The businessman has the choice of two deals, both of which will require the investment of the entire capital. Deal A offers a chance to double this capital, but it is a risky deal and there is one chance in five that not only will there be no profit but further that the original $10,000 will be lost. The mathematical expectation of deal A is:

$$E_A = (\%) \ (\$10,000) + (\frac{1}{5}) \ (-\$10,000) = \$6000.$$

The second deal is a much safer one. The capital is secured and a more modest 10 per cent profit is assured. The mathematical expectation is:

$$E_B = (1) \ (\$1000) = \$1000.$$

The application of Answer 4 leads to the decision: Take deal A. Moreover, the expectation of deal A is six times the expectation of deal B so there is a wide margin in favor of deal A. This advice, however, might be a little hard for the small businessman to swallow. What is the difficulty?

As I see it the difficulty lies in the fact that the small businessman is not exclusively concerned with making a profit—he also wants to stay in business. He cannot focus his attention on long-run results—if he is not careful there will be no long-run for him. Consequently, he would want a criterion which would not only provide some profit but which would also give some guarantee of short-run security. This is the motivation for rules which concentrate on what will happen if worse comes to worse—the loss-control criteria.

It would seem somewhat dangerous to go to the other extreme, however, and concentrate entirely on security since this may be self-defeating. Although survival, in business or everyday life, is a prime consideration the choice is *not* between taking chances and not taking any chances; some chances will have to be taken. Successful businessmen are not noted for an extremely pessimistic outlook (which is implied in the more extreme loss-control rules for action). If anyone adhered strictly to Answer 3 he would soon starve to death. He would never be able to take any other action than staying in bed with the covers pulled over his head.

Some compromise between profit and security is necessary. Such a rule is the dictum, "Minimize the maximum risk," which is an extension of Answer 5. This rule has been the criterion used in much of the research on Statistical Decision. For quite a while this rule for action provoked little objection, at least from the mathematicians. Its use facilitates mathematical analysis so that it was not only plausible but also convenient. A reaction has set in quite recently, however, and still more elaborate compromises have been proposed which attempt to control the losses and then maximize the expectation insofar as possible under this added restriction.

Still another approach is to try to deal with Case I by using maximum expectation, Answer 4, but modifying the expectation a bit. One way to do this is to argue that the difficulty arises from an inadequate analysis of the relevant values in the problem. If survival has some value, then this value should appear in the mathematical expectation. In other words, a term should be added which would be the product of the value of survival times the probability of nonsurvival.

A method which does not involve additional terms in the expectation and which has some historical development is a shift from values measured in monetary units to values meas-ured on the Utility scale described in the previous chapter. Un-

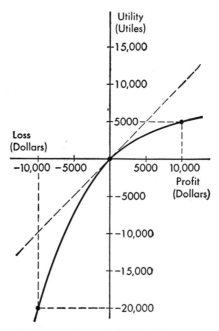

Fig. 6.01   Hypothetical Utility Curve

fortunately, as I have indicated, this Utility scale is still es-sentially speculative.

In Figure 6.01 an arbitrary Utility curve is illustrated. If the Utility of a dollar were constant then the dotted curve would describe the situation. I have shown the Utility curve as flattening off as the monetary gain increases. Income taxes might account for part of this effect so that $10,000 profit was not really worth twice as much as a $5000 profit. I have shown the curve as going down more sharply as the losses mount up.

This might be partially caused by the fact that if the capital is lost the businessman can be regarded as not only losing the profits on this particular deal but also the capacity to make profits on possible future deals.

Suppose now that the expectation of deal A is recalculated, using Utilities instead of dollars and cents. It becomes:

$$E'_A = (\tfrac{4}{5}) \ (5000) + (\tfrac{1}{5}) \ (-20{,}000) = 0.$$

The use of the criterion that the expectation be maximized will therefore lead to the decision: Choose deal B.

Conflict of Rules

Although I have raised this issue of choice of rules for action, I do not want to give the impression that this is a serious stumbling block to the applications of Statistical Decision. The choice of rule is tied very closely to the Probability and Value Systems. While I have separated the three components of a Decision-Maker for purposes of simplifying the exposition, it should be evident that in the construction of a Decision-Maker these three components are closely integrated.

In practice the situation is not as bad as the examples I have used in this chapter might indicate. Ordinarily the decisions obtained from the different criteria are quite similar. Even in cases in which different decisions are obtained this may be less annoying to the customer than it would be to the logician. When decisions are shifted it usually means that the decision is a fairly close one; the rules will therefore lead to good decisions even though they might not be the best possible. From what experience I have had in practical applications, I would say that these maxima or minima are relatively flat; in other words, even if the absolute maximum is not obtained there will be only a small loss involved in getting a value near the maximum rather than exactly at the maximum.

There has been a tendency in the past for research to concentrate on the absolute maximum, i.e., the very best. In this sense the "best" has been the enemy of the "good." Useful methodologies have been stigmatized as inefficient or crude when from a pragmatic standpoint there was really very little advantage to be obtained from the more complicated procedures that represented the "best" approach. One very real advantage of Statistical Decision is that it can provide a reconciliation between best and good. This advantage is lost, however, if the good is neglected and emphasis is placed entirely on the search for the best.

What this all means in practice is that nearly any reasonable criterion will lead to good decisions in the sense that if there are major advantages to one line of action this one will be picked out by the different criteria. On the other hand, if the decision is very close and it does not really make much difference which action is chosen, the different criteria may very well lead to different choices.

Even in situations in which there is a material difference between the lines of action in terms of consequences, the fact that different criteria lead to different choices of action is not necessarily bad. Thus in a gambling game such as blackjack the maximum expectation is possessed by the banker. The player has the advantage in terms of loss-control since he only risks his bet, whereas the bank sometimes has to pay off to a large number of players and thus has poorer control of its losses on a given hand. The house is in business for long-run profit so it regards the game as an instance of Case II, a routine decision, and it has the capital to pay off occasional heavy losses. The player who lacks this reserve may regard the game as an instance of Case I in which survival means that the player will be able to continue to play. Consequently, although the two criteria gave two different answers, both answers seem appropriate to the two different customers.

In the next two chapters I will deal with the maximum expectation criterion, but I have made this choice because I believe the criterion is a little easier to understand and because it does not involve any complicated mathematics.

Summary

Several possible rules for action are discussed and illustrated and the motivations for the rules examined. The two principal criteria are *maximizing the expected gain* and *minimizing the maximum risk*. While it is emphasized that the time is not yet ripe for the selection of any one rule as *the* rule for action, it is also pointed out that in practice the choice of rule is not critical.

CHAPTER 7

/ OPERATING A

DECISION–MAKER

The Saint Petersburg Paradox

Each of the components of the Decision-Maker has been briefly discussed, and now these pieces will be assembled into a machine for making decisions. I will try to illustrate the process by two simple little examples.

The first example is a coin-flipping game. This sort of example is especially convenient because it is easy to set up both the Predicting System and the Value System.

In this game a coin is flipped. If it is tails, the game ends. If it is heads, the banker pays out one dollar, and the coin is flipped again. This procedure is repeated on the second toss. The game automatically terminates on the third toss if it has not already been ended. The player pays one dollar for the privilege of playing. The decision to be made is: Should I play or bank the game?

The Predicting System is easily constructed providing we are satisfied that a fair coin is to be used (i.e., the probability of heads is equal to $\frac{1}{2}$ and so is the probability of tails). Let H stands for heads and T for tails. Then $P(T)$, the probability that the first flip comes up tails, is equal to $\frac{1}{2}$ and this is also the probability that the game ends with a single flip.

If the first toss is heads and the second toss is tails, then the game ends on the second toss. Let us consider the probability of this event, $P(HT)$. Since there is plenty of evidence that coin flips can be regarded as independent, the special multiplication rule (4.06) on page 72 can be applied:

$$P(H,T) = P(H)P(T) = (\tfrac{1}{2})(\tfrac{1}{2}) = \tfrac{1}{4}.$$

If the second toss is also heads the game goes on to the third toss and a repeated application of (4.06) gives:

$$P(HHT) = P(H)P(H)P(T) = (\tfrac{1}{2})(\tfrac{1}{2})(\tfrac{1}{2}) = (\tfrac{1}{2})^3 = \tfrac{1}{8}.$$
$$P(HHH) = P(H)P(H)P(H) = (\tfrac{1}{2})(\tfrac{1}{2})(\tfrac{1}{2}) = (\tfrac{1}{2})^3 = \tfrac{1}{8}.$$

This completes the Predicting System because we have found the probability of each of the possible outcomes. Next, a Value System must be constructed and here the usual dollars-and-cents scale seems appropriate. Suppose that the game is considered from the point of view of the player. Then the desirability of the outcome in which tails occurs on the first flip is zero since the player receives no payment. The desirability of the outcome HT is one dollar and so on. A table of probabilities and desirabilities can now be constructed:

Outcome	Probability	Desirability (in dollars)
T	1/2	0
HT	1/4	1
HHT	1/8	2
HHH	1/8	3

If the rule for action is maximize the expectation, then the expectation of the player, E_p, must be calculated:

$$E_p = (\tfrac{1}{2})0 + (\tfrac{1}{4})1 + (\tfrac{1}{8})2 + (\tfrac{1}{8})3 - 1 = -\$0.125$$

where the -1 is the price of playing the game. The expectation of the banker will simply be the negative of the player's expectation:

$$E_b = \$0.125.$$

This leads to the decision: Bank the game.

The player's expectation of $-\$0.125$ has the interpretation that the player will lose, on the average, an eighth of a dollar each time he plays the game. If he can play four hundred games in the course of an evening he will ordinarily leave some $50.00 with the banker. Perhaps this will teach him to abide by the time-honored rule: Don't play gambling games when your expectation is negative.

Las Vegas, Reno, and Monte Carlo make a steady profit because the customers either do not know this rule or else deliberately disregard it. Very few gambling houses, legal or illegal, will play fair games with their customers (i.e., games in which the expectation of both house and customer is zero). The house is in a business which is less speculative than most investment trusts or small businesses—only the customers are really gambling, not the house itself.

The coin-flipping game can be made more interesting by altering some of the rules. For example, the limitation that the game automatically ends on three tosses can be removed and the game allowed to continue until the first tail appears, whenever this may be. In this event there is no limit to the number of possible outcomes and the expectation is not so easy to calculate. The terms are:

$$E = (1/2)\,0 + (1/4)\,1 + (1/8)\,2 + (1/16)\,3$$
$$+ (1/32)\,4 + \ldots - 1$$

where the three dots indicate that there are infinitely many more terms but they have not been written down. The reader can test his understanding of this material by writing down some more of the terms.

Now even though there are infinitely many terms in this sum, a mathematician can add them up. If you are not a mathematician, you will have to take my word for it that the sum of all these terms equals one and hence the expectation turns out to be zero.

Therefore the maximum expectation criterion indicates a completely balanced choice as to whether to bank or play this modified game. However, the player risks only a dollar while the banker, if there is a long run of heads, will have to pay out a large sum of money. Consequently by the loss-control criterion the decision is: Let the other fellow bank the game.

A very curious result occurs if one further modification in the game is made. Suppose that the game goes on until the first tail appears and furthermore the banker's payments are altered. He must pay $1.00 for *HT*, $2.00 for *HHT*, $4.00 for *HHHT*, $8.00 for *HHHHT*, and so on, *doubling* the payment each time. This much increased schedule of payments is called the St. Petersburg game (or paradox). It leads to a very strange result.

Naturally the banker should be paid more as a stake because he must pay out more. How much should he demand of the player to make this a fair game with zero expectation?

The expectation now becomes:

$$E = (1/2) \, 0 + (1/4) \, 1 + (1/8) \, 2 + (1/16) \, 4 + (1/32) \, 8$$
$$+ \ldots - \text{stake.}$$
$$E = 0 + 1/4 + 1/4 + 1/4 + 1/4 + \ldots - \text{stake.}$$

Not even a mathematician can add up this infinite series because it has no upper limit. If the banker follows the rule against negative expectations, he should refuse to play the game even if the player offers him a stake equal to the present national debt.

This is a paradox because most people (including mathematicians) would be glad to bank the game for a million dollars, or even a thousand dollars. It looks as though something is wrong with mathematical expectations if they lead to unreasonable decisions.

Many explanations have been offered to resolve the paradox. It is interesting to note that the first proposal for Utilities instead of monetary units was suggested in order to resolve this paradox. Daniel Bernoulli argued that the logarithm of the payment, rather than the payment itself, was an appropriate measure of Utility of the payment (the expectation is finite if the logarithms of the payments are used). This ingenious solution merely led mathematicians to devise new versions of the game in which the expectation became infinite even if logarithms were used.

Actually the St. Petersburg game is not a genuine paradox. The difficulty arises because the very simple model of the game used to calculate probabilities omits the limitations of any real game—such as the banker's ability to pay—and if a more realistic model is constructed to include these limitations, reasonable (and finite) stakes are obtained. The moral of this story is that mathematical, like verbal, analogies can be carried too far (i.e., to infinity).

Some people have erroneously concluded that the whole difficulty with the St. Petersburg game is that the payments go up so fast (doubling each time). Here is another game, due to Feller,[1] with which you might like to experiment.

Feller's game: A coin is repeatedly tossed, and the total number of heads and tails is recorded. The banker pays one cent for each toss until the game comes to an end. The player pays a stake for the privilege of playing the game. The game comes to an end whenever more heads have been tossed than tails. Thus, if a head appears on the first toss the game ends. If a tail is followed by two heads the game ends on the third toss, and so on.

Hint: Play the game, do *not* bank it. It may save arguments to agree to play a fixed number of games, say ten, *before* commencing the play. You can afford to pay a considerable stake for the privilege of playing this game. For details see Feller's excellent book on probability. This very simple game has an infinite expectation if no limits are placed on the banker's ability to pay or on the number of games to be played. Even if played for pennies the losses can easily run into many dollars. It can be one of the most exasperating games ever invented. So don't pick a banker with a bad temper!

[1] Feller, W., *An Introduction to Probability Theory and Its Applications,* John Wiley & Sons, Inc., New York, 1948.

Business Decisions

Let us turn now to the sad plight of a manufacturer, Mr. M., whose factory makes plastic gadgets which contain small metal inserts. If these inserts are the proper size the gadget works; if they are oversized or undersized the gadget will not function, and the product must be scrapped. Lately Mr. M. has become convinced that entirely too many of the metal inserts are defective, and he calls a conference to discuss the problem.

"Something has got to be done about our scrap rate!" Mr. M. announces. "All the profits are going into scrap. I want some suggestions."

"We've had a bad batch of inserts lately," Purchasing admits, "but no other supplier gives us a price on inserts. We've howled and the supplier has checked his production processes and has got them back into control. On the whole his quality has been pretty good for the price."

Mr. M. glares. "So you suggest that we go ahead as usual— well—" (Mr. M. pauses as he remembers his blood pressure and his doctor's instructions), "well, how about other suggestions?"

"I think we should inspect all the inserts before we use them," Production declares. He's made this suggestion before, but Costs has always vetoed it.

"It doesn't cost much to inspect one insert," Costs chimes in, "but to inspect *every* one will knock down the profits a whole lot more than a little scrap. But we might inspect a sample from each lot and ship the bum lots back."

"No soap," growls Production. "What are my boys supposed to do while the inserts go shuttling back and forth across the state?"

After Production and Costs have restated their positions six times without modifying them one iota there is a lull.

"This is getting nowhere," Mr. M. points out rather grimly.

There is a silence so profound that one can almost hear Mr. M.'s ulcers growing. Finally a junior engineer, fresh out of college and quality control courses, ventures a suggestion.

"We might take a sample and decide, on the basis of the sample, whether or not to 100% inspect the lots. That way we'd only have to inspect part of the lots, mainly the bad ones which we would want to inspect anyway."

"That sounds O.K.," nods Production. "How do you do it, Junior?"

"Well," Junior launches into the topic, "we get out the AOQL charts and—"

The others listen to this statistical gibberish with increasing impatience. Mr. M. looks unhappy—a bad sign. Finally he breaks into the oratory:

"We don't want a lecture. How much does all this cost?"

"I'd have to figure it out by my charts—" Junior says apologetically.

"Just scrapping a few gadgets now and then would be cheaper than all this rigmarole," contributes Costs.

"If we gotta inspect we might as well inspect them all," adds Production, whose original enthusiasm is much dampened by the lecture.

"O.K.," Junior interposes desperately to save his brainchild. "Let's get the costs on all three methods." And Junior writes down on a pad of paper:

A_1: No inspection.
A_2: 100% inspection.
A_3: Sample inspection.

"What's the usual quality on inserts?" Junior asks Purchasing.

"Depends on whether the supplier is in control or not," Purchasing answers. "In control we get 2% defectives, out of control maybe 10%."

"How much of the time is the manufacturing in control?"

"Most of the time—say four out of five lots."

"O.K.," says Junior. "Now how much does it cost to scrap a gadget?"

"About two bits—25 cents," Costs replies.

"So let's figure costs on the basis of a hundred inserts to make it easier," Junior begins. "That means we lose a quarter apiece on the two bad inserts or 50 cents when production is in control. And we lose $2.50 on the ten bad inserts when production is out of control, so that on the average the scrap costs, with no inspection, would be:

$$E_1 = (4/5) \ (0.50) + (1/5) \ (2.50) = 0.40 + 0.50 = \$0.90$$

per hundred inserts."

Mr. M. groans softly.

"Now let's see what happens with 100% inspection. How much does it cost to inspect an insert?"

"The last time we tried it—before we gave it up—it cost about a penny per insert to inspect it when tool and labor costs are figured in," replies Costs with just a suggestion of a smile of satisfaction.

"So if we 100% inspect we avoid scrap but it costs us a dollar per hundred inserts to inspect. So $E_2 = \$1.00$."

"That's what I said before," Costs says with a smile. "You lose money by inspecting."

"Now suppose that we pass the good lots, those with 2% defective, and 100% inspect the bad lots, those with 10% defective. What would this cost?" continues Junior, ignoring the interruption. "It costs 50 cents for scrap in the good lots and a buck for inspection in the bad lots or an over-all cost of:

$$E_3 = (4/5) \ (0.50) + (1/5) \ (1.00) = 0.40 + 0.20 = \$0.60."$$

Junior paused. Mr. M. stares at the 60-cent figure with new interest.

"Wait a minute," Costs objects. "What about the sampling costs?"

"And how the hell do you know which are the good lots?" demands Production. "Do you use a forked-stick divining rod?"

"This isn't a real scheme yet," Junior says hastily. "I just wanted to show that it was possible to save money by separating the two kinds of lots. We'll have to do the separation by a sample inspection plan, say by inspecting 10% of all incoming lots. This would add 10 cents to the cost per hundred and make the total 70 cents."

"How does this sampling business work?" asks Mr. M., who is warming up to the scheme.

"I can't give a plan right off, sir," Junior admits. "It takes a while to work out a good one, but I can give an example of how such a plan would work. Suppose ten samples are taken at random from each lot of one hundred. These samples are inspected and the following rule is set up: If there are no defectives, pass the lot without further inspection; if there are any defectives, inspect the rest of the lot.

"First, let's see what happens in good lots. We now need to calculate the chance that there are no defectives or, what is the same thing, the chance that all the inserts are good. The chance that the first insert is good is 98/100, the chance that the second insert is good is also about 98/100, and so on for all ten in the sample. Since these are all independent events, or nearly so,

$$P \text{ (All ten are good)} =$$
$$\underbrace{P \text{ (First is good)} \; P \text{ (Second is good)} \ldots P \text{ (Tenth is good)}}_{\text{ten terms}}$$

$$P \text{ (All ten are good)} =$$
$$\underbrace{\left(\frac{98}{100}\right)\left(\frac{98}{100}\right)\left(\frac{98}{100}\right) \cdots \left(\frac{98}{100}\right)}_{\text{ten terms}} = \left(\frac{98}{100}\right)^{10} = 0.81 \text{."}$$

Junior takes a minute to whip out the value of 0.81 on his slide rule.

"Next, consider what happens in bad lots. The only change is that the probability that an insert is good is now only 90/100, so

$$P \text{ (All ten are good)} = \left(\frac{90}{100}\right)^{10} = 0.35$$

and we can set up a table which tells the story."

Junior writes down the following table on the pad:

Quality of Lot	*Probability of*	
	Passing the Lot	*100% Inspecting the Lot*
Good (2% defective)	0.81	0.19
Bad (10% defective)	0.35	0.65

"For good lots," Junior continues, "we lose 50 cents in scrap when we pass the lot and 90 cents in added inspection costs if we 100% inspect. So this gives:

$$(0.81) \ (0.50) + (0.19) \ (0.90) = \$0.576$$

as the average cost of the scheme, apart from the original sample, when the lot is good. For bad lots we get

$$(0.35) \ (2.50) + (0.65) \ (0.90) = \$1.40$$

"To get the expected cost, E_4, for this sample scheme we note that 80% of the time we will lose $0.576 per hundred and 20% of the time we will lose $1.40 per hundred, and we will spend 10 cents per hundred for the sample inspections, so:

$$E_4 = (0.80) \ (0.576) + (0.20) \ (1.40) + 0.10 = \$0.8528$$

or about 85 cents per hundred, which would save a nickel per hundred over not inspecting!"

"But that nickel will be eaten up by inspection costs because it costs money to take a random sample." Costs is unconvinced. "Besides, the figures are all guesses—"

"If we run the scheme maybe we can figure a gimmick to cut inspection costs," Junior insists. "Anyway since we get inserts in lots of ten thousand, I'll bet we can get by with a couple of hundred in the sample and still give decent separation. In addition we'll always have a tab on the quality of incoming lots so we can yell before we ever get badly hurt."

Mr. M. only smiles. There is a really profound silence. Mr. M.'s ulcers have stopped growing.

Levels of Decision

The fable of Mr. M. really involves two separate decision problems. There is the executive decision: What inspection

scheme should be used? There is also a lower-level decision if
Junior's scheme is employed: Should a given lot be passed or
100% inspected? This latter decision is almost an automatic
process. A sample of inserts will be collected and inspected and
the defectives counted. If there are more than so-many defectives the lot will be 100% inspected. In this sense the decision
is objective—it is made by the data and the human factor is
essentially eliminated from the process.

Objectivity of decision is an important goal in science and
is partly responsible for the current popularity of modern
statistics in scientific research. Statistical methods allow the
data to "speak for itself" with a minimum intrusion of human
preconceptions and biases. There is a very practical advantage
to this mechanization: Scientists will be led to the same conclusions if they start from the same data and premises. Not only
does this produce the agreement of individuals so essential to
effective group action, but it tends to reduce the amount of
energy wasted in futile scientific controversies.

In the past, and even today, it is not uncommon for scientists
to disagree violently on the conclusions to be drawn from a
given body of data. But although there may be a complete
deadlock at the data level, it may be possible for the scientists
to agree at the next higher level, i.e., on the *rules* for drawing
inferences from data. If agreement is reached on these rules, and
these rules are applied to the data, then agreement on the interpretation of the data may be obtained.

I think that Statistical Decision can play much the same role
outside the boundaries of science; that is, it *could* be a method
for reaching group decisions. The agreement of two or more
individuals is often an important aspect of everyday decisions.

It may be easier for a group to agree on probabilities and desirabilities than on actions considered per se. If probabilities
and desirabilities are still too controversial then it may be possible to agree on the next level—Prediction and Value Systems. In any case, these concepts of Statistical Decision may
at least serve to break down the main problem into a number

of smaller, and possibly simpler, problems. The attempt to think in terms of numbers instead of words may in itself help to clear the atmosphere. Somehow the use of words always seems to inject irrelevant or emotion-charged issues into a discussion. I will consider these issues again in the last chapter.

Summary

The functioning of a Decision-Maker is studied in two very simple situations, a gambling game and an industrial inspection problem. Some potentially valuable features of the statistical Decision-Maker are noted.

CHAPTER 8

SEQUENTIAL DECISION

Decision Chains

The types of decisions which you may be called upon to make are probably quite unlike the very simple examples of the last chapter. To meet more complex and realistic decision problems, it will be necessary to know the technical details of Prediction and Value Systems—details that I have been avoiding. Moreover, a thorough knowledge of the symbolic language of science, as well as specialized information about the field of application, may be required.

The St. Petersburg game is simple because the probability mechanism and rules of the game are man-made and because there are three centuries of experience which can be utilized. The case of Mr. M. is not quite so simple because, although there are some twenty years of experience with industrial-sampling inspection, each individual application encounters a situation more or less unique insofar as probabilities and costs are concerned. In practice these quantities (which I manufactured for the example) would have to be determined from available past experience or possibly from a trial run of the sampling scheme; that is, from an experiment whose main purpose would be to acquire the needed experience.

Both of the examples have dealt with repeatable events and the costs and probabilities for such events can be obtained in a straightforward fashion. Many decisions, however, deal with novel situations in which past experience is scanty and in which even the possible courses of action are not evident. If Statistical

Decision is to have a broad field of application it must be capable of dealing with problems of this nature. Hence the conceptual basis of Statistical Decision will have to be broadened or generalized so as to encompass more complex decision problems. The easiest way to see what generalization is required is to take a look at a more difficult situation.

An emergency ambulance brings a dangerously ill patient into a hospital. At the time that the patient is admitted there are obviously hundreds of possible courses of action which might be taken. These would range from putting the patient into a bed to performing a major operation. At the time of admission, however, it is not going to be possible to make the choice of action because there is not enough information to make an adequate decision. The line of action actually followed would be to postpone any final decision and to concentrate on obtaining the necessary information. The first steps are to take a history and make an examination of the patient.

From this information it may be possible to make a diagnosis. A diagnosis is simply a classification by cause of illness. The practical advantage of a correct diagnosis is that it greatly simplifies the decision problem. If the patient is suffering from pneumonia, then the relevant past experience will be that dealing with pneumonia. This information will, in turn, suggest a list of possible courses of action. The course of action which has been most successful in this past experience might be the administration of antibiotics.

On the other hand, as is often the case, there might be several diagnoses which could be made from the history and preliminary examination. It would then be necessary to obtain more information before coming to a decision. Blood tests and other laboratory tests might be performed in an attempt to eliminate the alternative diagnoses.

The process of diagnosis is a decision problem, but it is only a step in a larger decision problem. If a diagnosis which satisfies the members of the staff is made there will still be other decision problems associated with the choice of therapy. Relatively few diseases have specific remedies, i.e., therapies which will cure the disease nearly all the time. Most diseases may be treated in any of several ways, and none of these therapies will work all the time. For example, there may be a choice between drugs and an operation. In such a case, a second remedy may be tried if one remedy fails.

Even if the patient responds to treatment there are other decisions which must be made such as: When is it safe to discharge the patient? It is characteristic of most practical decision problems that they involve not just one decision but rather a *series* of decisions. Such a series can be called a chain.

Decision chains occur in the actual problems encountered in science, business, or everyday affairs. Military operations also involve *sequences* of decisions and often simultaneous sequences at different levels. Thus at the staff level, strategic decisions must be made or changed as new information comes in; at the field level, these decisions must be utilized to make tactical decisions; and at the level of the G.I., these tactical decisions must be used to make vitally important personal decisions when the consequences of a bad decision may be fatal.

One of the advantages of Statistical Decision over its predecessors is that this sequential nature of the problem is recognized and is incorporated directly into the structure of the theory.

There is more to Sequential Decision than the job of hooking up a chain of Decision-Makers. Some very difficult questions arise when machinery is linked together in a series. In some ways these difficulties are analogous to those encountered when the components of a radio circuit are hooked together. The performance of one set of tubes not only affects what happens further along the line, but sometimes the effects may travel backwards along the chain. Peculiarities of a loud speaker, for example, may affect the amplifier section, and sometimes surprising phenomena, such as loud wailing noises, will cause the equipment as a whole to perform very poorly even though the individual components have performed well when tested separately. This phenomenon, called *feedback* by the communications engineers, is a key topic in cybernetics.[1]

Although the construction of a Sequential Decision-Maker involves technical difficulties above and beyond those encountered in one-stage Decision-Makers, a very rapid exploration of the subject is currently in progress. This work, I hope, will supplement the present Sequential Decision-Makers (only a few of which have passed the developmental stage).

"Sequential" is currently used in two senses—a narrow one and a broader one. In the narrow sense, the word deals with the situation in which experience is collected in little units (observations) one at a time and the information at each stage is used to make the choice between a terminal decision (such as pass or 100% inspect) and a decision to take still another observation. The broader usage of the word allows for such alternatives as collecting some entirely different data or doing an experiment to see if the efficiency of the collection process can be improved.

Many practical decision problems are sequential in a still wider sense. The decisions may relate not only to the process of collecting the data which go into the hopper of the Decision-Maker but to any other stage in the process as well. For example, it may be worthwhile to study the methods of implementing the recommendations. Operations analysis [2] is concerned with this problem (mainly in the military field). Thus even if the Decision-Maker recommends that submarines should be attacked by air-surface teams equipped with given weapons, there are many other decisions necessary to implement this verdict. For example, there may be various patterns of fire that might be used, and a choice among these is necessary.

The decisions might even involve the Decision-Maker itself. Thus one course of action might be "Stop work on this project of evaluating the services of public-health nurses until an ade-

---

[1] Wiener, N., *Cybernetics*, John Wiley & Sons, Inc., New York, 1948.

[2] Morse, P., and Kimball, G., *Methods of Operations Research*, John Wiley & Sons, Inc., New York, 1951.

quate value system can be constructed." Or it might even be "Don't bother with Statistical Decision at all in this problem since it would cost more to develop an adequate predicting system than we could hope to gain by making the right decision."

Sequential Inspection

In this section Sequential Decision in the narrow sense will be considered. In the narrow sense the sequential concepts are involved largely in answering the question, "When do I have enough data to make a decision?" This is often an important question in practice and, although the sequential answer has been applied mainly to industrial inspection problems, there is a large area of scientific research in which these sequential concepts might prove fruitful.

Suppose that I go to the market to buy some grapes. If I take a grape as a sample, I hope to improve my decision by bringing in additional data. If the grape is sweet, then I purchase a bunch; if it is sour I postpone purchase. These decisions are called *terminal* decisions because when they are made the decision process comes to an end. The sequential approach allows me a third course of action: If the grape is "in between" I might feel that I still did not have sufficient information to make an adequate decision and that I should take a second grape to obtain this information.

The costs of samples enter very directly into sequential processes. If I sample one grape the proprietor of the fruit stand may not object; if I take two, he may frown; if I take three or more, I might precipitate an unpleasant argument. This would have to be balanced against the consequences of getting "stung" on my purchase.

If my sequential concepts are broad, there might be an additional alternative. I might feel that the information I really required was not merely a second sample of the grapes but, say, a sample of the grapes offered by a rival merchant across the street.

Now let us turn to the corresponding problem which faces

our old friend Mr. M., who is purchasing metal inserts for the plastic gadgets that he manufactures (Chapter 7, page 123) . The technical complexities of Sequential Decision prevent me from giving a simple example of the process so what I shall do instead is to give an outline of the steps which are followed in setting up a sequential scheme.

Sequential Processes of Inspection

The first step is to gather together the necessary prior information. This will mean that the following costs and consequences must be examined: (1) the cost of sampling, (2) the cost of allowing a defective part to enter the production process, and (3) the cost of rejecting a lot (i.e., the cost of 100% sampling) . In addition to costs the prior probabilities must be determined from knowledge of the production processes used in fabricating metal inserts and also from the past experience with the quality of parts delivered.

When this information is assembled the construction of a sequential sampling scheme can begin. The construction is a technical job involving much mathematics and computation. The following outline gives only the skeleton and I shall give a reference to a publication where the "meat" may be found:

I. Draw a graph with one axis representing the number of good pieces (i) and the other axis representing the number of defective pieces (j) .

   A. Any given stage in the sampling process will correspond to some point on the graph.

   B. Any actual series of samples may be represented by the zigzag line joining a series of points.

II. For any point on the graph (which may be denoted by two numbers i,j) the probability that the shipment contains a given proportion of defectives, $p,$ can be computed by Bayes rule (see page 81) .

III. If the sampling is terminated at any given stage (i,j) the cost information, combined with the results of step II, can be used to calculate the *expected cost* of either of the two possible *terminal* decisions. Therefore, calculate the expected cost of decision if the shipment is rejected and also the expected cost if the shipment is accepted.

IV. Rule: The terminal decision at any stage will be the one with the smallest expected cost. Let E_{ij}^t be the minimum expected cost for the stage (i,j) of a terminal decision.

V. If the sampling is continued at the stage (i,j) and another piece is inspected there will also be an expected cost of decision. Let E_{ij}^e be the expected cost of decision if the sampling is not terminated.

VI. Rule: Continue the inspection if E_{ij}^e is less than E_{ij}^t. Otherwise terminate the process and make the decision in accordance with the rule given in step IV. Let E_{ij}^* be the smaller of E_{ij}^e and E_{ij}^t or in mathematical notation

$$E_{ij}^* = \text{minimum } (E_{ij}^e, E_{ij}^t).$$

VII. The above rules specify the sequential process. To present the rules in a simple form, each point on the graph may be colored as follows:

A. Color the point white if $E_{ij}^e \leq E_{ij}^t$.

B. Color the point red if $E_{ij}^e > E_{ij}^t$ and if step IV leads to rejection of the lot.

C. Color the point blue if $E_{ij}^e > E_{ij}^t$ and if step IV leads to acceptance of the shipment.

Although the construction of the sampling plan is quite complicated the execution of the plan requires a minimum of intellectual prowess. After each sample the inspector counts the number of good pieces found so far, (i), and the number of defectives, (j), and locates the corresponding point on the graph. The color of this point then tells the inspector what to do (for example, if the point is colored white the inspector takes another sample).

If this is still too much of a strain on the abilities of the inspector, a machine can easily be constructed so that the inspector has only to punch one key if the last piece inspected is good and another key if the piece is defective. A loud-speaker then tells him what to do next.

If the process of inspection can be made automatic by the use of X-ray inspection or some other device, the entire decision can be made mechanically and the resulting robot takes over the job of a purchasing agent! Statistical Decision leads to the possibility of technological unemployment at a lower executive level.

When the scheme is placed in operation it should, in the long run, lead to minimum costs. It may produce a substantial reduction in costs compared to a single sample plan such as the one discussed in Chapter 7. This is likely to happen if the costs of inspection are high—a situation which might occur in destructive inspection (where the part must be destroyed in the process of inspection). Test firing of bullets is one example of a destructive inspection method, eating grapes is another example.

This discussion is incomplete because the actual calculation of quantities like E_{ij}^e has not been mentioned. Such calculation may be done by an ingenious method due to A. Wald. Remember that the quantities like E_{ij}^t can be calculated directly, using Bayes rule, and this method can also be used to obtain the probability of getting a defective in the next sample if i good pieces and j defectives have been obtained so far. Let this probability be p_{ij}.

If the sample is defective the next stage will be $(i, j + 1)$ and the expected cost of decision will be $E_{i,j+1}^*$. If the sample is good the next stage will be $(i + 1, j)$ and the expected cost of decision will be $E_{i+1,j}^*$. In either case it will cost an amount, say c, to take the additional sample. Consequently the expected cost of continuing the sampling process will be

$$E_{ij}^e = p_{ij}E_{i,j+1}^* + (1 - p_{ij})E_{i+1,j}^* + c.$$

At first glance we seem to have accomplished nothing by this formula since the E^e's depend on E^*'s which we do not know. In practical problems, however, the sequential process eventu-

EXAMPLE OF A SEQUENTIAL PLAN FOR MEDICAL RESEARCH

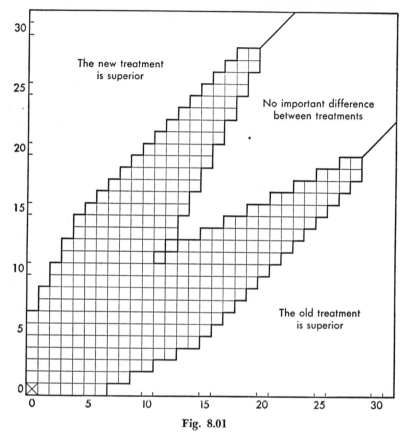

Fig. 8.01

Instructions for use of above
chart appear on facing page.

INSTRUCTIONS FOR USE OF SEQUENTIAL CHART

The plan is designed for clinical experimentation where a) the patients enter the study over an extended period of time but where it is possible to *pair* consecutive entrants, b) there are two treatments under study (*old* and *new*), and one individual in the pair is assigned (alternately or at random) to each treatment, and c) after treatment the patients are classified as *cured* or *not-cured*.

Use of the Plan: Each pair of patients constitutes a sub-experiment whose outcome is plotted on the above chart (Fig. 8.01) in accordance with the three rules given below. The plotting starts from the "✕" in the lower left-hand corner of the chart.

PLOTTING RULES

1. If both patients are cured or if neither patient is cured, nothing is plotted.
2. If the old treatment cures and the new fails, mark an "✕" to the *right* of the last entry on the chart.
3. If the new treatment cures and the old fails, mark an "✕" *above* the last entry on the chart.

After each entry is plotted a decision is made. This decision will depend on whether or not the last entry is outside of the heavy lines (barriers) bounding the chart.

DECISION RULES

1. If no barrier is crossed, continue the study.
2. If a barrier is crossed, stop the study and make the statement (or take the action) given on the chart for that particular barrier.

ally comes to an end and at this stage (by the definition of E^* in step VI) $E^* = E^t$, and we can find E^t. The formula can therefore be used to work backward step by step and find all the E^e's by an *iterative* process. A worked example of this sort of scheme can be found on page 117 of Wald's book, *Statistical Decision Functions*.[3]

The moral of this story is that although the technical difficulties in Sequential Decision are formidable, the mathematicians can devise ways and means to overcome them. By the time they are finished the Decision-Maker can be operated by almost anyone.

Narrow Sequential Schemes in Science

At first glance the sampling inspection scheme presented in the previous sections may seem far removed from scientific research, but actually a scientist often faces virtually the same problem. Medical men, for example, may wish to determine whether a new treatment offers any advantage over a standard therapy. When the treatment is given to a patient, the results are often described as "success" or "failure," classifications which are obviously quite similar to the non-defective and defective categories of the industrial problem.

The purposes of the doctor and manufacturer may also be parallel. The manufacturer wants to use the information obtained by inspecting a sample of metal inserts in order to determine the action which should be taken on the entire shipment of inserts (i.e., whether to pass or 100% inspect the lot). The doctor wants to use the information obtained on a short series of patients in order to recommend the therapy that should be given to the *population* or class of patients who suffer from a specific disease. Like the manufacturer who has two courses of action with respect to the entire shipment of inserts, the doctor has two courses of action with respect to the population

---

[3] Wald, A., *Statistical Decision Functions*, John Wiley & Sons, Inc., New York, 1950.

of patients: he can recommend either the new treatment or the standard therapy.

At this point some major differences arise between the *actions* of manufacturer and the doctor. The shipment of inserts is an easily defined group of objects, whereas the patients who suffer from a specific disease constitute a more tenuous collection of individuals. Moreover, the manufacturer has control over the shipment, whereas the doctor does not have control over all patients with a given disease. Consequently the manufacturer can enforce his decision; if he says "100% inspect the lot," he can be reasonably confident that this action will be taken. The doctor, however, can only *recommend* to other doctors that they follow the new treatment; he cannot compel them to do this. His problem is more complicated in that he must convince his colleagues that the new treatment is superior. Therefore the problem of the doctor is not merely one of selecting the best treatment, but also of *demonstrating* the superiority to a somewhat skeptical audience.

A second distinction lies in the value systems involved in manufacturing and medicine. In the industrial problem the cost of a wrong decision is evaluated in terms of dollars and cents, and a good cost accountant or production analyst can estimate the costs of decision. In the medical problem, however, it is not a simple matter to set up a cost scale. If the new treatment is abandoned, although it could have saved ten additional lives per hundred patients, what is the cost of this mistake?

The lack of an adequate Value System in the problem is a serious obstruction to the application of Decision-Makers of the type which I have emphasized so far. A temporary expedient is to use a simple Value System in place of a more realistic one. To some extent the use of this simple Value System may be justified by the shift in point of view from choice of action to demonstration.

In spite of these distinctions between industry and science, there is enough common ground so that the Decision-Makers developed in one field have been successfully used in the other with relatively minor modifications. In both the industrial and medical examples that I have given here, there is this fundamental question of taking action with respect to a large aggregate of individuals (patients or inserts) on the basis of a sample. The question stands out clearly in the simpler industrial problem, but unfortunately it is occasionally overlooked in medical problems.

At present there are only a few instances of narrow sequential plans, like the inspection plan, which are used in science. In ten years I think that there will be a much wider use of such schemes.

Broad Sequential Schemes in Science

When Sequential Decision in the wide sense is considered, there is no such dearth of examples. Most comprehensive research projects are inherently sequential, each stage of the study laying the groundwork for, and sometimes suggesting, the next stage. The sequential concept is *not* the discovery of statisticians; they have simply *systematized* this idea, an important step in harnessing an idea and putting it to work.

Let us suppose that a research team is searching for an antibiotic which will be effective against a strain of polio virus. The end product of the search will be, if all goes well, a recommendation of some chemical to be used in therapy. Before this stage of selecting an antibiotic is reached, however, a long and complex chain of preliminary decisions must be followed.

The first step is to take advantage of previous experience, to search the medical and technical literatures for information. If the team is to use laboratory experimentation as the primary tool, it will be necessary to standardize techniques and determine the accuracies of various measurements.

The second link in the decision chain is to choose the candidates for testing those antibiotics which might work. Next the experiment must be planned and performed. When this experiment is finished the results may then be used to select the candidates for further study, another decision problem.

After the unpromising candidates have been weeded out,

efficient methods of administration and optimum dosage must be determined. By proceeding stepwise the scientist eventually arrives at the terminal decision recommending one or more antibiotics for use against the virus.

This laboratory experimentation must then be followed by further testing, possibly by the clinical staff of a hospital. Even this may not be sufficient, however, and an extensive cooperative study involving hospitals all over America may be undertaken (as was done, for example, in connection with penicillin and syphilis).

The actual conduct of research is not always a straight-forward process; sometimes a line of research ends up in a blind alley, and a new start must be made. Sometimes a promising lead is overlooked and not exploited for many years. The various specialized techniques employed in the application of Statistical Decision to scientific work are designed to avoid blind alleys and to reveal promising leads. Detours will still occur, even when Statistical Decision is used, but there will be fewer of them.

I do not want to give the impression, however, that Statistical Decision will substitute for the creative imagination which is the mark of a top-flight scientist or that it will enable a complete mechanization of the process of scientific research. Rather it is a powerful tool like a microscope or analytical balance. Modern research workers, especially in the biological sciences, have found that they must learn to use statistical methodologies just as they must learn microscopic techniques. Like a microscope, the methods of Statistical Decision can be inefficiently used or even misused. Unlike the microscope, the processes of Statistical Decision are intellectual rather than physical; they represent a quantitative logic which enables a scientist to take effective action toward the accomplishment of the purposes of his research.

Statistical Decision is a powerful instrument in the process of discovery. It is not, however, an automatic process of discovery. It cannot lead to the choice of the best course of action if this action has been omitted from the list of possible actions.

It may, however, assist in an additional investigation to determine possible courses of action.

The principles of Statistical Decision are useful even when it is inconvenient to go through all the technicalities of the construction of an actual Decision-Maker. The mere qualitative analysis of the problem may lead, without numerical work, to an improvement of the research process. The qualitative outlining of the steps toward decision forces the scientist to systematize his planning and to think in terms of the components of decision, to envision what prior information is needed, what values and purposes are involved, and what the next step in the research process might be.

It has been my own experience that the most profitable part of my consultative work has been in the supplying of a conceptual *framework* which the research worker can use to clarify the planning of his project. On many occasions my scientific friends, after assimilating these principles, were able to answer for themselves the questions they had come to ask me. I believe most consulting statisticians would concur with these remarks and would agree that the most important part of their job lies in the formulation, rather than technical solution, of problems presented by the research worker.

Summary

Complex decision problems require not one but a series of Decision-Makers. The linking together of a chain of Decision-Makers leads to the concept of Sequential Decision. In the narrow sense "sequential" refers to a plan in which, at each stage, a decision is made as to whether to continue the experiment or to stop experimentation and make a terminal decision. In the broad sense, the direction or path of the experimentation is also determined by a stepwise plan. An example of a narrow sequential plan for industrial sampling is indicated, and a broad sequential plan for a scientific research project is described. The utility of the concepts, as well as the techniques, of Sequential Decision is emphasized.

CHAPTER 9 / **DATA**

The Fuel

In the previous chapters I have described the *internal* structure of the Decision-Maker. Now I want to discuss the *external* relationships, the manner in which Statistical Decision is coupled to the real world. Until an adequate linkage with the real world is provided, the mechanism is only an intellectual toy.

The Decision-Maker is tied to reality by both the input and output stage. The output, recommendations for action, will only be of practical value if the customer actually puts these recommendations into effect in the real world. Problems arise when the customer implements the recommendations—problems which may be overcome by Sequential Decision or by such techniques as Operations Analysis—but in general the output coupling is rather straightforward. I want to focus attention on the other link, the input, the insertion of data into the mechanism.

Data may be regarded as the fuel of the Decision-Maker. This fuel must be of good quality if the mechanism is to function properly. Ordinarily Statistical Decision does not use raw data —it operates on rather highly refined information. Unless considerable care is devoted to the process of refining data, even the fanciest chromium-plated Decision-Maker will operate at low efficiency. In this chapter I want to tell you a little about the operation of a data refinery.

I cannot overemphasize the importance of good data to the

successful operation of a Decision-Maker. Some customers have
the erroneous impression that an elaborate statistical technique
will compensate for poor quality data. It is true that a high-
powered, efficient technique can squeeze the last drop of information out of the data—but it can neither supply information which is lacking nor eliminate misinformation. In fact, it
is generally true that a more elaborate analysis requires *higher*
quality data. A *single* item of bad data may disrupt some of the
extremely elaborate statistical devices.

Another point to be made is that the job of collecting good
data demands just as much intelligence, foresight, and imagination as the job of designing Decision-Makers. The price of
good data is eternal vigilance. Some theoretical folks tend to
look down their noses at the scientists who collect data. When
these theoretical people are faced with a practical problem,
their naive attitude toward data frequently leads them into
some amusing boners. It is also possible, of course, to go too far
in the other direction; in fact, this attitude is even more common. The scientist becomes so engrossed in the desperate ac-
cumulation of huge stacks of data that he never stops to think
what he will do with the data after it has been collected. When,
at last, the scientist does get around to the analysis of the data he
may find that very minor flaws in his collecting or recording
techniques have rendered his data worthless. The consulting
statistician often has to play the villain's role in the last act of
this scientific tragedy—it is a very unpleasant part of his job.

Evaluation of Data

When we sit down to make a decision we start with a tremendous supply of data. We, ourselves, have years of personal
experience and, if we take the trouble to go to a library, we
can avail ourselves of the accumulated experience of centuries.
Nearly all this experience will be irrelevant to our decision,
however, so the first problem which we must face is that of
trying to separate a few kernels of grain from a great pile of
chaff.

The first requirement of good data is relevancy.

Even when the separation of the relevant data is accomplished, a second sifting is necessary. This second screening involves the *reliability* of the data. I find it very annoying that when I think about a topic my memory is likely to provide me with a hodgepodge of hearsay, gossip, anecdote, and folk lore. This vague, dubious, but colorful information seems to be readily retained in my memory, but if I want facts and figures I have to rely on some form of written memory.

Now why do I regard hearsay or folk lore as unreliable? One reason is that this type of data often turns out to be *biased*. I shall be using this word "bias" in a somewhat more general sense than its ordinary usage. In everyday language we frequently use the word to denote deliberately dishonest information. Propaganda and advertising are often biased in this sense. Deliberate bias may range from the concealing of unfavorable information to the falsification of data.

Another common meaning of bias is in the sense of preference or prejudice. This sort of bias is honest in that the individual believes his own data. Thus in scientific research one occasionally finds an author who is intent on proving some favorite thesis and who picks and chooses from the available data in such a way as to come out with "proof" of his contentions. This same type of bias also tends to occur when the success or failure of some new method is evaluated subjectively by an enthusiast of that method.

In scientific usage the word bias is applied to situations in which no intention or prejudice is involved, to a measuring instrument, for example. A steel measuring tape may be biased. The tape would be biased *relative* to a caliper if, say, it gave readings consistently larger than those given by the caliper. Sometimes we speak of an absolute bias instead of a relative bias, but this means only that the instrument used for comparison is taken as the *standard*. Bias, as used in this book, is not to be regarded as an emotional epithet.

The second requirement of good data is freedom from bias.

A third concept closely associated with the reliability of data is repeatability or concordance. If it is claimed that a can contains 13 ounces of milk, then I should find if I measure the contents in a graduated flask that my measurement is close to 13 ounces. This should also be true if other people make the measurement.

In scientific research an experiment which leads to remarkable new results will be accepted only if these results can be duplicated by other research workers who repeat the original experiment. This rule has avoided many scientific wild goose chases; it has imparted a continuity to the progress of science. On a few occasions this rule has resulted in some delay in the recognition of important new research, but the net effect of the rule has been favorable.

I think that we use this same concept of repeatability in every-day matters. One of my friends may insist that so-and-so, a political personality, is very popular. To justify the remark my friend may point out that he has talked to five people and they all thought that so-and-so was a fine fellow. Almost automatically I enumerate the people whom I have encountered with opinions about so-and-so, i.e., I repeat my friend's experiment. In the same way we are inclined to believe an account of an accident if the witnesses agree, and our suspicions are aroused if there is conflicting testimony.

A third requirement of good data is repeatability or concordance.

These three criteria for good data—relevance, freedom from bias, and repeatability—do not exhaust the list. Moreover, in the last analysis the final criterion for data is the pragmatic one, i.e., that the use of the data in a Decision-Maker produces decisions which lead to favorable consequences. The three criteria that I have listed, however, are very useful in rejecting faulty data. In Chapter 12, we will formulate these criteria in the more precise symbolic language.

The Critical Mind

Technical concepts, such as the above criteria, are useful in evaluating data, but perhaps the best protection against faulty data is the development of a critical attitude towards data. The best consulting statisticians and research workers of my acquaintance have developed this critical faculty to a high degree —it is something of an occupational disease. Even after working with large masses of data for many years (with much of this data from research laboratories) the statistician finds it very difficult to avoid the new pitfalls which constantly appear. Consequently an analyst finds that his safest mental state is to be "from Missouri."

So the most useful advice that I can give you concerning data is to suggest that you try to cultivate a critical mind, that you learn to winnow out the information which you receive. This screening ability is rightly emphasized as a prerequisite of a scientist, but it is also important in any other field where decisions must be made.

One characteristic which I have noted in my acquaintances who have a highly developed critical ability is that they scrupulously avoid dogmatic points of view. On the other hand, the credulous scientists whom I have encountered have nearly always exhibited a mental inflexibility. Our educational methods are deficient insofar as developing intellectual elasticity is concerned; in fact, it often takes several years of experience to overcome the rigidity produced by graduate training.

A second characteristic which I have noted in individuals who possess a keen critical mind is that these individuals have a wide range of interests and experience with data. Apparently this breadth of view helps them to spot incongruities in the general picture which are not apparent if each aspect of the data (i.e., collection, recording, etc.) is scrutinized separately.

Therefore there are three steps that I would recommend for the development of a critical mind: (1) Avoid dogmatism; (2) acquire a wide range of knowledge and experience; and

(3) appreciate the technical tools which have been developed for the evaluation of data.

Private and Public Data

The problems which arise in connection with data can be subdivided into four categories: Classification, collection, recording, and summarization. The problems of classification are associated with individual observations, whereas the problems of the other three categories are associated with aggregates of observations.

An observation is a description of some phenomenon. This description is ultimately based on raw or sensory data. Items of raw data are inherently *private;* that is, these items can only be used by the individual who has experienced the sensation. Statistical Decision is necessarily based on *public* data, i.e., information which can be communicated. Public data has already undergone at least one stage of abstraction, for the sensory impressions have been translated into verbal or numerical form. I think that this point is well worth remembering because many things can go wrong in this very first step. In the evaluation of data, therefore, this first step must be given careful consideration.

Suppose that I am observing some phenomenon such as the bird on my window sill. Information comes in through the various channels of my sensory apparatus) but if I want to make a note of the phenomenon I will reject most of this information as irrelevant. I would not write down that I am smelling the tobacco I happen to be smoking because I feel that this has nothing to do with the phenomenon I am describing.

I actually may write down: "There is a pigeon on my window sill." Note that in this statement I have made several *classifications.* Although I might think that I was merely recording an impression of an external phenomenon, the situation is much more complicated than that. My past experience with respect to language, birds, and architecture has also entered this description. In fact there are many ways, even in this very simple case in which I, as the observer, have stamped the characteristics of my personality upon the observation.

Moreover, I may have introduced into the data errors associated with aberrations in my sensory equipment, errors related to my past experience, imperfections in language, and so on. These various defects need no elaboration here; the philosophers and, lately, the psychologists have gone into the matter at length. Suffice it to say that this item of data, "There is a pigeon on my window sill," is born under a cloud!

These defects of data are, like death and taxes, something that we have to learn to live with. At some point in the production of data the human measuring instrument, with all its faults, is going to be involved. Although we cannot eliminate the human observer we may profitably inquire: How can the detrimental effects be minimized?

I think that the answer to this question is straightforward: We must try to arrange things so that the human plays as small a role as possible in the gathering of data. If the human observer has a fairly complicated role we can try to break this task up into a number of simple *operations*. The answer that I have given above is really an informal statement of the famous principle of scientific objectivity.

Objectivity and Subjectivity

When the human observer has a complex role in the gathering of data, the adjective subjective is often applied to the data. From my previous remarks it follows that the difference between objective data and subjective data is a matter of degree, not *kind*. Thus if a physicist records a pointer reading, we regard the measurement as objective. The task of the human instrument is simple. Ten other physicists can repeat the task and they will write down numbers which will be approximately the same as the original reading.

If an art expert is asked to give an opinion on a painting, however, we would regard his answer as subjective data. We have called upon the observer to play a very complex role. Ten other art experts may repeat the task, but it is highly unlikely that the ten answers will be the same.

It is hardly surprising that objectivity is closely associated with repeatability and freedom from bias. If the role is simple enough an observer can not only obtain results which agree well with his own previous results, but in addition he will tend to agree with other observers. This repeatability makes it relatively easy to detect individual biases and even to correct them. Note that our standard for bias is based on the rule that whenever an overwhelming majority of observers are in agreement they are, *ipso facto,* right. A color-blind dissenter might insist that grass is gray, not green. Since the great majority of observers agree that grass is green, the observation of a color-blind man would be regarded as erroneous. Furthermore, this error would be regarded as a personal bias.

The majority rule breaks down in subjective data because it is so hard to get a clear majority. Since no standard for bias can be set up, we are willing to acknowledge the influence of the observer on the data. We sometimes forget this influence of the observer in objective data, i.e., we feel that green is associated only with the grass, not with the observer.

Most scientists prefer to work with objective data whenever possible, and in some scientific circles the word "subjective" is a form of profanity when applied to a scientific paper. While I heartily concur with this passion for objectivity, there is one serious danger in this attitude. The first criterion for data, relevance, is occasionally overlooked. This has happened in studies of the effect of meteorological conditions on plant growth. It is easy to measure rainfall by an objective method, such as a rain gauge, *but* plant growth depends on the amount of water that gets to the roots, not on the water that runs off or is dissipated in other ways before it gets to the roots. The rain gauge data turn out to be very nearly irrelevant when the statistical techniques for determining relevance are employed. Meteorologists are now aware of this difficulty and are currently searching for measures of rainfall which will be both objective and relevant. Social scientists must be especially wary of this pitfall which, to give it a name, might be called *the fallacy of irrelevant objectivity.*

Classification

The first stage of the data refinery is the conversion of private data to public data. The transition from sensory impressions to verbal classifications or numerical measurements is not an easy process, although it is often taken intuitively. Perhaps it is because of the intuitive nature of the process that the inherent difficulties are quite often overlooked.

When I see a large dog crossing the street I may say to myself: "That dog is a collie." This classification is so automatic that I would not ordinarily stop to consider just how I made it. If I were challenged on this classification, how could I justify my designation? I might say: "That dog satisfies the definition of a collie." But this statement would only lead to the further question: What is the definition of a collie? If I go to my *Webster's Collegiate Dictionary* I find two definitions. One is a demonstrational definition: a picture of a collie. The second is a verbal definition: "A large dog of a breed originating in Scotland, used for generations in herding sheep."

The demonstrational definition might be useful. I could point to the actual dog and then to the picture and say, "See, there is a very close similarity—that proves the dog is a collie." The verbal definition is not very helpful since I would doubtless have a very hard time proving that the dog in the street had Scotch ancestors or that these ancestors herded sheep.

Still a third type of definition is possible—an *operational* definition. In an operational definition the classification would be made by following a specified series of actions. If I were sufficiently goaded by my challenger, I might suggest the following set of actions: (1) Check the dog license number, (2) determine the owner, (3) locate the owner, (4) obtain the pedigree if possible, and (5) use as the classification the statement on the pedigree.

Alternative operational definitions could be framed which might be based on the opinion of a veterinarian or on a series of measurements on the dog itself. The choice of an operational definition would depend on the purpose of the investigation, the means available for investigation, and the degree of agreement which could be obtained concerning the operational definition itself.

Generally speaking, the most effective approach to the problem of classification is to try to set up an operational definition. One evident advantage of such a definition will be that it will reduce the role of the human observer and hence provide more objective data. A second advantage of operational definitions is a semantic one. All of us have encountered definitions in which the concept that is being defined turns up in the definition itself. Operational definitions provide one way of getting out of this sort of vicious circle. I might add that I have found that difficulties in scientific experimentation frequently turn out to be semantic problems.

What I particularly want to emphasize is that improvement in a classification process requires close study of the process. Improvement is *not* obtained by clever manipulations of words or even by prolonged rationalizations. In particular it does not involve merely the setting up of a clever verbal definition. Improvement of classification is a subject for research, not speculation.

Frequently extensive experimentation is necessary to construct an adequate operational definition of a classification. The proposed definition must be used by various individuals and the results examined for relevance, repeatability, and freedom from bias. Some of the procedures will be mentioned in Chapter 13.

Problems of classification arise in almost every human endeavor—in medical diagnosis, in the specification of the quality of goods, in administration, and even in sports where, for example, it is often a moot question whether a pitched baseball should be classified as a ball or a strike.

A *measurement* may be regarded as a classification by numerical values. Thus a measurement of weight given as 157 pounds may be considered as indicating that the individual is in the class of humans who weigh more than 156.5 pounds but at most 157.5 pounds. The shift from verbal classification to numerical measurement will be discussed later.

Collection

That the gathering of data is not an indiscriminate or haphazard process is a point which has been missed by a long succession of philosophers, commencing with Bacon. Details of the collection process (such as the specification of where, when, and how the observations will be made) are not very glamorous and hence are often overlooked. Nevertheless, a close attention to these details "pays off"—neglect of these details is often fatal.

Systematic observation and scientific success are closely associated. Occasionally unsystematic observations may provide valuable clues, but the exploitation of the clues requires carefully planned procedures for collecting data.

The basic idea associated with the collection of information is the concept of *control*. To illustrate this concept I want to consider how we might go about the investigation of the effects of a new fertilizer on the yield of corn. As you will see, the design of such an investigation is rather complex—a far cry from unsystematic, everyday observations. Yet the first clues concerning the use of fertilizer on field crops (one of the most important technological advances in history) probably came from unsystematic observations; sharp and intelligent observers noted that the grass was more luxuriant in the vicinity of animal droppings.

We might start our design of a test for the new fertilizer by considering the resources that are available to us. We have, say, a large field, a supply of homogeneous seed, and a quantity of the new fertilizer. We might merely spread the fertilizer, plant the seed, and see what happens, but it will pay us to see what information can be obtained and how we might use this information *before* we actually perform the experiment.

If we spread our fertilizer over the entire field we will have no standard for comparison. When we calculate the yield we will obtain a number, but this number, by itself, will not tell us much. What we need to do is to fertilize part of the field with the new compound and the rest of the field with some standard compound so that we will be able to make a comparison. This is one type of control, i.e., control of the factor under study.

We know that there will be other factors relevant to crop yield as some parts of the field may be more advantageous than others with respect to soil, drainage, etc. If we were to apply the new fertilizer to the advantageous areas the comparison would be misleading. Hence we would like to control the factors other than those under study.

One way we might do this would be to divide the field up into blocks. We might expect that conditions would be more homogeneous within a block than within the field as a whole. This subdivision of the field into blocks represents an application of the principle of local homogeneity.

In order to obtain a comparison we would have both the new and the old fertilizers represented in *each* block. So we must divide the blocks into plots. Now it is evident that the yield on a plot will depend on how much area there is in the plot. This factor we can control *directly* since we can divide the field to suit ourselves. We would plan the subdivision so that all plots are of the same size. If the shape of the plot were important (it might be with a row crop), we could also specify that all the plots have the same shape. In collecting observations we want to insure that, insofar as possible, the observations will be *comparable*.

If we divide each block into two equal plots then the question arises: Which fertilizer goes on which plot? If we ourselves make the assignment it is always possible that some conscious or subconscious bias will operate so that we assign the new fertilizer to what we feel is the most favorable plot (it would be just as biased if we leaned over backwards in the assignment). What we need now is some way of controlling the *experimenter* and one obvious way is to flip a coin to make the assignment. This is an application of the principle of randomization.

We may still feel that we have not controlled an important factor, say the acidity of the soil. If we were worried about this factor we might use still another control device, the principle of auxiliary measurement. To use this device we would take measurements of the soil acidity on each plot. The use of these auxiliary measurements requires an advanced statistical technique (analysis of covariance).

At some point we may feel that we have controlled the major extraneous factors, but we realize that there are many other factors which we have not controlled. Practical limitations of our resources may prevent further efforts at control, so we can lump these other factors into what is generally called experimental error. We may then try to use *statistical control* for the experimental error.

It should be noted that we can never really have *control* in any absolute sense, although some factors may be controlled to a high degree. We may succeed in limiting some of the detrimental effects, but we never eliminate them altogether.

As you can see there is more to the job of collecting data than the mere aggregation of observations. The collection processes should be systematic, carefully planned, and conscientiously controlled.

Recording

The various devices for recording data are extensions of the human memory. Like memory, these devices involve three phases—insertion of the data, storage, and recall. Any recording device must be judged by its performance on all three phases: pen and ink notes are convenient with respect to insertion of the data, they can be stored, but difficulties arise when the recall phase is reached.

The details of recording are even less glamorous than the

details of collection processes, yet they are vitally important. Consider, for example, the printed form which will be used to record the data. The design of such a form might appear a suitable occupation for an "ink-stained drudge," but actually the process is a very tricky one. Minor flaws in the printed form may well lead to the unhappy result that a large amount of data, collected at great expense, will turn out to be quite useless.

It may seem like a very small thing to specify carefully the dimensions (such as inches or centimeters) of the measurements that are recorded, but I have seen cases in which records which omitted these details were unusable. In another case an ambiguity in the identification of the individuals who were included in a study led to the scrapping of an experiment which had already taken two years of hard work.

Clerical errors and incompleteness may also have serious effects. Sometimes editing can overcome these defects but this is usually possible only if the editing is continuous and the suspicious entry is caught early. If three years pass before any editing is attempted, it may be impossible to undo the mischief or else it may be very expensive to trace back to original sources. Incompleteness is especially frustrating. No matter how good the form may be, there will be gaps in the data if the form is not filled out properly (and this generally takes some supervision). It is especially disconcerting to start out with records on hundreds of people and then find that, because of deficiencies in the recording form or in the recording itself, only a handful of records are complete enough to provide the information desired.

Another source of frustration is to have good, complete data but to find that it is inaccessible. If it is necessary to go through extensive files to locate the few records which are pertinent to a problem it may be too expensive to make the required search. It is primarily with respect to *recall* that the modern punched-card methods offer a great advantage. The newer machines make it possible to search thousands of records in a relatively short time. However, even this modern equipment is not a complete answer to the problems of recall. For one thing, the equipment is designed for routine administrative purposes in which only a limited recall is necessary. The billing of customers, for example, will involve the cards for only one month. A study of hospital records may involve the accumulated punched-cards for decades, and the number of cards in such situations may be up in the millions. Sorting large numbers of cards— or even finding room to store them—may be difficult and expensive.

The newer electronic devices offer hope that current problems of memory may be solved. Just at present the memory of even the best of these devices is not very impressive; in many respects the human brain is a much better all-around instrument. But the day is coming when the collective experience of mankind will be so voluminous that, without mechanical assistance, sheer bulk will render it unusable. Students in this future era will have to rely on mechanical memories rather than their own, and this will have a considerable influence on the nature of education in the future.

Summarization

Systematic collection and recording of data are not unmixed blessings. True, it is possible to obtain much more imposing aggregations of data in this way, but such an overwhelming mass of data may very well confuse rather than clarify the issues. Part of the data may seem to conflict with the rest of the data and consequently it is often harder to make decisions from a mass of data than from a very sparse supply of information.

A body of data may also be difficult to interpret simply because the human mind has very definite limitations. I can compare one number with a second number but I cannot readily compare one set of twenty numbers with a second set of twenty numbers. Something must be done to boil down the data, to summarize the information in terms of a few numbers or statements.

This summarization is another stage of abstraction, for we must go from symbols to statements about symbols. The transition brings up problems of relevance in another form. If a mass of data is condensed into a few summary statements, some of the information in the data is bound to be lost. Our problem is to design our summary procedures so that we will lose as little *relevant* information as possible. It might seem remarkable that a *thousand* numbers can sometimes be summarized by just *two* numbers and these *two* numbers may contain nearly all of the relevant information. A method of summarization which can avoid loss of relevant information is called, in the trade, a *sufficient* summarization.

Many different quantities are used in the summarization of numerical data: Ratios, averages, indices, and index numbers. We have already had occasion to use ratios (for example, the proportion of coin tosses in which heads appear). Averages are commonly used in everyday affairs, the arithmetic mean being the most familiar. Statisticians have evolved some fancier types of averages (such as moments) which are useful in special situations. Indices and index numbers are also prominent in every-day affairs, especially cost-of-living indices.

The summarization of data is discussed at great length in most elementary textbooks on statistics. I shall not go into the technical aspects here.

Summary

In this chapter I have outlined the steps in the transition from raw sensory data to refined data. Standards for good data are discussed and the importance of a critical mind is emphasized. Classification, collection, recording, and summarization of data are stages in the refining process and each is briefly described. It is repeatedly pointed out that the chain of steps involved in the operation of a data refinery will be no stronger than the weakest link.

The decisions that come out of the Decision-Maker will reflect the quality of the data which we put into the machine.

CHAPTER 10

/ **MODELS**

The Symbolic World

The data refinery starts with raw data—the sights, sounds, and smells of the real world—and passes the information through several processes of abstraction. The end product, refined data, may then be pumped into the Decision-Maker.

The Decision-Maker itself operates in the symbolic world. A course of action is selected by a symbolic mechanism and then the process of abstraction is reversed—the recommendation is translated into physical action in the sensory world.

The effective use of a Decision-Maker requires some knowledge about both worlds, sensory and symbolic. Experience with data is needed for an appreciation of the symbolic mechanism. Similarly an understanding of the symbolic picture (i.e., the model) is required for an appreciation of data. This latter remark may strike you as curious. Perhaps it will seem less odd when you have finished this chapter.

Before I consider the rather elaborate *statistical* models, I want to devote some attention to the broad concept of a *model*. Models are vitally important in scientific work and, in my opinion, in any intellectual endeavor. An understanding of the nature and role of a model is prerequisite to clear thinking.

In ordinary language the word "model" is used in various ways. It covers such diverse subjects as the dolls with which little girls play and also the photogenic "dolls" who occupy the attention of mature men. I shall be concerned here with model in the sense of replica (as in a model airplane).

Physical Models

There are several kinds of model aircraft. Solid scale models resemble the actual planes in general appearance (shape, markings, etc.). The flying model aircraft not only resemble the originals in appearance but, to some extent, in *function* as well (i.e., they are capable of free flight). Some very elaborate models are essentially simplified versions of real aircraft; they have gasoline engines, operable controls, and may even have radio-control mechanisms which allow the plane to be directed from the ground.

A boy who is interested in aviation can learn about the subject from the construction and operation of such flying models. In much the same way a scientist who has constructed a model of some natural phenomenon may learn about this phenomenon from a study of his model.

The model aircraft is easier to study than a full-sized aircraft for various reasons. It is more convenient to handle and manipulate. It is also simpler than the original, and principles of operation may be more apparent. There is some danger of oversimplification, of course, and some characteristics of a real aircraft would be overlooked if all attention were focused on the model.

As a matter of fact, adult scientists use model aircraft to learn about the performance of full-sized aircraft. They build carefully scaled replicas and test these models in wind tunnels. This is a much more economical process than to build a full-sized airplane and then to test *it* in a wind tunnel (a mammoth wind tunnel is a fabulously expensive piece of equipment). This type of argument by analogy has proved quite successful and is used all the time by aircraft engineers.

I do want to emphasize that the aircraft engineers do not trust the method entirely, that they carefully test the full-sized aircraft as well as the model. In other words, it does not follow that one can *automatically* obtain useful information about the original phenomena from the study of a model. Whether a model will be useful or not will have to be learned from experience, by comparing the performances of the original phenomenon and the replica.

The model represents a process of abstraction. The real aircraft has many properties or attributes such as shape, weight, and so on. Only a few of these properties are duplicated in the model. The wind tunnel model, for example, duplicates only the shape. However, the aerodynamic performance depends largely on this one characteristic; the other properties are more or less irrelevant.

This is an example of an effective process of abstraction. It allows us to focus our attention on a much simpler phenomenon without much loss from the fact that many details have been neglected.

This particular type of abstraction, the construction of a physical model, is used in various branches of science, engineering, and industry. Models are used to design ocean liners, bridges, water supply systems, and all sorts of products from automobiles to stage scenery. Not all models involve a change in size. In aircraft construction, for example, a full-sized model of a part of a plane is sometimes constructed out of wood in order to insure that an absent-minded designer does not put components in places which cannot be reached for repairs. In this situation the relevant factor is size, and the mock-up (as it is commonly called) eliminates other factors such as weight, function, and so on.

Abstract Models

In the scientific world physical models are occasionally used for instructional purposes. In a planetarium you will generally find a model—little spheres which revolve on wire arms around a big sphere—which presents a picture of the astronomer's conception of the solar system. This sort of model is often used to demonstrate a phenomenon such as an eclipse. A rather similar physical.model is sometimes employed to explain the atom to the general public. The solar model and the atom model illustrate one striking and sometimes confusing characteristic of models; two very diverse phenomena can sometimes be repre-sented by similar models.

The solar model which you can see in a planetarium has had a very interesting history. Nowadays we think of the sun as a giant globe with a large family of little spheres circling around it. We locate ourselves on the third little sphere (counting out from the sun), and this notion does not cause us any mental anguish. In earlier days the picture was quite different and the earth was regarded as the center of the system. Of course if we go back still further there are all sorts of fabulous models which involve giants, turtles, and sea serpents. The history of astronomy is the story of the evolution of a model.

Did you notice that in describing the solar model I was actu-ally taking a further step in abstraction? I was going from a physical model to a *verbal* model. The little balls were re-placed by their symbols, the words "little balls."

All of us are accustomed to using verbal models in our think-ing processes and we do it intuitively. Verbal models have played an important role in science, especially in the prelimi-nary exploration of a topic and presentation of results. Verbal models are subject to a variety of difficulties, some of which I have discussed earlier, and most scientific fields have advanced (or are trying to advance) to the next stage—symbolic models of a mathematical nature. Astronomy was one of the first sub-jects to make this transition to the symbolic model. It should be noted that *until* this stage was reached there was really no reason to prefer a model with the sun as a center to a model with the earth as a center.

Symbolic Models

In a symbolic model the balls and wire arms of the physical model of the solar system are replaced by mathematical con-cepts. Geometrical points are substituted for the balls. The next problem is to replace the wire arms which hold the balls in place. Now the wire arms have fixed lengths, and these lengths can be stated numerically. If all of the little balls revolve in the same plane, only one additional number is needed to locate the geometrical point. This number would be the angle between the wire arm and a stationary arm which would serve as a reference point.

Hence two numbers—the radius (length of arm) and an angle—will fix the location of the geometrical point just as effectively as the wire arm fixes the location of the little sphere in the physical model. Actually the astronomer's model is much more complicated than the symbolic model which I have described, but the general principle of construction is the same.

Now suppose that the astronomer wants to use his model to predict eclipses. He will have to take observations to obtain specific numbers to use for the radius and angle. These empirically determined quantities are substituted in the mathematical model and, after various manipulations, the astronomer announces: "There will be an eclipse of the moon visible in the northeastern part of North America on such-and-such a date and at so-and-so time."

It is at this point that a comparison of alternative models can be made. If the predictions are borne out, the successful model can be used for future predictions. If, on the other hand, the eclipse does not occur at the specified time, the scientist must begin looking for another model.

The Ptolemaic astronomers set up a mathematical model of the solar system with the earth as a center. They first considered that the other astronomical bodies moved in circles. When this picture did not lead to adequate predictions the Ptolemaic astronomers decided the paths of the heavenly bodies were epicycles. If you would like to visualize an epicycle, imagine two gears, one large and standing still and the other small and rolling around the rim of the large one. An epicycle is the path of a tooth of the small gear.

This complication led to a little improvement in prediction, but the forecasts were still quite unsatisfactory so the model was complicated still further. This time the astronomers postulated that the paths of the heavenly bodies were epicycles *on* epicycles, literally a "gears within gears" situation.

If you think that this is getting too complicated consider the sad plight of the astronomers. *They* had to make the calculations which go along with this model of the solar system. Nonetheless it was many years before the simpler model with the sun at the center of the solar system was widely accepted.

There is a moral in this epicycle story. Scientists occasionally become attached to a model even though it does not give adequate prediction. They try to use the model by cutting off a piece here or adding a piece there. This patchwork can go on for many years, and the resulting crazy quilt may prevent the development of new and more efficient models. After all, when it takes a scientist ten years to master a complex model, he has a vested interest in it, and he sometimes is hostile to labor-saving devices which may deprive him of his job. "Epicyclitis" is a symptom of senility in a scientific field.

Mathematical Models

It might be puzzling to understand why the astronomers should go from a nice simple physical model with little spheres on wire arms to a symbolic model with all sorts of queer mathematical signs when, if sufficient care were taken in the construction of the physical model, it would be possible to use it directly in order to predict eclipses. The astronomer's choice is a matter of taste. From the astronomer's point of view it is the mathematical model which is the *simple* one and the physical model with balls and wire which is complex. Since the physical model is made out of metal it not only has attributes which are intended to simulate the solar system, but it also has a lot of attributes which depend on the materials used in its construction and the way in which it is made. Thus the wire arms can be geared to rotate at an appropriate speed but the mounting and drive arrangements of the model are attributes of the model and *not* attributes of the solar system which it is supposed to represent.

Even though great care is lavished on the construction of the physical model the predictions which would come out of it would depend on friction, vibration, and other characteristics of the *model*. Hence the prediction would be rendered inaccurate by the entrance of attributes other than the ones which were deliberately built into the model to simulate the solar system.

In a *mathematical* model, on the other hand, the material of the model itself—in this case the symbolic language—does not ordinarily contribute such extraneous and undesirable attributes. If we want friction in the mathematical model we can put it in symbolically, but otherwise this friction will not appear in the model and hence cannot disturb our predictions. In the physical model the process of abstraction tends to introduce new and irrelevant details, while in the mathematical model the process of abstraction does not.

In this sense, therefore, a mathematical model is simple whereas a physical model is complex. It may strike you as curious that I should say that Einstein is working with an extremely simple model in his theory of relativity, while a schoolboy is working with an extremely complex model when he builds an airplane. If you think it over carefully, however, you may see the justice of the statement.

Now and then a mathematical model gets beyond the resources of the mathematicians who construct it, so a physical model is substituted to obtain an answer. This is done in the Monte Carlo method, a device for solving mathematical problems by having one of the giant brain computers play gambling games with itself. However, such devices are used for computational convenience rather than conceptual simplicity.

The construction of symbolic models is an important part of the job of the scientist, and the great advances in science are those in which a useful new model is introduced. In physics the powerful model devised by Isaac Newton is one landmark, the relativity model of Einstein is another, and the quantum models are a third landmark. In chemistry the gas laws, the mass action laws, and the periodic table are all the end results of successful models of atomic and molecular processes. In biology the evolutionary model of Charles Darwin (a verbal model) has been developed into a mathematical model by R. A. Fisher and Sewell Wright. Another important biological model is the one which describes genetic inheritance. In medicine the models are mainly verbal, but they are of great importance. Harvey's model of the circulatory system, and the various models of the reaction of the human body to invading organisms have influenced the development of the modern treatment of diseases.

Effective verbal models which describe the transmission of disease have been useful in the eradication of many of the epidemic diseases which used to terrorize humanity. Efforts are currently in progress to translate these verbal models into mathematical ones (epidemic theory), but the earlier models have been so successful that a modern investigator is often hard put to find enough data to test his new mathematical models!

Currently, there is research under way which is attempting to devise mathematical models for sociological phenomena, such as the growth of cities, and for psychological phenomena. Norbert Wiener in *Cybernetics*[1] deals with a mathematical model associated with the operation of the human brain.

One of the key steps in the progress of a field of knowledge toward scientific maturity is the fabrication of models which enable successful prediction in that field. A tremendous amount of imagination and insight is needed for the creation of new models, but they are only half of the story. The mere creation of models is not enough; the models must survive exacting tests, they must meet the pragmatic criterion, they must work.

This brings us back to data. The test of the model involves data from the real world. Without adequate data the construction of models is a mathematical pastime. Purely speculative mathematical models may be as useless as purely speculative verbal models. For example, I might construct a very fancy mathematical model to describe the mechanism of transmis-

---

[1] Wiener, N., *Cybernetics*. John Wiley & Sons, Inc., New York, 1948.

sion of some virus disease. No good diagnostic test may be known for the disease, and consequently the available data may be quite unreliable. If a doctor comes along with a quick, cheap, and effective skin test for this disease, it may then be possible to get adequate data to test my fancy model. Until this happens my model is just another mathematical game. After the development of the skin test, the model may turn out to be useful in the understanding and control of the disease or, as is more likely, it may turn out to be a complete waste of time.

Progress in science is based on this constant interplay between model and data. Sometimes there is a tremendous amount of observational data available but no satisfactory model, so that little progress is made. This was the situation in astronomy before the heliocentric model and it also has occurred repeatedly in the biological sciences. At other times there are elaborate models but little adequate data. Something resembling this situation occurred in economics where an elaborate mathematical theory was developed which did rather poorly when tested with actual data.

Occasionally a scientist not only works out the model but also obtains the data. Darwin and Galileo accomplished this feat. More often one man, such as Brahé, gathers good data and another man, such as Kepler, supplies the model. When this division of labor occurs it is rather pointless to say that the model-maker is a greater scientist than the data-grubber, for the advance depends on teamwork.

Advantages

Why should a model be used? The real answer to this question is that this procedure has been followed in the development of the most successful predicting systems so far produced, the predicting systems used in science. It is simply a matter of going along with a winner.

Some of the advantages of model-making might, however, deserve a separate statement. A big advantage of a model is that it provides a frame of reference for consideration of the problem. This is often an advantage even if the preliminary model does not lead to successful prediction. The model may suggest informational gaps which are not immediately apparent and consequently may suggest fruitful lines for action. When the model is tested the character of the failure may sometimes provide a clue to the deficiencies of the model. Some of the greatest scientific advances have been produced by *failure* of a model! Einstein's work was the outgrowth of the Michelson-Morley experiment in which the aether model led to unsuccessful prediction.

Another advantage of model-making is that it brings into the open the problem of abstraction. The real world is a very complex environment indeed. An ordinary apple, for example, has a great many properties—size, shape, color, chemical composition, taste, weight, ad infinitum. In making a decision about the apple, such as whether to eat it or not, only a few of these characteristics are considered. Some degree of abstraction is necessary for decision.

The model-maker must, therefore, decide which real world attributes will be incorporated in the model. He may decide that the size of the apple rather than shape is important to decision. He may, if he is setting up an inspection plan, concentrate on the number of worm holes. If he is interested in the velocity of a falling apple, on the other hand, he may include only the weight of the apple in his model.

By making this process of abstraction deliberate, the use of a model may bring such questions to light. Moreover, it may suggest preliminary experiments to determine which characteristics are relevant to the particular decision problem under consideration.

Once the problem is expressed in symbolic language there is the advantage of the manipulative facility of that language. The symbolic language also offers advantages in communication. It allows a concise statement of the problem which can be published. Moreover, it is more easily integrated with the other scientific work which is also in symbolic language.

Another advantage of mathematical models is that they often provide the *cheapest* way to accomplish prediction. Sometimes it is possible to reach the same results by the sheer mass of data —by a "brute force" attack on the problem—but the mathematical route is generally more economical.

One reason for this is that a newly-minted Ph.D. in mathematics can be hired (alas) for a salary which could not entice a good plumber. A Ph.D., a pencil, and some paper may be all the equipment necessary to handle the symbolic manipulations of the model. Only a very small proportion of the millions currently spent for research goes into model-making. Even when the scientists are well paid, most of the money goes into the process of collecting data.

Disadvantages

The use of models also has some drawbacks. The model is subject to the usual dangers inherent in abstraction. A mathematically feasible model may require gross oversimplifications. There is no guarantee that an investment of time and effort in constructing the model will pay dividends in the form of satisfactory prediction. No process, however, can provide such a guarantee.

The symbolic language is also subject to limitations. It may be beyond the ability of a mathematician to manipulate the symbolic language so as to obtain useful results. In such cases it may be more efficient to use direct methods. In gambling-game problems, such as the game of solitaire, it may be easier to play a large number of solitaire games and determine the probabilities by the Direct System than to embark on a mathematical analysis of the probabilities.

There is another very grave danger in the use of models. After a scientist plays for a long time with a given model he may become attached to it, just as a child may become, in the course of time, very attached to a doll (which is also a model). A child may become so devoted to the doll that she insists that her doll is a real baby, and some scientists become so devoted to their model (especially if it is a brain child) that they will insist that this model *is* the real world.

The same sort of thing happens with verbal models, as the semanticists point out, when a word and its counterpart in the real world are regarded as the same thing. This identification in the world of words has led to unhappy results which are reflected in the real world. The behavior of individuals who are unable to distinguish between words and the real world may become so bizarre as to lead to the classification "insane."

Now things are not this bad at the scientific level largely because of the self-corrective features of the sequential process of model-making which provide a periodic return to the real world after each excursion into the symbolic world. The test of the model acknowledges, as it were, the supremacy of the real world. If the model fails to predict what will happen in the real world, it is the model that must give way. This is the standard of scientific sanity.

When this standard is not admitted, a conflict between a model's predictions and happenings in the real world will sometimes lead instead to the rejection of the real world. This course is the prelude to disaster. To guard against such disasters it is well to remember the following rule for working with models: A model is neither true nor false.

The standard for comparing models is utility, i.e., successful prediction. The evaluation of a model is therefore dependent on the situation in which it is to be used; it is not *intrinsic* (i.e., dependent only on the model itself). If this point is understood several apparent paradoxes in science disappear.

One such paradox is the simultaneous use of two contradictory models. An example of this paradox occurs in the field of physics in which a *wave* and a *photon model* for light are both accepted. Wave theories are used when *they* provide successful prediction, and in other situations the photon theory is employed. Hence the paradox arises only if the models are identified with the real world.

Another paradox is the occurrence of scientific revolutions which (unlike political revolutions) do not interrupt the orderly development of the area. If models are not identified with the real world, the revolution is merely the substitution of a refined model for a cruder earlier model. Most of the time the older theory continues to be useful in the original applications; it is only in extended applications that the newer theory gives better prediction. The older theory is often a special case of the new theory. This explains why, despite the revolutionary work of Einstein, the older Newtonian physics is still used. In designing a dam or bridge, for example, both models would lead to essentially the same predictions (or in other words, the predictions are indistinguishable at the practical level).

One class of scientific workers does not worry about the testing of its models. They are the mathematicians. Their only interest (as long as they are functioning as mathematicians) lies in symbolic derivations from the models. Their business is to provide models in which the symbolic implications are worked out—anyone who wants to use the model for real world predictions will have to test it first. Nevertheless, the mathematicians serve a useful purpose in society (though a pure mathematician would strenuously deny it) by providing the scientists with ready-worked models. Often the models created by mathematicians are not used for years, or even centuries, but the literature of mathematics is a sort of Sears-Roebuck catalogue of models which may be consulted whenever a special type of model is needed. Unfortunately it takes some mathematical sophistication in order to use this catalogue.

As long as the model is completely divorced from the real world the criterion of utility cannot be used. Instead the mathematicians employ an *intrinsic* standard, *consistency*. Various attempts have been made, all unsuccessful, to extend this standard to the real world. The only result which these attempts have accomplished is to confuse matters and cause an identification of models and the real world.

Role of the Model

The disadvantages inherent in the use of models can be avoided to a large extent by a judicious balancing of the two processes, model-making and data collection. The relationship between these two aspects of Scientific Method deserves careful consideration; it provides one of the main keys to scientific success, and it also involves several notions which can be carried over into our thinking about everyday problems. The relationship can be represented diagrammatically by Figure 10.01.

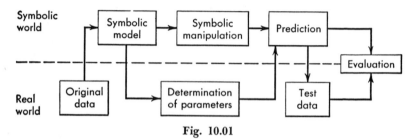

Fig. 10.01

The model itself should be regarded as arbitrary; it represents an act of creation like a painting or a symphony. The model can be anything its creator desires it to be. In practice, of course, it is generally stimulated (and therefore affected) by data from the real world (which is labeled "Original data" in Figure 10.01). Artistic creations also use sensory data. Even in abstract canvases there is some influence from the original data (sensory experience). If the modern artist paints the portrait of a woman, it may not look like a human being to me. But presumably the dabs of paint have some relationship to the woman, though it may require an expert to understand this relationship. Similarly, a physicist's mathematical model of the atom may be far removed from any material substance; again only an expert can appreciate it.

In many cases the symbolic representation used in the model is chosen because it was successfully used in previous models, because it seems plausible to the creator, or because it is convenient. However, some very useful models are based on assumptions which are not evident from common sense or—as in the quantum model—are actually repugnant to common sense.

I would not consider it very plausible to be seated at a desk in Los Angeles and then suddenly to find myself at a desk in Baltimore. It is even less sensible for this jump to have been accomplished in no time at all and without passing through any intermediate point in the process. Yet electrons jump around in this remarkable manner in the quantum theories of physics. Models which embody this curious behavior lead to successful prediction.

Scientists are generally pictured as coldly logical creatures with no disposition to embark on wild flights of fancy. But the geniuses of science have at least as much imagination as any other creative artist. In some respects the symbolic language of science allows greater freedom for expression than the printed word, musical notation, or oil paint.

There is one very important respect in which the scientist differs from the artist, however. The model itself may be arbitrary, but once it is constructed it must meet exacting and carefully specified tests before it is acclaimed as a masterpiece. In the artistic world the criteria for judging the finished product are vague and unsystematic.

There is a second respect in which science and art differ. In art the portrait is the end of the job; in science it is just the beginning. Once the model has been created there are two lines of development—one in the symbolic world and the other in the real world.

In the symbolic world the implications of the model are pursued by manipulations of the symbolic language. If I am interested in the behavior of a pendulum I can set up a mathematical model in which the bob of the pendulum is replaced by a geometrical point. The cord or arm of the pendulum is replaced by a symbol, L, which can be interpreted as the length of the cord. The Newtonian laws may be applied to this model and, by manipulations of the symbolic language, I may derive as a consequence of my model a relatively simple relation between the period (the length of time it takes to complete a full swing) and the length, *L*. All of this takes place in the symbolic language.

In the real world the numerical value for the length must be obtained. This quantity, *L*, is often called a "parameter." The word "parameter" is merely mathematical jargon for a symbolic quantity, such as *L*, which may be associated with some measurable quantity in the real world. The process of measuring the length of the cord would therefore be called the "determination of the parameter." In most problems there will be more than one parameter involved.

The two paths from the model now join again when the numerical value from the real world is substituted in the formula (derived by symbolic manipulation) in order to obtain the period. The period is found, mathematically, to be proportional to the square root of the length, *L*. If my pendulum is 4 feet long it is easy to calculate that the period will be about 2.2 seconds. This statement is made as a prediction.

In order to test this prediction it is necessary to return once again to the real world. I set up my pendulum and time the swings. I find that the period as determined experimentally is about 2.2 seconds. Perhaps I go ahead and try a whole series of different lengths and the agreement between prediction and experiment seems to be good.

As a consequence of this agreement, I am encouraged to use my mathematical model for prediction purposes and also in the design of clocks or other equipment which utilizes a simple pendulum.

The reader may find it worth while to consider another example, such as the astronomical model of the solar system, and trace through the steps in Figure 10.01 in order to clarify his own ideas on the role of the model.

One striking characteristic of the relationship between the model and the data is the periodic return to the real world which is indicated in Figure 10.01. It should be noted that the original data used in the construction of the model may be quite useless for the determination of parameters or testing the model. Hence the return to the real world may not mean merely the collection of additional data, but it may require collection of data of a completely different *type* from the original data.

Now a reader who has forgotten his elementary physics may have wondered why I did not include the weight of the bob as well as the length of the cord in the model of the pendulum. An interesting feature of the mathematical model of the pendulum is that if this additional factor, weight, is included in the symbolic structure, it will cancel out in the manipulations. In other words, the model implies that the period of the pendulum does not depend on the weight of the bob, i.e., the weight is irrelevant in this particular problem. The same thing happens if other factors, such as the way in which the pendulum is set into motion, are included in the model. Thus the symbolic model has served the useful purpose of focusing our attention on the length of the cord. It has therefore suggested an efficient way of experimenting on the pendulum; the *model* has told us what *data* need to be collected.

The little story about the pendulum had a happy ending, for the model was satisfactory. However, few scientists are so fortunate or clever as to devise a useful model on the first attempt. If prediction from the first model turns out very badly the scientist will have to start over again. The way in which the predictions break down sometimes provides valuable information which can be used to construct a second model.

The role of the model as given by Figure 10.01 is therefore only a part of a larger sequential process. This sequential role is indicated by Figure 10.02.

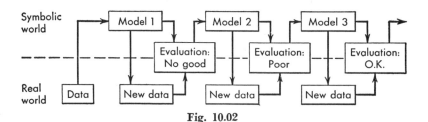

Fig. 10.02

The evolution of a successful model generally follows the above pattern. The first shots are often very wide of the mark, but by gradual stages the scientist zeros in on his target. There is really no end to the sequence. Even after a model has years of successful usage (i.e., Newtonian models in physics), a situation may come along which will not be adequately predicted by the model. A new model must then be developed.

Some readers may find this viewpoint rather unpleasant because they would like this sequence to stop somewhere (i.e., at the truth). Nowhere in the scientific world has this stopping place been attained, although now and then the models have survived for many years. The attitude that the truth had been attained was often a barrier to progress.

A Model for Data

The mathematical model for the solar system or for a pendulum can be used for prediction and then tested against actual data. In this test it is not expected that the data and prediction will agree *exactly*. In the pendulum example the predicted period of a 4-foot pendulum is 2.2 seconds. If a 4-foot pendulum is constructed and the period is measured with a stopwatch or other timing device, the periods so measured will be about 2.2 seconds, but there may be some departure from this figure.

Note that these departures of the data from the predicted value have received no allowance in the mathematical model for the pendulum. In order to *evaluate* the model, however, this behavior of the data must be taken into consideration. This may be done intuitively by an argument such as "the departures from the predicted value are very small and quite negligible for practical purposes." A more sophisticated approach is to set up a second model, a model to deal with the measurement data.

Such a model would be a *statistical* model; it would characterize the measurement process itself in mathematical terms. One parameter of this model might be interpreted as the *precision* or repeatability of the method of measurement and this might be estimated from new data collected for this purpose. Many scientific measurements are given in the following form: 2.22 ± 0.10 seconds. The number after the plus-and-minus sign relates to the precision of the measurement. Thus 2.22 might be the average period calculated from a series of measurements on the period of the pendulum. The 0.10 second might indicate that the average is only reliable to $\frac{1}{10}$ of a second. We would not be very surprised, therefore, if we had gotten 2.32 or 2.12 seconds as our average period. Consequently, there is no reason to feel that the data contradict our predicted value of 2.2 seconds. If, on the other hand, we had found the average period to be 3.22 ± 0.10 seconds, we would feel that something was wrong either with the model or with the data.

When we set about constructing a mathematical model which will describe data we immediately are confronted with the problem of including, in the mathematical formulation, the well-known inadequacies of data. Thus the inadequacies of the measuring instrument must appear in the model: it must include such things as sensory lapses of the human measuring instrument; various errors introduced by the inanimate instruments as microscopes, telescopes, or clocks; and, in biological work, where an animal is used in the measurement process, all sorts of additional sources of variation due to the animal.

Then there will be incompleteness of the data due to the various steps in abstraction. Some of the data may be irrelevant; some of the relevant factors may have been neglected. Also, only part of the available data may have been collected and only part of this data actually used. In short, any real data will be inadequate and incomplete, and these deficiencies must be included in the model.

It would be hopeless to try to catalogue all the things which might go sour in the process of collecting and utilizing the data, to analyze all of the factors which might operate to influence the experimental results. About all that is possible is to consider broad categories of deficiencies and to include these broad categories in the model.

Now how can these inadequacies, and the resulting uncertainties, be handled mathematically? As you might suspect, this is accomplished by the introduction of the concept of probability into the model. In fact, the notion of probability can be regarded as the distinguishing feature which sets statistical models apart from other mathematical models.

Statistical Models

The role of a statistical model is in many respects quite similar to that of any other mathematical model. The diagrammatic representation is indicated in Figure 10.03.

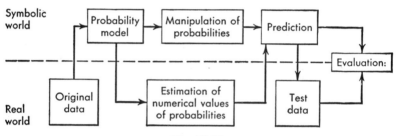

Fig. 10.03

The gambling game models which were introduced earlier are instances of statistical models. Occasionally a simple model of this type can be applied to situations in everyday experience. Suppose that I am interested in the proportion of male babies in 10,000 records of live births. There are two outcomes possible when a baby is born (just as in a coin flip) —the baby can be a boy or a girl. I might therefore think of sex determination as analogous to the process of flipping a coin.

One distinction between the coin toss and sex determination is that while the mechanism for determining heads and tails on a coin is fairly well understood, the corresponding mechanism for fixing the sex of a baby is not well understood. Consequently it would be specious to argue that each sex was equally likely. There is, in fact, a large amount of data to show that this is not the case. Hence if a symbol, p, is used in the mathematical model to indicate the probability that a baby will be male, it may not be assumed that $p = 1/2$.

Consequently, one of the things that will have to be done in order to use the model is to obtain data which will enable us to estimate the value of this parameter, p. Perhaps a number such as $p = 0.52$ will be determined from this excursion into the real world.

A second chain of reasoning stays in the symbolic world. Taking the probability as p that a live baby will be a boy, we must answer the question: What will happen in 10,000 births? I will not burden you with the manipulations of probabilities required to answer this question. The mathematics involved in calculating the probabilities for each of the 10,001 possible outcomes becomes too tedious, even for a statistician, and in practice a mathematical approximation which yields useful results with little effort is employed.

With the aid of this device, and substituting the value $p = 0.52$, we can obtain a prediction of the following form: The probability that there will be between 5100 and 5300 male births in the sample of 10,000 is equal to about 0.95. In other words, if I am convinced that the model is a good one and that my value of $p = 0.52$ is also reliable, I would be very confident that the actual data should show between 5100 and 5300 live male births.

This particular model has taken into consideration only one source of variability in the data on live birth—the variation due to sampling. Now in practice there are a number of other inadequacies of the data which might very well cause trouble. The reporting procedures may introduce difficulties. In a well-run department of vital statistics in the Western World the tabulation of births may be done rather carefully. On the other hand, if my 10,000 live births were reported by tribal chieftains in a colonial administrative district there might well be a tendency to forget female children.

The problem of *evaluation* of the statistical model is a tricky one. If I found 4957 boys in the sample of 10,000, I could not say that this result was *impossible* insofar as my model was concerned. The model itself allows a very small chance of this sort of sample.

To a large extent the users of nonstatistical mathematical models can dodge the problem of evaluation by making the evaluation intuitive and simply stating that the agreement of prediction and data is either satisfactory or unsatisfactory. In statistical models one must come to grips with the problem—though I shall postpone this topic for discussion in Chapter 13. A major part of a statistician's job lies in the no-man's-land between the symbolic world and the real world, and in particular he must evaluate the predictions of models relative to actual data.

Summary

The key role played by models in scientific thinking is illustrated by several examples. The notion of a model for data is introduced and leads to the concept of a statistical model. The advantages and disadvantages of models are considered. Special stress is laid on the distinction between models of the real world and the real world itself.

CHAPTER 11 / SAMPLING

Samples

The data which will form the basis for practical decisions may be incomplete, unreliable, or inaccurate. Consequently the model representing this data must somehow reflect these inadequacies. This raises the question: How can a mathematical model (which is precise and consistent) be used to describe something as confused and erratic as data?

The statistician's answer to this question brings in a concept which has been mentioned before but which has not received the attention it deserves. I am referring to the notion of a *sample,* a bread-and-butter word to workers in my particular trade.

Formally, a sample is simply a part, or subset, of an aggregation of individuals. In statistical jargon this aggregation is called a *population* or *universe.* The simplest sort of population is a finite collection of individuals, such as a deck of cards or the students in a class in school. A sample from such a population would be a group of individuals selected from the larger group —a bridge hand, or those students whose last names start with the letters A to M.

Now there is nothing novel in this notion of a sample. People have made decisions on the basis of the information in samples long before statisticians arrived on the scene. People were judging a bunch of grapes by sampling a few grapes or accepting merchandise by examining a portion of the shipment before the advent of civilizations. The contribution of the statistician has been to systematize these intuitive concepts and convert vague general advice into a specific methodology.

People have long been aware that the information in a sample is necessarily incomplete and that if a person relies on this information he will occasionally make decisions with unpleasant consequences; a sample of merchandise may be good, but the shipment may be of poor quality. All of us have encountered what might be called the "fruit-stand" effect—the goods on display (i.e., those which can be conveniently sampled visually) are not representative of the goods which are actually sold. The vendor has arranged his stock in a deliberately deceptive fashion or, in technical parlance, he has provided us with a biased sample.

Everyday experience has led us to such concepts as a fair sample or a representative sample, and these phrases often appear in daily conversations. In everyday usage these phrases have a vague and often ambiguous meaning, so the first necessary step is to try to clarify these ideas. When this step is taken the next problem is to set up methods which will lead to fair or representative samples.

Populations

Before we consider these questions, however, I want to indicate how the concept of a sample can be used in constructing a model for data. The general procedure is to consider that any actual set of data represents a sample from some population. This procedure may best be illustrated by some examples.

Suppose that a new drug which may be useful in the treatment of some specific malady is developed. An experiment is designed and carried out in which half of the patients who are diagnosed as having the specific malady are given the new drug and the rest of the patients in this category are given some standard therapy. The experiment runs for, say, a year and at the end of this time it is desired to come to some decision about the new drug. This decision is to be based on the data in the experiment.

The patients who were given the new drug represent a *sample* of the *population* of patients with a given diagnosis who were available during the time period of the experiment. Let us suppose that the patients were assigned to the therapies by the use of some randomization mechanism. Then, hypothetically, there would be a large number of possible assignments, each of which might have led to a different experimental result from the one actually observed. So we can consider our actual data as one sample selected from many possible samples.

In a larger sense the entire population of patients specified above represents a sample from a *superpopulation*. The particular year in which the experiment took place can be viewed as a sample drawn from a population of years. Moreover the patients coming to a given hospital may be regarded as a sample of the patients in a locality who suffer from the specified malady. These patients, in turn, are a sample from the population of the country. Therefore the set of observations in the experiment can be viewed as a sample from a number of wider and wider populations.

This illustrates the principle that any set of data can be regarded as a sample from a population (or even from many populations). In constructing a model for data we try to represent, symbolically, the probability that our sample would be drawn from some population. If a randomization mechanism is used in the process of drawing the sample, we may be able to use models quite similar to the ones discussed earlier in connection with gambling games.

Since I have indicated that a given sample may be regarded as having been drawn from any of several populations the question naturally arises: What population is used in the model? This question does not have a simple answer because it depends on what general information is available, how the data were obtained, and what courses of action are open to us. If the choice of action lies between a recommendation that the new therapy be used routinely for patients with a specified diagnosis in a given hospital and a recommendation that the new drug be dropped, then the population affected by these courses of action would be the patients coming into the given hospital in the future. We might regard the patients in the experiment as a fair sample of the population of patients coming to the given hospital.

On the other hand, we might want to make a recommendation which would apply more generally, and in this event the population which might be affected by the recommendation might include people in other hospitals in the city, or even people in the rest of the country, or, conceivably, in the world. Notice, though, that the wider the population, the more difficulties we might have in justifying to others (and to ourselves) that the experiment represents a fair sample of the wider population. In particular, past experience may have shown that the nature of the malady differs from one section of the country to another. In this event it might be misleading to regard the sample as representative of the population in the country. The use that can be made of information in a sample will depend on how the sample is drawn and this, in turn, affects the choice of the hypothetical population.

Hypothetical populations, while convenient conceptually, lead to some difficult problems. If I flip a coin ten times the results of this little experiment can be regarded as a sample, a sample of possible tosses of the coin. However, this latter population is not finite since there is no limit to the number of coin tosses. Although it is a little harder to say just what we mean by a sample from an infinite population, the mathematical theory is generally easier, and most statistical theory deals with such infinite populations. Thus we frequently regard a series of measurements, say heights, as a sample from an infinite population even when the populations affected by our actions may, in fact, be finite.

Fair Samples

The concept of a fair sample arises in everyday experience and is fundamental to the whole concept of sampling. It will therefore pay us to examine closely the meaning of the words "fair sample." To do this let us return to the fruit-stand vendor who puts the choice apples in his display and serves his customers out of a box containing the remaining apples. This we feel is a very unfair business practice, but when we try to point out just what is unfair there are some difficulties.

Suppose that the fruit vendor is so upset by our allegations that he selects his sample of fruit as follows. He assigns a number to each apple in the shipment and writes this number on a slip of paper which he puts in his hat. He mixes up the slips and draws, say, one hundred slips. He then puts into his display those apples whose numbers have been drawn. It may turn out that, although 10 per cent of the apples are rotten, all of the apples chosen for the display are good.

Is his sample a fair one? You might feel that the display is still not representative of the rest of the apples and hence must be branded as unfair. Perhaps you would feel that about 10 per cent of the apples in the display must be rotten before the display sample could be judged fair.

The difficulty with this criterion for a fair sample is that it requires a knowledge of the *population* before the *sample* can be judged. In practice, of course, we rarely know the nature of population (for if we did we would hardly bother to take a sample) so that the criterion cannot be applied. Hence, any standards for a fair sample which depend on a comparison of the sample with the population being sampled will be of no practical use. The way out of this impasse is to consider that the designation fair refers not to the *particular* sample but to the *method* used in drawing the sample.

Thus if a vendor selects his display fruit by a randomizing mechanism and happens to get all good apples in the display sample I would regard this sample as a fair one. I would take this attitude because I think that the method used for selection is a fair method.

The question then arises: What is a fair method of sampling? The problem occurs quite often in everyday affairs. There may be a group of people, and it may be necessary for one of them to undertake some chore. A common solution to this problem is to draw lots or use some other randomization device to draw the sample (i.e., to select the individual who will have to do the chore). The use of a randomization mechanism gives each individual in the group the same chance of appearing in the sample, and consequently this method is generally considered to be fair.

The same idea, translated into the language of probability, is basic to much of the statistical theory of sampling. The above method of selecting an individual to do the chore is called a *simple random sample* in the trade. The word "random" refers to the mechanism employed and the word "simple" is used to distinguish this method from more complex methods which also use some randomizing mechanism.

Note, too, the relationship between a fair sample and the concept of freedom from bias which was discussed earlier in connection with data. The scientist who picks and chooses his data so as to demonstrate a pet theory is not using a method of selection that gives all items of data the same chance of appearing in his sample (i.e., the actual material to be used in this argument). Statisticians usually use the phrase "unbiased sample" rather than "fair sample."

Repeatability

While fair sampling methods are desirable, there are other characteristics of sampling methods which must be considered. Suppose that some administrative decision requires information about the commercial peach crop in a locality. Previous experience may indicate that the easiest way to obtain this information is to estimate the number of fruit trees in the area. It may also be known that there are 500 commercial fruit growers in the area and (to take an extreme case) that there is one big grower who has as many trees as all the other growers put together.

To obtain the desired information quickly and cheaply a sample of, say, 50 growers would be interviewed, and the trees reported by these growers would be totaled. This figure would be blown up by a factor of 10 to obtain an estimate of the total number of trees in the area.

But if we take a simple random sample of the growers we are immediately in trouble. If the big grower appears in the sample our estimate will be much too large. On the other hand, if the big grower does not appear in the sample our estimate will be much too small. In other words, a simple random sample will always give a very poor estimate here.

The obvious thing to do is to put the big grower into a class by himself and include him automatically in the sample. A simple random sample of the other growers could be taken, their total inflated by a factor of about 10, and this number added to the reported total of the big grower in order to obtain an estimate.

Since there might well be disparities in the sizes of the 499 smaller orchards, it could be argued that the same principle of separation ought to be applied to the 499 others. This could be done if, as might well be the case, there were acreage figures for all farms in the locality. The growers could be classified by the acreages of their farms, and each acreage class (or stratum) could be considered separately. This method of classifying and then taking a random sample of each class is called *stratified random sampling* and is widely used in practice.

With this method it is no longer necessarily true that all individuals in the population have the same chance of appearing in the sample. Nevertheless the method can be a fair one if the results from the different strata are properly combined.

Now in what way does stratification improve the estimate of the number of peach trees? To answer this question we can imagine that the simple random sampling and stratified random sampling methods were both used repeatedly on the same population.

The simple method would give estimates which were either much too high or much too low. In other words the estimates obtained by the simple method would be scattered over a wide range. On the other hand, the estimates obtained by the stratified method would be much less scattered. We therefore say that the stratified method gives better repeatability or concordance. If we have a choice among various fair sampling methods we would want to choose a method which gave good performance by the standard of repeatability.

Economy

It costs time and money to gather data and, in practice, considerations of economy are important in the choice of a sampling method. In the peach tree problem we might find that the big grower did not know how many trees he owned. In this case we might try to estimate the number of trees on this large farm by a sampling method. Thus the farm itself would be a sample, and we would be sampling with a sample. This device is called *sub-sampling*.

In certain practical situations (such as when we want to take a sample of records from a file), there is still another technique which may provide substantial savings in time and money. This is the method of *systematic sampling*.

A systematic sample is one which is drawn by a carefully prescribed process which does not include a randomizing mechanism. A systematic sample of a card file could be obtained by a rule such as: Pull every twentieth card in the file. A systematic sample of households could be drawn by a rule such as: Interview the people in the house closest to the northwest corner of each block.

Systematic samples have a number of advantages. They are generally easier to take, and hence the survey will be easier to administer. For a given number of observations the systematic method may provide greater repeatability than a simple random sample. However, systematic sampling is not always a fair method.

In sampling houses, for example, the rule mentioned above will lead to the selection of corner houses most of the time. In some cities corner houses are subject to double taxation, and the owners of such houses are in a higher economic class than their neighbors on the block. Wealthier individuals tend to hold more conservative political opinions, so if we were making a public opinion survey the use of this method might put a bias into our results.

This sort of bias can sometimes be avoided by combining systematic with random sampling, i.e., constructing a method which gives systematic selection up to a point and then uses a randomization device to pick the actual sample. In the theory of sampling various combinations of the devices of systematic, stratified, and random sampling have been explored and evaluated with respect to freedom from bias, repeatability, and economy. Very complicated schemes have been developed to handle special problems—say, a sample of the entire population of the United States. One of these methods is area sampling which is used by government agencies. This method does well insofar as freedom from bias and repeatability are concerned but, unfortunately, tends to be rather expensive.

In practical applications numerous special problems arise. How can a population of fish in the ocean be sampled? How can flies, mice, or rocks be sampled? How can migrant workers, smog, or grain in a freight car be sampled? The topic of sampling is a very broad one indeed.

Haphazard Samples

If a person is asked to choose a number between zero and nine, the answer he gives is a personal choice. This is quite a different matter from the selection of a number by a randomization mechanism. Even though the individual might feel that he picked the number at "random," his choice would not be random in the sense in which I am using the word. In fact, it is well known that numbers selected in this personal fashion tend to be odd numbers such as three or seven.

I prefer to call a sampling system involving such personal choices a *haphazard* method and limit the word "random" to methods which employ a randomization mechanism.

Haphazard sampling methods provide us with most of the data which we have, not only in everyday life, but in science as well. Even if the sampling methods previously discussed are used, part of the selection may be haphazard. Thus if questionnaires are sent out to a random sample of people there will ordinarily be some individuals who do not return their questionnaire. Personal choice has therefore entered the selection of the sample. However, current sampling techniques strive to make the influence of personal choice as small as possible.

These remarks are in line with earlier comments on the principle of minimizing the role of the human instrument. It is very much easier to study the characteristics of a randomization device than to learn about the corresponding characteristics of personal choices. It is always a difficult matter, for example, to determine whether or not a haphazard method is biased.

A classic example of a haphazard sample is the presidential election poll of 1936 conducted by the *Literary Digest*. Over 10,000,000 straw ballots were sent out and of these 2,376,523 were returned (a very large sample indeed). The results indicated a Landon landslide (370 electoral votes for Landon), but Landon secured just 8 electoral votes in the actual election.

The trouble arose because individuals in the lower economic classes had very little chance of appearing in the *Literary Digest* sample. While the later public opinion polls attempted to avoid the methods which led the *Literary Digest* to disaster, they continued to exhibit a similar, but smaller, bias. This persistent bias was large enough so that in the close election of 1948 the "scientific" poll takers were unanimously wrong in their predictions.

I want to discuss the reasons for the 1948 debacle briefly because anyone who accepts the principle that the proof of the pudding is in the eating might consider the failure of the poll takers as evidence that there is not much in sampling theory.

The point is that public opinion polls conducted by private organizations have continued to use haphazard methods for drawing their samples, largely for reasons of economy. The actual method employed is called *quota sampling*. In this method the person collecting the data, the *enumerator*, goes to some public place such as a bus station or railroad depot (*his* choice) and then picks out people (again *his* choice) in various age, sex, racial, and economic categories. The quota method is therefore a haphazard method—although this point has been concealed by fancy statistical formulas and scientific double talk.

The majority of sampling experts have been pointing out for a long time that the quota method is riddled with biases and that the estimates of the reliability of the method were unduly optimistic. What is more, the estimates of reliability failed to take into account several important sources of error which are not simply sampling problems. For example, public opinion is not static so that, even if percentages are correct at the time that a poll is taken, the situation may be changed by election day. Several studies of the pollster's techniques were made prior to the 1948 election and the various deficiencies were duly noted. Despite these studies the pollsters only seemed to realize the limitations of their methods *after* the election of Truman in 1948 and the resulting well-deserved horse laugh by the public.

I do not want to give the impression that haphazard samples are useless. Quite often the only available data for a decision are collected in a haphazard manner. The mathematical models developed for random samples are frequently the only models available so that in practice one has to use such models for haphazard data. But the user must proceed with caution and should try to appreciate and investigate the limitations of his methods.

Sampling Models

Now we are ready to return to the problem of constructing a model for data. The three concepts which we needed were *sample, population,* and *sampling method.*

The first step in setting up the model is to regard any collection of data as a sample from some population. The second step is to try to specify the population. This step is a creative one. We start with past experience concerning the population sampled (or similar populations) and try to characterize this population symbolically. It may require considerable ingenuity to construct a mathematical model for this population. The unknown characteristics of the population will appear in the model as parameters.

The third step requires the fabrication of a second model— a model of the sampling method. If the method of sampling is one of the standard methods, the model will be available in the literature. If a haphazard method of sampling is employed, the construction of the second model may be a difficult problem.

By putting together the model of the population and the model of the sampling method, and by manipulating the symbols, it may be possible to derive the probabilities associated with the various possible samples from the population. If the samples fall into classes, it may also be possible to derive the probability that a sample will fall into a given class.

The actual construction of a model for data will depend on three key factors:

(1) What we know from past experience (or are willing to assume) about the population sampled, i.e., our previous information concerning the subject field of the particular data.

(2) What we know (or are willing to assume) about the sampling method, i.e., the way in which we obtained the data.

(3) What we want to decide from the data, what we want to say or do on the basis of the data.

These principles will be illustrated in the next chapter when we will use them to construct a statistical model for measurement data.

The introduction of the concept of a sample enables us to construct models which will exhibit properties analogous to the properties of data which were discussed earlier. The incompleteness of data is intrinsic in the very notion of a sample. The biases of data are closely associated with the method of sampling and the populations involved.

The repeatability of data is tied to the repeated sampling of a population. In the peach tree example it was pointed out that repeatability depends on the sampling method. It should be noted that the repeatability also depends on the population. If, in the peach tree example, all of the orchards were of the same size (a characteristic of the population) it would make no difference whether a simple random sample or a stratified random sample were used—in fact, haphazard methods would also give good estimates. The lack of repeatability, i.e., the variability, or scatter, can be regarded as arising partly from the population and partly from the sampling method, and there are methods for partitioning the variation. These methods are discussed in Chapter 14.

The elaboration of the concept of a sample is, in my opinion, one of the main contributions of the statisticians. Without this concept, a method for making decisions from data soon runs into trouble. In the older forms of pure logic, for example, the theories of induction lacked the concept. A favorite example of the early logicians was the induction that all swans are white. It was based on a process of enumeration: This swan is white, so is this one, and so on. Therefore all swans are white. The example was dropped from logic texts when black swans were eventually discovered. The difficulty arose because the population of swans sampled was the population of European swans while the population of inference was much wider.

This same type of fallacy is encountered daily in print, on the air, and in conversations. In fact, some people have been so impressed by the persistence of this particular fallacy that they go to the other extreme and insist that all generalizations are false. Generalizations are useful in making decisions, however, even if they may not be strictly true. What is needed is a method for arriving at generalizations which can be used for practical purposes. The application of the concepts of sampling allows us to make generalizations of this type.

Summary

The concepts of sample, population, and sampling method are discussed. Some sampling techniques which provide fair samples are mentioned and a contrast is drawn between these methods and *haphazard* methods. Consideration is given to the way in which sampling concepts can be used to provide a model for data.

/

CHAPTER 12

MEASUREMENT

Models for Decision

The model for Statistical Decision which I presented in the first few chapters of this book described a decision situation in which only a limited number of actions was possible and each action had only a few possible outcomes. If you think back to the car vs. bus example of Chapter 2 you will recall that there were just two actions and only three possible outcomes: home early, home late, and accident. If we wanted to construct a more realistic model of the decision situation we might consider a finer classification of transit times than early and late; i.e., we might wish to consider the *measurement* of transit times in minutes.

If we do measure transit times in minutes, there will be a very large number of possible outcomes in place of early and late. The transit time might take anywhere from, say, twenty minutes to six hundred minutes. At first glance it might appear that this transition from classifications of transit times to measurements (and the corresponding increase in the number of outcomes) would have the effect of enormously complicating the calculations required for decision. Quite often the effect of this transition to measurements, however, is actually to simplify the technical part of the decision problem.

The technical simplification comes about, as you might expect, for purely mathematical reasons. When it is possible to substitute continuous (smooth) curves for discrete (disconnected) points, the mathematician is able to use powerful tools, such as calculus, in his manipulations of the symbolic model. Perhaps you do not regard the introduction of calculus as a simplification of a problem, but, as has been noted in connection with physical models, simplicity is relative.

With the help of calculus and still fancier mathematics (such as point-set theory) it is possible to construct much more flexible models for Statistical Decision than the elementary ones which I have presented. The use of advanced mathematics allows us to widen the scope, the range of applications, of Statistical Decision.

I will not discuss these advanced models in this book, but I do want to describe the transition from classification to measurement. This discussion will also serve to tie together and to illustrate the concepts associated with data, models, and sampling which have been introduced in the last three chapters.

Ordering

The basic idea in the transition from classifications to measurements (such as heights, weights, yield of corn in bushels, etc.) is *order* or, in other words, relationship between the classifications. Some classifications have no apparent order. For example, individuals might be asked in a survey whether they preferred ice cream, cake, or candy. If we were making up a table to present the results of this survey, there would be no obvious order in which this table should be arranged. There is no reason why we should not tally the cake lovers between those who prefer ice cream and those who prefer candy, or, in fact, make any other arrangement of the three categories.

On the other hand, if I am classifying patients suffering from a given disease as mild, moderate, and severe there is a natural ordering of these categories. We would feel that the mild cases would more nearly resemble the moderate cases than they would the severe cases. Various degrees of ordering of classes are possible; thus at one end of the scale would be the classification of desserts and at the other end of the scale would be numerical measurements. If we weigh three children we may find that A weighs 60 pounds, B weighs 50 pounds, and C weighs 65 pounds. Not only is there a natural ordering—C is heavier than A who is heavier than B—but we can go still further and say that there is less difference in weight between A and C than there is between A and B. Numerical measurements involve a very *strong* ordering of the classes.

A second characteristic of numerical measurements is that the classifications can be made finer and finer. In the example given above the weights were given to the nearest 5-pound category, but they might have been given to the nearest pound or the nearest half-pound. In any actual process of measurement there is a practical limitation to this process of subdividing categories (for example, the scale used in weighing may only read to the nearest ounce), but, hypothetically at least, the subdivision could be carried still further if we had better equipment.

If the midpoints of the weight classes were marked along a line, and if the process of subdivision were continued indefinitely, there would at first be a set of isolated points. Then gradually these points would become so dense that the set of points would eventually appear to be a *continuous* straight line; that is, the gaps would be filled up and pencil points would flow together into a solid line.

There is more to the construction of a good measurement scale than strong ordering or fine subdivision. There are such matters as the choice of endpoints and units. There are also questions involving the relationship between measurement scales, and the actual scale may be chosen so as to provide simple relationships.

A Measurement Prototype

Now let us turn our attention to the job of constructing a mathematical model for measurement data. In order to have a specific example in mind let me suppose that I have just measured the length of a room with a steel measuring tape and have obtained the numerical value of 14 feet 2 inches. This information is to be used to make some decision. Perhaps I am planning to order some wall-to-wall carpeting, so that it will pay me to devote some thought to the interpretation of this quantity, 14 feet 2 inches.

First of all, I will regard this particular measurement as a sample from some population. The question is: What population? In this example I will take as my hypothetical population the population of measurements which I might obtain if I were to repeat my measuring process. Conceptually there would be no limit to the size of this hypothetical population.

Next, I must try to specify this hypothetical population mathematically. First, however, I might try to give the specifications in verbal form. I can start by asking myself: What do I know from past experience about measurements of this type?

One thing I know is that all of the numerical values in the hypothetical population will *not* be the same; I might get 14 feet 3 inches if I measured a second time and 14 feet 1 inch if I tried again. Although there will be a scatter effect in my measurements, I also know that there will be some clustering. I would tend to get, say, 14 feet 2 inches much more often than I would get 13 feet 6 inches.

These remarks are rather vague, and I might try to make them more definite by using the concept of a *frequency distribution*. I might imagine that I repeated my measurement process a very large number of times—a thousand times—and that I counted the number of cases in which I measured 14 feet 2 inches, 14 feet 3 inches, and so on. If I let y stand for some distance, and $N(y)$ represents the number of measurements in which this distance was obtained, then I could plot $N(y)$ against y and obtain a picture of the frequency distribution. In Figure 12.01 I have drawn the *type* of frequency distribution which I might expect to obtain from the thousand measurements.

I have drawn this particular distribution on the basis of previous experience with numerical data; it represents a *prototype*. I would not really expect to get this particular distribution if I measured the room a thousand times, but I would expect to get a frequency distribution of the same general character.

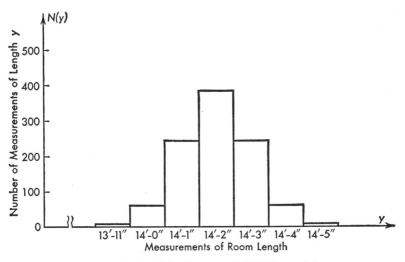

Fig. 12.01   Hypothetical Distribution of 1000 Room Measurements

This prototype has the following characteristics:

(1) The distribution rises to a single central peak (mode). Technically such a distribution is called *unimodal*.

(2) As one moves out from the central peak in either direction the distribution tapers off regularly.

The frequency distributions of most measurement data have the two above characteristics. Not all measurement distributions, however, show a third characteristic of Figure 12.01—symmetry. In Figure 12.01 if one moves out a given distance from the central peak, the height (ordinate) will be the same whether one goes to the left or to the right. This assumes, for example, that one would get the measurement 13 feet 11 inches as often as one would get 14 feet 5 inches. This characteristic of symmetry (or near symmetry) is quite common in measurement data, and most measurements of distance show this symmetry. Therefore, I will include this as a third specification of the prototype:

(3) The distribution is symmetrical about the central peak.

Mathematical Model

In order to construct a mathematical model we would want to describe the population, or really the prototype of the population, in terms of a formula. It is mathematically convenient to replace the discrete distribution of Figure 12.01 by a continuous distribution (as in Figure 12.02). To do this we imagine that the one-inch intervals are successively subdivided ad infinitum.

There is a wide choice of mathematical curves (functions) which could be used to represent the prototype. If specification (3) is removed, an even wider choice is possible. The actual selection is arbitrary, though of course the resulting model is subject to test against data. In practice, only a few mathematical functions have been used, and by far the most popular function is the *normal distribution*.

The normal distribution is a symmetrical, bell-shaped distribution with mathematical properties which make it especially convenient when the model is to be manipulated symbolically. The equation of the curve may look formidable to the uninitiated, but it is simple to a mathematician. I want to give this equation because it brings out some important points.

Let y denote some particular measurement of length. We can consider that we have subdivided length classes until the class intervals are very short (call the length of an interval dy). We may then want to know what the probability is that a measurement will fall between y and $y + dy$. I will denote this probability by $dP(y)$. The normal equation then becomes:

$$(12.01) \qquad dP(y) = \frac{e^{-\frac{1}{2}\left(\frac{y-\mu}{\sigma}\right)^2}}{\sqrt{2\pi\sigma^2}}\, dy$$

where e is a constant with value approximately 2.718, π is your old friend from the formula for the area of a circle and is

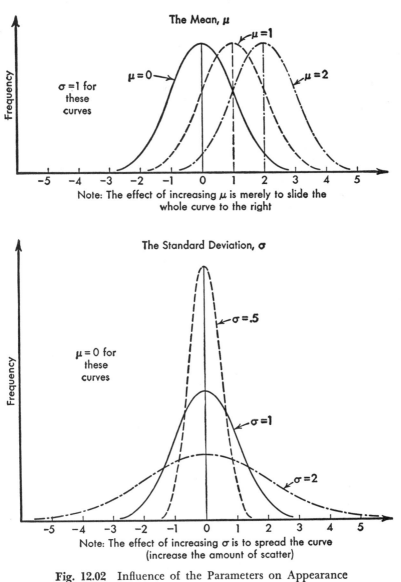

Fig. 12.02 Influence of the Parameters on Appearance of the Normal Distribution

approximately equal to 3.1416, and μ and σ are *parameters*.

These parameters have an interpretation in terms of the appearance of the curve. The quantity μ (the Greek letter *mu*) is often called the *expected value* or *mean* and is the numerical value of y where the curve reaches its peak. If we were to take an infinitely large number of measurements of the room and average them, then we would obtain this value, μ. Since μ refers to this central value of the curve it is sometimes called the *location* parameter. The other parameter, σ, is called the *standard deviation* and represents the extent of *scatter* of the measurements in the population.

The effect of substituting larger and larger numerical values for μ is merely to slide the entire curve over to the right without changing the shape of the curve. The quantity σ can take only positive values. If σ is small the curve is sharply peaked and the tails are small. If σ is large, the peak flattens out and the tails become larger. In other words, if σ is small it means that the measurements would cluster closely around the central value, while if σ becomes large it would indicate that the measurements were more scattered. The appearance of the normal curve for different values of the parameters is indicated in Figure 12.02.

The parameters μ and σ can also be interpreted in terms of bias and repeatability. Consider the population of repeated measurements with a steel tape. If we have some method of measuring the length of a room which is generally acknowledged to be much superior to the use of a steel tape, then this method can be taken as a standard. Let the numerical value obtained by this superior method be μ^*. Then if $\mu = \mu^*$ the steel tape method is said to give *unbiased* measurements. On the other hand if, say, μ is greater than μ^*, the steel tape measurements would be biased upward.

The repeatability or concordance of measurement data is evidently related to the amount of scatter in the observations which, in turn, is measured by the parameter σ. Consequently, as long as we are dealing with a normal model the concepts of bias and repeatability can be stated symbolically in terms of the parameters μ and σ.

Since μ and σ are *population* parameters they will, in practice, never be known *exactly*. However, they can be estimated from data and these estimates used in assessing the bias and repeatability of a method of measurement. In technical publications the word "accuracy" is sometimes used as a synonym for lack of bias and the word "precision" is used instead of repeatability.

So much for the mathematical model of the population measurements. I shall further assume that the actual measurement was a *random* sample from a normal distribution and consequently the probability of the sample is given by equation (12.01). If I used a sampling method which involved personal choice (for example, if I discarded any measurement that I didn't like) then equation (12.01) would not necessarily hold.

Use of the Model

The mathematical model will only provide *numerical* probabilities when the two parameters, μ and σ, have been determined numerically. This determination takes us back to data, i.e., to previous measurements which I have made with the steel tape. The parameter σ can be estimated from such data, and I will suppose that the estimate of σ is 1 inch. The parameter μ cannot be estimated from previous data unless I have already made measurements of the length of this particular room. However, from previous information, I may have satisfied myself that the steel tape was not *biased*. Notice that μ would then have the interpretation that it was the true length of the room, or, in general, the true length of whatever was measured by the steel tape.

Although I can use my model to evaluate my method of measurement with respect to bias and repeatability, I cannot use it to calculate numerical probabilities (such as the chance of getting a measurement in the 14 feet 2 inches class) because I have no estimate of μ. In spite of this, there is some useful information which can be obtained from the combination of the model and previous data. I can establish that most of the time (about 95 per cent of the time) my measurements will be within 2 inches (2σ) of the "true" length of the room (μ).

The use which can be made of the above statement depends on the decision situation. If I am buying a small carpet 13 feet long, an error of 2 inches in my measurement would hardly matter. On the other hand, if I am buying wall-to-wall carpeting a 2-inch error could be quite serious, and I would be reluctant to make a decision on such unreliable data.

What can be done in this latter situation if I do not have any method of measurement available which is superior to the steel tape? One possibility would be to take a series of measurements and then to average them. This will solve my problem providing I am careful that the observations are independent or, in practical terms, that I do not let the results of my previous measurements influence my later ones.

Now I face the question: How many measurements will I have to make? To answer this question I can proceed as follows. Let me call the number of measurements which I will need n. I take these n measurements and calculate their average. Next I must construct a model for samples from a population of the averages of n measurements. Fortunately this takes very little work because of some interesting properties of the normal distribution.

It is possible to derive mathematically that the *average* of a series of normally distributed observations is itself normally distributed. Moreover, this new normal distribution has the same location parameter as the population of individual observations, namely μ. The amount of scatter of the *averages* will be less than the scatter of an individual observation. We usually use the term "Standard Error" when we refer to the degree of scatter of an average (or, in fact, any *combinations* of the original observations). The standard error of an average of n measurements can be shown to be equal to the standard deviation of an individual observation (σ) divided by the square root of the number of observations $(\sqrt{n})$.

It is now necessary for me to decide, on the basis of the decision situation, how much precision I wish in my estimate of the length of the room. After due consideration I specify that I will be satisfied if most (95 per cent) of the time my estimate will be within half an inch of the actual length of the room. It can be shown (using the assumptions made previously) that about 95 per cent of the time an average will be within two standard errors of the actual length of the room. Hence, my specification is equivalent to the requirement that two standard errors should be equal to one half inch or one standard error equal to one quarter inch.

To find n, the number of measurements needed, it is only necessary to solve the equation

$$\frac{\sigma}{\sqrt{n}} = \frac{1}{4}$$

where I know that $\sigma = 1$. Hence I should take sixteen measurements if I want to meet my specifications.

There is one very remarkable property of the normal distribution which I want to emphasize. Perhaps the prototype that I chose was not a good model for the individual measurements. Perhaps I should have used a prototype with two peaks instead of one or an unsymmetrical prototype. In this event, the use of the normal model could very well have led me astray if I were to act on the basis of a single measurement. But—and this is really amazing—*even* if the prototype was *not* normally distributed, the *average* of sixteen observations would be very nearly normally distributed! I would not be led astray by my model if I were to act on the basis of the average of a number of observations.

These last remarks need a little qualification. A mathematician can sit down and devise a fantastic prototype for which this last remark would be wrong. In practical applications, however, such pathological distributions are quite rare, although there are some famous examples in economics and biology (i.e., the distribution of income) .

The normality property of averages also applies to totals and, in certain situations, even to counts. It provides one very good reason why the normal model is so successful in practical applications.

The Normal Distribution

The normal model for measurements has been used in nearly every field of human activity in which measurements are made. Originally it was applied to astronomical and land-survey observations, and subsequently it was used to describe measurements in various branches of physics and chemistry. When the biologists began to make measurements they borrowed many techniques from the physical sciences—most of which did not work out very well. The normal curve, however, was successfully used in medical research, in agricultural field studies, and other biological applications. In price studies in economics, in mental measurements in psychology, and in various other applications the use of the normal model was fruitful. In view of this breadth of application it is not surprising that the normal distribution acquired the status of a "Law of Nature" and that a mythology grew up around this ubiquitous model.

Individuals and textbooks, unable to distinguish between myth and math, have accepted the model as an article of faith. To my way of thinking it is dangerous to identify a model with the real world, so I want to devote a little attention to the question: Is the normal curve a fact of nature?

First of all, I do not feel that characteristics which we put into the data when we construct operational definitions or make calculations should be regarded as facts of nature. Such characteristics look to me like artifacts of man. As I noted earlier, there is a tendency for averages to be normally distributed irrespective of the population sampled; hence, the normality of the distributions of averages does not constitute evidence that individual observations are normally distributed. A similar effect holds for other quantities than averages, such as the scores on a test.

This problem of artifacts in data is a thorny one. For instance, it can be shown that if a series of observations is smoothed by a common technique called mean moving averages there will be a tendency for the smoothed data to show well-marked *cycles* even if the original observations are samples from a random number table. Mean moving averages are often used on economic data (such as a time series of stock market prices) and many investigators have spent their time chasing will-o'-the-wisp cycles which they themselves have put into the data by their computational methods.

In studying the question as to whether or not the normal distribution provides a good approximation to a population, it is therefore necessary to limit consideration to frequency distributions of *individual* measurements. When this is done one often encounters markedly nonnormal populations. On the other hand, one also meets frequency distributions which are unimodal and symmetrical, and the normal distribution provides a good approximation. With a very large amount of data one can generally point out minor ways in which even the unimodal and symmetrical frequency distributions depart from the theoretical normal curve. Such minor deviations are unimportant in practice, but they do constitute evidence against the normal distribution as a fact of nature. One crusader against the myth of normality has a standing offer of $100.00 for any collection of data with over one thousand observations which will meet the standard statistical tests of normality. So far as I know he has had no takers.

There is one proviso in the offer—the operational definition of the measurement should *not* have been deliberately constructed in such a way as to lead to a normal distribution of the observations. Some psychological tests, for example, have been carefully normalized.

Most of the current statistical techniques are based on the normal model. Extensive tables have been constructed not only for the normal curve itself but for some derivative distributions which arise when normal data are *manipulated*. For example, the chi-square distribution (which will be discussed in the next chapter) tells us what happens when the original observations are first *squared* and then averaged. In practical work, such auxiliary distributions are needed, so one has the choice of using the normal model or constructing a whole set of new tables for some other model—not an attractive alternative. Consequently, almost everyone uses the normal model.

This is not quite as bad as it sounds because even if the population sampled is markedly nonnormal there are a number of tricks of the trade which can be used to transform the original population into a more nearly normal one (insofar as computations are concerned).

Steps to Prediction

In the last four chapters I have tried to sketch the workings of what I have previously called an advanced Probability Predicting System. The normal model which I have just described in an example of an advanced system. Most of the technical part of Statistical Decision deals with these advanced systems.

In my discussions I have tried to describe, step by step, the way in which we can bridge the wide gap between raw, imperfect data and the final stage—numerical probabilities associated with outcomes. The gap may be thought of as a wide river with two islands in the middle. When we go from raw to refined data, we construct a span between the real world and the nearest island. When we devise a mathematical model for data based on the concept of a sample, we link the symbolic world with the other island. Finally, by using both the mathematical model and the refined data, we create a bridge between the two islands and open the way for traffic between the symbolic world and the real world.

The building of the bridge is a long, hard job. The creation and testing of models, the gathering and refinement of data, the evolution of a workable predicting system constitute a sequential process which may take years or even centuries. I cannot, therefore, present Statistical Decision as a quick and easy highroad to success.

There is one consolation. Once a good predicting system has been evolved, the use of this system in future decisions may be quite easy. The collection of data and the manipulations of the model may become routine. This routine may be tedious, it may require some computational effort, but, whenever there is sufficient demand, a machine can be designed to take over the chores. Hence at the *operational* stage it may be both quick and easy to go from data to prediction. The Predicting System can grind out good forecasts for the administrator or executive, or it can be coupled to the later stages of the Decision-Maker so that wise decisions are made automatically, decisions which are virtually "untouched by human brains."

Summary

The transition from classification to measurement is described and a verbal prototype of a population of measurements is presented. The normal distribution is used to translate the verbal prototype into a mathematical one. The use of the mathematical model is illustrated. The interpretation of the normal model, the most important model in statistics, is briefly discussed.

CHAPTER 13

/ **STATISTICAL INFERENCE**

Beyond the Sample

The Great Detective studies the knife wound in the murder victim's back and announces: "The murderer is left-handed." You are introduced to a middle-aged gentleman and, after the routine introductions, there is a brief but uncomfortable pause before you ask: "Have you read so-and-so's latest book?" A medical scientist examines the records of his experiment and says: "The new treatment is superior to the old one."

These three episodes have one thing in common: they involve the process of *inference,* the procedure for going from a sample (data) and structural knowledge (model) to a statement. In all three cases, the statement goes beyond the sample. The Great Detective has not seen the murderer with a knife clutched in his left hand. Similarly, you are not sure that the middle-aged gentleman will be interested in so-and-so's book, but you think from the gentleman's appearance that this book is a likely common ground for conversation. The doctor has seen the results of the new treatment for a sample of patients, but his statement is not limited to this particular sample.

All of us are accustomed to making inferences in everyday life, but we usually do the job intuitively. What I want to do now is to try to analyze an intuitive process to see if it can be stated in terms of the concepts of sample, model, probability, and so forth. If this can be done, perhaps the logical structure of the intuitive inference will be revealed.

To do this, I shall try to expose the inner workings of the Great Detective's brain as he forges the chains of inferences which lead him, at the end of the book, to the identity of the murderer.

Let us suppose that the Great Detective has just arrived on the scene of the crime and is busy examining the haft of the knife in the victim's back (i.e., he is gathering data). He notes the angle at which the haft protrudes and various other clues.

The Great Detective's brow furrows as he considers the alternatives: the killer must have held the knife in his left hand or else he thrust home with his right hand. In effect, the Great Detective is setting up a list of alternative statements (hypotheses) which he might make:

H_o: The murder weapon was held in the right hand.
H_a: The murder weapon was held in the left hand.

The sleuth now considers what might be expected *if H_o* were true. Taking this hypothesis to be true, what sort of wound might be expected? This is a *conditional* argument; the sleuth makes no assertion at this point but merely considers what might have happened *if* the murder weapon had been held in the right hand.

The Great Detective now draws on his prodigious knowledge and past experience. He is well acquainted with the pattern of behavior of a killer who holds a knife in his right hand (i.e., the detective can set up a *model* for human behavior), and this information leads him to deduce (i.e., derive from the addition of H_o to the model) that a specific type or class of knife wound would result. The Great Detective therefore considers all possible types of knife wounds (samples) and, under the hypothesis that the murderer used his right hand, the criminologist can divide the set of all possible knife wounds into two classes, say likely and unlikely.

In the same manner, the detective can take the hypothesis H_a (a left-handed knife thrust), and under this hypothesis he can again divide the set of all possible knife wounds into those which are likely and those which are unlikely. This classifies the set of possible wounds into four categories: (1) Wounds which would be expected if the killer were right-handed but would be unusual otherwise, (2) wounds which would be expected if the killer were left-handed but which would be unusual otherwise, (3) wounds which might be expected if the thrust were *either* right-handed *or* left-handed, and (4) wounds which would be unlikely to have been made by a thrust (i.e., might be made by a thrown knife). Notice that this entire classification process does not involve the actual wound yet, and could be performed before the victim is seen.

The Great Detective in his examination of the actual wound is trying to classify it into one of the four predetermined categories. He concludes that the nature of the wound is such that it falls in category number two—that this wound is one of the types of wounds which would be expected from a left-handed knife thrust but which would be unusual, or even impossible, if the killer used his right hand.

In view of this the Great Detective rejects H_o and affirms H_a. He announces: "The murderer is left-handed."

To recapitulate the steps in this inference:

(1) A list of statements or hypotheses is set up. These statements go beyond the sample.
(2) A list of all possible samples is made.
(3) Under a specific hypothesis (i.e., conditionally) the list of all possible samples is divided into two sub-lists, expected samples and unusual samples.
(4) If the actual sample is on the unusual list, the corresponding hypothesis is rejected.
(5) By a process of elimination the hypotheses are rejected one by one. If one hypothesis remains which cannot be rejected, this hypothesis is affirmed.

Note that there might be some wounds of which the Great Detective might be unable to make a statement of either hypothesis. This would happen for wounds which might be expected either if the thrust were right-handed *or* if the thrust were left-handed.

The above pattern of inference is, I think, a fairly common one and, as we shall see, is also the pattern of statistical inference.

Now let us jump to the end of the book and watch the Great Detective at work again. In the intervening chapters the sleuth has gathered more and more clues (data). By the time the denouement is reached a list of suspects has been built up. This list of suspects is a list of hypotheses. If the suspects are numbered (1, 2, 3, etc.), and if i is any one of these numbers then the i-th hypothesis is:

H_i: The i-th suspect is the murderer.

For convenience, the set of various clues which the Great Detective has unearthed might be called S (for sample). The question facing the Great Detective is: "*If* the i-th suspect is the murderer, what is the chance that this set of clues, S, would have been obtained?" In symbolic terms this question might be rephrased as: What is the numerical value of $P(S \mid H_i)$? I hope that you will recall that $P(S \mid H_i)$ is the probability of the sample *if* the i-th hypothesis is assumed, a *conditional* probability (see page 70).

Casual detective story readers, such as myself, will miss most of the clues and will not know what to do with the clues which are spotted. The Great Detective, however, has the previous experience and models necessary to utilize all of the clues in order to evaluate quantities such as $P(S \mid H_i)$.

The climax comes when all of the suspects are seated in the very room in which the deed was done. The Great Detective now explains to the suspects (and to the casual readers) just why it is very unlikely that the sample of clues, S, would have been obtained *if* the murderer were the second suspect. Thus he demonstrates that $P(S \mid H_2)$ is practically zero. In the same way he proceeds through the list of suspects and shows that in the sample of clues there are one or more clues which renders it highly unlikely that suspect number 3, 4, or 5 could have committed the crime.

By this process of elimination the Great Detective narrows his list down to suspect number 1. For suspect number 1, $P(S \mid H_1)$ is not near zero; in fact, it is a large quantity. Consequently, the Great Detective announces: "Suspect number 1 is the murderer!"

Faced with such relentless logic the fictional criminal (suspect number 1) either breaks down and confesses verbally or else whips out a gun and tries to escape (effectively a confession). The Great Detective, from his models of human behavior, has already anticipated this attempt and corners suspect number 1, who then jumps out a window or perishes in some suitably gory fashion.

Rules for Inference

If you will examine other inferences—for example, those which lead you to choose a particular topic to start a conversation with a stranger—I think you will find the same logical pattern as the Great Detective's. When you are introduced to a stranger you set up a list of alternative statements such as: "X will be interested in books" or "X will not be interested in books." The appearance of the stranger is the sample. Social stereotypes provide the model. If the stranger is a serious-looking, middle-aged gentleman you infer that he will be interested in books.

I do not mean to imply that you follow the deliberate process outlined above. You probably make social inferences so automatically that you have no awareness of the process of inference itself. In fact, it would be silly to try to make every social inference by a formal procedure when intuitive methods will do the job quite well.

When we consider the inference of the doctor concerning the efficacy of a new treatment, however, there is a strong incentive to try to develop a formal process. True, the doctor can glance at his experimental results and intuitively reach the inference that the new treatment is superior, but this inference —unlike the social inference—is for public rather than private consumption. The doctor must convince not only himself; he must convince other doctors.

If the doctor justifies his inference by a remark, "That's the way the experimental results look to me," other doctors may say, "Humph! That's not at all the way *I* would interpret the results!" If different scientists look at the same data and, intuitively, reach opposite conclusions, it is difficult to resolve the argument. Not only must the discussion take place at a verbal level, but, further, the justifications will necessarily be vague and subjective. Such a situation is hardly satisfactory for a scientific problem.

Since it is so hard to resolve the situation when doctors disagree, it is easier to meet the problem by attempting to avoid the disagreement in the first place. For this we might try to convert the procedure for inference previously discussed into a more definite and objective *rule for inference*. Then if the doctors can agree in advance on the rule for inference, there should be no disagreement on the conclusions.

As you might suspect, the construction of a *quantitative* procedure for inference will involve the various principles discussed in the last four chapters. The sample is characterized by counts or measurements, the model is specified symbolically, and the verbal categories of likely or unusual are replaced by numerical probabilities.

The construction of a rule for inference is quite analogous to the construction of a rule for decision. A Decision-Maker makes a choice between possible actions. Now we want an Inference-Maker to select a statement or hypothesis from a list of possible statements. Since making a statement may be regarded as an action, a theory of decision includes inference as a special case. Inference-Makers are simplified versions of Decision-Makers.

An actual problem in medical research may serve to exemplify the above notions. Consider a doctor who wishes to compare a new treatment for a given allergy with a standard treatment for that allergy. The doctor may feel that the efficacy of the treatments can be measured by the amount of protective substance (antibody) in the patient's blood. The amount of antibody would actually be determined by a fairly complicated titration procedure, and the measurement obtained would be called a *titer*.

The plan of the experiment might call for half the patients to receive the new treatment the first year and the standard treatment the second year, while the other half of the patients would receive the treatments in the opposite order. Due precautions would be taken to insure that neither doctor nor patients knew which treatment was received (such a plan is called a double-blind experiment). The purposes of these and other precautions, such as randomization, would be to guard against biases and to control known sources of variation.

After completion of the experiment the patient's titer on the standard treatment would be subtracted from the patient's titer on the new treatment. For the i-th patient this *difference* between treatments could be denoted by Y_i. Evidently the Y_i's would serve as a measure of the relative efficacy of the two treatments. If the new treatment were better, the Y_i's would tend to be positive. If the standard treatment were better, then the Y_i's would tend to be negative. If there were no difference in the efficacy of the treatments then the Y_i's would tend to be small positive or small negative numbers. The Y_i's would not be expected to be *exactly* zero because an individual's titer may change a little over a period of time even if he always receives the same treatment.

Now suppose that the doctor has carried out a carefully planned experiment on ten patients and that he has obtained ten numbers (Y_i's). He would like to make a statement about the relative efficacies of the two treatments. What the doctor needs is a rule for inference by which he (and anyone else who might wish to check on his results) can, from the observations, make a statement about the relative merits of the treatments.

In order to obtain such a rule for inference the doctor can fol-

low in the footsteps of the Great Detective—he can take exactly
the same five steps (page 214) that the Great Detective took.

Step 1: Draw up a list of possible statements.

In the doctor's case there might be two hypotheses which
would be of interest:

H_o: There is no difference in the efficacies of the two treatments.
H_a: There is a difference in the efficacies of the two treatments.

The designation H_o is commonly used for the null hypothesis
(i.e., an hypothesis of no difference), while the symbol H_a usually represents an alternative hypothesis. Here the alternative
hypothesis would be that the treatments were different.

I want to caution you against too literal an interpretation of
these hypotheses. From past experience I can safely say that two
different treatments would not be *exactly* equal in effectiveness
—just as no two peas in a pod are literally identical. Hence if
H_o were interpreted strictly, it would not be necessary to do an
experiment; we could simply assert H_a. Rather H_o should be
interpreted as stating that the two treatments are equally effective for all practical purposes, and H_a implies some appreciable
difference between the efficacies.

If I assume that the Y_i's are normally distributed (page 202)
and if μ is the expected value or mean of the normal distribution, then the two hypotheses can be translated symbolically as:

$$H_o: \mu = 0$$
$$H_a: \mu \neq 0$$

where the equal sign with the line through it means *not* equal.
This symbolic statement of H_o can be interpreted in terms of an
infinitely large hypothetical experiment. Thus if the treatments
are equally good and if the number of patients is increased without limit, then the average of the Y_i's will tend to be zero. In
other words, there would be no consistent difference between the
standard and the new treatments.

Step 2: Specify all possible samples.

It will not be necessary (or possible here) actually to list all possible samples. It will suffice to know that, conceptually at least, Y_i may take any value, positive or negative. The possible samples therefore comprise all combinations of the ten Y_i's.

Step 3: For each hypothesis (Step 1) specify the expected and the unusual samples.

Roughly speaking, the expected samples (if H_o were true) would be ten numbers, some of which would be positive and some negative and most of which would be numerically small (i.e., near zero). Unusual samples under the null hypothesis (H_o) would have most of the observations of the same sign and probably some numerically large quantities. On the other hand, if the alternative hypothesis is true, then the designation of the samples is, essentially, reversed. That is to say—what were the unusual samples become the expected samples under the alternative hypothesis.

In a later section I shall discuss just how we can specify the usual and unusual samples more definitely. At this point the vague definitions will suffice to indicate that the set of all possible samples *can* be divided into two subsets which might be called expected and unusual.

Step 4: Determine whether the actual sample falls in the expected or the unusual class (under H_o).

Once the two classes are adequately specified, the above step requires only that the experimenter examine the sample and possibly perform some computations to determine how the actual sample should be classified.

Step 5: If the sample falls in the unusual class then H_o is rejected.

In actual practice when H_o is rejected it is customary to assert H_a—that is, to make the statement: "The two treatments have different efficacies." Here then is a definite and objective way to progress from data to inference. If the doctors can agree to use this procedure, they should all arrive at the same conclusion provided they start from the same data. The role of the human in this process is merely to see whether the actual sample falls in the expected list or in the unusual list. This rule puts no strain on human abilities.

Standards for Inference

Before we can continue with the construction of an Inference-Maker, it is necessary to lay down some specifications for the machine. To set the specifications we must consider the question: What do we want from a rule for inference? The answer to this question might be: We want a rule for inference which will not lead us astray, that is, will not lead us to make assertions which future investigators will show to be erroneous. In short, we want a rule for inference which will enable us to avoid mistakes in our inferences.

I hardly need to point out that we cannot expect a rule for inference to be infallible. We will have to expect that the rule will lead us astray occasionally. We can, however, demand that the rule must make mistakes only rarely. Let me therefore set up this condition as a tentative standard for our Inference-Maker: *A satisfactory rule for inference should make mistakes only rarely.*

Although this standard may seem simple, this simplicity is deceptive. Two words require careful definition: "mistakes" and "rarely."

First of all let us consider what we mean by a mistake. The first difficulty that arises is that we can make several different *kinds* of mistakes. Suppose that there is no difference in efficacy between two treatments, *and* that our rule for inference leads us to assert that there is a difference. Clearly we have made a mistake. I shall call this a Type I mistake.

On the other hand, let us suppose that there really is a difference of some practical importance *and* that our rule for inference does not lead us to assert that there is a difference. Once again we have made a mistake, but a different kind of mistake. I shall call this a Type II mistake.

Notice that if we make a Type I mistake, this constitutes a "sin of commission." We have asserted something that isn't true. On the other hand, a Type II mistake is a "sin of omission." We have failed to make a statement that would have been true.

Legally, "sins of commission" are considered more serious than "sins of omission"—one cannot be hanged for failing to throw a life-preserver to a drowning man. Statisticians have taken the same attitude and have tended to concentrate on avoiding "sins of commission" (Type I mistakes).

There are some further complications in the definition of "mistakes," but I shall return to this point a little later. First let me consider the definition of "rarely." As might be expected, the vague verbal definition is replaced by a numerical one. Thus in the biological sciences the word "rarely" is usually understood to mean "5 per cent of the time." In what follows I will generally refer to control of Type I mistakes at the 5 per cent level, though the research worker can choose *any* level he wishes.

One might think that the Type II mistakes would be controlled in the same fashion, i.e., set at a preassigned numerical level, but unfortunately this can only be done for a special class of statistical techniques (sequential methods). For the more frequently encountered statistical techniques, it is possible to control only one type of mistake at a time. Thus if the Type I mistake is controlled at the 5 per cent level, the best that we can do is to *minimize* the Type II mistake. Unfortunately, for small samples the percentage of Type II mistakes may be quite large.

Let me restate these conditions as standards for Inference-Makers:

Specification 1: Control the risk of a Type I mistake at 5 per cent.

Specification 2: Subject to the first specification, make the risk of a Type II mistake as small as possible.

The above two specifications are nearly enough to enable us to construct Inference-Makers. There is one further difficulty, however, which again involves the definition of a "mistake." Since this point is something of a semantic tangle (see Chapter 4, page 70) , I would advise the casual reader to skip ahead to the next section. However the reader who is actually concerned with statistical methods would do well to stay with me and struggle with this messy point—and perhaps wrestle with it on his own.

What I wish to do now is to distinguish between an *error* (as the word is used in statistical literature) and an actual mistake. This distinction involves the difference between a compound probability (A occurs *and* B occurs) , and a conditional probability (A occurs *if* B has occurred) . Some readers may wish to review the discussion of compound and conditional probabilities in Chapter 4 before proceeding. In order actually to make a Type I mistake, there must be no difference between treatments, *and* we must assert that there is a difference. On the other hand, the risk of error in the technical sense of the word involves the conditional probability—the probability that we assert that the treatments are different *if* there is no difference between treatments.

Although the conditional and compound probabilities sound very much alike, they are quite different in their meanings and may also be quite different numerically. However there is a relationship between the two probabilities, a relationship which follows from the multiplication rule (page 70) .

$$P(\text{reject } H_o \text{ and } H_o \text{ is true}) = P(\text{reject } H_o \mid H_o) \, P(H_o) .$$

When properly interpreted, the above equation provides the key to an understanding of current Inference-Makers. The left-hand side of this equation represents the risk of making a Type I mistake. The first term on the right-hand side indicates the risk of a Type I error (in the technical sense) . The numerical value of this probability is determined by the rule for inference that is used and can be set at any preassigned value (more or less). The second term on the right-hand side, $P(H_o)$, is the probability that there is no difference between treatments (i.e., H_o is true). This second term, the *prior* probability, is the one which causes all the trouble.

The prior probability itself is blameless—it is a perfectly respectable probability with a sensible interpretation in terms of a series of experiments. However a numerical estimate of this prior probability may be obtained only from a series of experiments; it cannot be obtained from a *single* experiment.

Sir R. A. Fisher, creator of most of the current statistical methodologies, has advocated the principle that the analysis of experimental results should be *self-contained*. In other words the inference from a set of observations should involve those observations alone and should *not* involve any prior data. There is a great deal to be said in favor of this principle, and it has been widely accepted. But if the analysis is to be self-contained, the prior probability cannot be estimated and hence is an unknown quantity; the risk of a Type I mistake cannot be assessed; and there is an impasse.

The way out of this impasse which has been taken by most statisticians is to adopt the loss-control philosophy and argue as follows. The *worst* situation, insofar as making Type I mistakes is concerned, is for the treatments studied *always* to have the same efficacy. If a rule for inference is formulated which will lead to Type I mistakes only 5 per cent of the time even in this *worst* situation, then the rule can be "safely" used in any situation.

In the *worst* situation the risk of a mistake is the same as the risk of error since $P(H_o) = 1$; therefore, if the risk of a Type I error is fixed at 0.05, the risk of a Type I mistake will automatically be controlled. In practice, then, the specifications for an Inference-Maker are given in terms of the errors rather than the mistakes.

Specification 1: Control the risk of a Type I error at 5 per cent.

Specification 2: Subject to the first specification, make the risk of a Type II error as small as possible.

The distinction that I have drawn between errors and mistakes may be clarified by considering two series of experiments. The first series is the work of Dr. Dub who has no luck or skill in selecting treatments for testing, that is, all the treatments which he chooses are no better than standard treatments, so $P(H_o) = 1$. When Dr. Dub uses standard Inference-Makers he makes Type I mistakes 5 per cent of the time. On the other hand, Dr. Sharp always manages to select treatments with a real advantage over standard therapies, so $P(H_o) = 0$. Although Dr. Sharp uses statistical methods where the Type I error is 5 per cent, he *never* makes a Type I mistake. Thus despite a fairly widespread belief to the contrary, there is nothing in current statistical methods that *condemns* a research worker to make mistakes 5 per cent of the time.

Significance Tests

The next problem—and this is a technical one—is to construct actual rules for inference which will meet these two specifications. Although this is a job for a specialist, the *principle* of construction is so simple that I can give it here.

First of all, we suppose that there is no difference between treatments (H_o is true), and we shall therefore be working with conditional probabilities of the type $P(S \mid H_o)$. Under this hypothesis we want to divide the set of all possible samples into two parts—the unusual samples (technically the critical region) and the remaining samples. The job is to construct the critical region so that the rule for inference determined by this critical region will meet the two specifications given above.

I shall suppose, for simplicity, that a model has been set up and that, with the assumption that H_o is true, the numerical values of parameters of the model are known. In this case, we can calculate for any particular sample, say S_i, the numerical value of $P(S_i \mid H_o)$. We then proceed to do just this for all possible samples.

Next, I will suppose that there is a specified difference between the two treatments (i.e., H_a is true), and that I can calculate the numerical values of $P(S_i \mid H_a)$. Therefore, associated with any sample, S_i, I will have two numbers,—$P(S_i \mid H_a)$ and $P(S_i \mid H_o)$—and these two numbers can be used to calculate the *probability ratio* (p.r.) associated with S_i. The probability ratio is:

$$\text{p.r. } (S_i) = \frac{P(S_i \mid H_a)}{P(S_i \mid H_o)}.$$

Now what does this probability ratio mean? If the ratio is large (somewhat greater than one), it says that the probability of the sample *if H_a* is true is greater than the probability of the sample *if H_o* is true. This is more or less what we mean when we regard a sample as unusual under the null hypothesis. Consequently it would be sensible to construct the list of unusual samples (critical region) by the following rules:

(1) Rearrange the list of all possible samples so that the first sample, S_1, has the largest probability ratio, the second sample, S_2, has the next to largest ratio, and so on down the list.

(2) Beside the i-th sample in the list write the number $P(S_i \mid H_o)$.

(3) Starting at the top of the list, add the quantities $P(S_i \mid H_o)$ until the total comes to 0.05 (or as near to this value as possible). We might, for example, have to add a number, c, of the conditional probabilities until

$$P(S_1 \mid H_o) + P(S_2 \mid H_o) + \cdots + P(S_c \mid H_o)$$
$$= \sum_{i=1}^{c} P(S_i \mid H_o) = 0.05.$$

(4) The critical region (i.e., those samples where we will reject H_o) will be the list of samples $S_1, S_2, \cdots, S_c$.

I have given the rule for constructing a critical region when we want $P(\text{Type I error}) = 0.05$. If we wished to control the Type I error at 1 per cent instead of 5 per cent we would include samples until the sum in the equation above (3) were equal to 0.01.

These rules lead to a rule for inference which meets our first specification because the type I error is the chance of rejecting H_o *if* H_o is true. We will reject H_o only if our sample falls in the critical region and, if H_o is true, the chance of this happening is

$$\sum_{i=1}^{c} P\left(S_i \mid H_o\right),$$ which has been fixed at 0.05.

The rules also insure that the second specification, i.e., that P (Type II error) is as small as possible, is met. I will not try to demonstrate this point although the proof is easy and does not involve any fancy mathematics. Since the proof is an exercise in the translation of common sense into mathematics, I suggest that you try to make the proof for yourself. The trick is to consider what happens if any change is made in the critical region given above. For the new critical region the first specification must still be met $[P\left(S \mid H_o\right) = 0.05]$ but $P\left(S \mid H_a\right)$ is altered. Since the new critical region includes samples with a smaller probability ratio, you can show that the quantity $P\left(S \mid H_a\right)$ can only be *decreased*. This quantity, $P\left(S \mid H_a\right)$, is called the power of the test and represents the chance that a Type II error will *not* be committed.

Testing Two Treatments

The principles of constructing a significance test discussed in the last section will now be used to obtain an actual technique. What I wish to show is that although the construction of a test of hypotheses is rather complex, the end product is very simple to use.

Consider once again the testing of two treatments for allergy. The results of this experiment consist of ten numbers $(Y_i\text{'s})$, which have been obtained by subtracting the patient's titer on the standard treatment from the corresponding titer on the new treatment. The details of the design used (page 218) would influence the actual analysis, but in what follows time effects, etc., would be neglected.

To keep matters as simple as possible I am going to make two assumptions about the model. I will assume that the Y's are samples from the *normal distribution* (discussed in the previous chapter). This is not a very drastic assumption because I know that *if* I draw two samples from the *same* population of measurements, then regardless of the nature of the population, the *difference* will be symmetrically distributed. Hence the normal distribution should provide a fairly good approximation.

My next assumption will not be generally true. I am going to assume that from past experience we *know* the precision of the measurements. In other words, I shall assume that the standard deviation of the normal distribution, σ, is known to me and, further, that this standard deviation of the Y's is numerically equal to *one* $(\sigma = 1)$. This second assumption can be avoided and is not used in the standard statistical methodologies which deal with this problem.

The two standard hypotheses:

H_o: There is no difference in the efficacies of the two treatments
H_a: There is a difference in the efficacies of the two treatments

are equivalent to the following statements about the location parameter, μ, of the normal distribution of the Y's:

H_o: $\mu = 0$
H_a: $\mu \neq 0$

In other words, if there is no difference between treatments then we would expect that *in the long run* the average value of the differences between counts (Y's) would be zero.

Under the null hypothesis we can write down at once the probability that, for the first pair of patients, the difference between the counts will be between Y_1 and $Y_1 + dY_1$,

$$dP\left(Y_1 \,|\, H_o\right) = \frac{e^{-\frac{1}{2}Y_1^2}}{\sqrt{2\pi}}\, dY_1$$

where this formula comes from formula (12.01) on page 202 $(\mu = 0$ and $\sigma = 1)$.

Assuming that the Y's are *independent*, it is a very simple matter to write down the probability of the *sample* (i.e., the probability of Y_1 *and* Y_2 *and* the other Y's up to Y_{10}). It is only necessary to multiply successively the quantities like $dP(Y_1 \mid H_o)$. Using S for sample, and taking advantage of the fact that e^a times e^b is equal to e^{a+b}, we have

$$(13.01) \qquad dP(S \mid H_o) = \frac{e^{-\frac{1}{2}(Y_1{}^2 + Y_2{}^2 + \cdots + Y_{10}{}^2)}}{(\sqrt{2\pi})^{10}} \text{ (product of } dY\text{'s)}.$$

This result when properly interpreted can save us a great deal of work. Notice that the only way in which information from the sample enters equation (13.01) is in the sum of squares of the Y's. Let

$$T = Y_1^2 + Y_2^2 + \cdots + Y_{10}^2.$$

What formula (13.01) tells us (though I cannot go into all the details here) is that if we construct a rule for inference based only on T it will be just as good as any other rule for inference which considered all possible samples of ten observations. In other words, we can concentrate our attention on the *single* statistic, T, instead of having to worry about ten numbers.

Even with this simplification we could not literally carry out the procedure for constructing a critical region described in the last section. For one thing, there is no limit to the number of possible samples (i.e., values of T) which might be obtained. The procedure can be followed in principle by using calculus —I shall not go into this—and in this way it is possible to obtain such quantities as $P(T \mid H_o)$ and $P(T \mid H_a)$. There are two points concerning $P(T \mid H_o)$ and $P(T \mid H_a)$ which I think can be determined without mathematics. When there is no difference between the treatments we would expect the Y's to be small and consequently we would expect the T's to be small. Broadly speaking, if T is large, $P(T \mid H_o)$ will be small, while if T is small, $P(T \mid H_o)$ will be large. When there *are* differences between treatments then we would not expect T to be small. Hence if T is small, $P(T \mid H_a)$ will also be small.

The probability ratio, $P(T \mid H_a)/P(T \mid H_o)$, will therefore be large when T is large and small when T is small. In constructing our critical region we would therefore include those samples in which T is large. The critical region can be described rather simply; it consists of those samples in which T is greater than some constant, K (i.e., $T > K$).

The constant K will have to be chosen to meet the specifications for the rule for inference. The probability that a sample would fall in the critical region is equivalent to the probability that T is greater than K. In symbolic terms this condition on K is simply

$$P(T \text{ is greater than } K \mid H_o) = 0.05.$$

This equation takes some fancy mathematics to solve but it turns out that for ten patients the value of K is 18.3.

The construction of the test may be difficult, but the test is very easy to use. All that needs to be done is (1) to calculate T (which will mean squaring the Y's and adding the squares), and then (2) to see if T is greater than 18.3. If it is, this rule for inference says to reject H_o, that is, the doctor would state: "There *is* a difference between the two treatments." If the doctor uses this rule for inference in a series of experiments, and if there *never* is any difference between his treatments, the rule for inference will lead him astray only 5 per cent of the time.

Suppose, however, that T is less than 18.3. What can be said in this case? The consensus of opinion among statisticians seems to be that we should say nothing at all. Some statisticians would make a statement such as "No difference between treatments has been demonstrated," but this statement says nothing about the parameter μ and is a *description* of experimental results, *not an* inference. Consequently, this sort of statement can be made without risk of error of inference.

Some research workers have wanted to make the statement "There is no appreciable difference between treatments" if their value of T was smaller than 18.3, but this is risky in the sense that there may be a large error of the second type associated with this statement. Most statistics texts have warnings in boldface type against the making of such statements.

While such warnings are well justified from the standpoint of avoiding statements which are likely to be erroneous, it is not entirely satisfactory to refuse to make any statement. True, as long as we deal with statements it is plausible to allow situations in which no statement is made, but when we think in terms of action this easy way out is no longer possible. Some sort of action will have to be taken in the situation.

If the doctor who has studied the two treatments comes out with a T less than 18.3, he must make a decision as to his next step. Perhaps he will abandon work on the new treatment. In any event, the information in the experiment will be used to select a future course of action.

The *statement* "There is no appreciable difference between treatments" would be associated with the *action* "Abandon work on the new treatment." It is rather academic to refuse to make the statement but to take the corresponding action. I shall come back to this point later on in this chapter.

The Role of Significance Tests

I hope that the little mathematical manipulations in the last section have not discouraged you. The main reason for including this material was to provide a sample of the technical phase of the subject. The Inference-Maker thus obtained is the closest approach to an *operating* mechanism that I can give in this book.

Inference-Makers of the type just discussed are very useful in the process of Statistical Decision. For one thing, they serve to fill in a gap in my discussion of models. You may recall that I postponed consideration of the last step in the role of the model, the *testing* of the model. The techniques of statistical inference may be used to deal objectively with the question: Does the model adequately predict the test data? If the sample (test data) falls in the unusual category (critical region) then we reject the model.

Many statistical textbooks spend so much time working up to a discussion of tests of significance that such tests would seem to be the *ultimate* goal of statistics. Theoretical presentations also tend to give this impression. However, insofar as the construction of Decision-Makers is concerned, significance tests are only a *preliminary* technique.

If we want to set up a prediction system we will have to choose a model as a basis for the system. Significance tests will help us to *choose* the model, but from the standpoint of decision our eventual purpose is to *use* the model that has been selected. This detracts in no way from the importance of tests of significance because the first links in the chain are just as critical as the later links. I do want to emphasize, however, that significance tests are not a stopping point but are, instead, a starting point for an investigation.

Perhaps if we consider the doctor and his two therapies this issue will be clarified. Suppose that the doctor performs a significance test and rejects the hypothesis that the two treatments are equally effective. This is hardly a stopping point. Granted that the two treatments are different, this immediately raises the question: Which treatment is better and how much better is it? Later in this chapter I will discuss the statistician's answer to this sort of question, but even if the answer is given we still have not reached a stopping point. We will want to answer questions regarding our future actions such as: Should the superior treatment be given routinely in this hospital?

Although it is convenient to treat each stage in the process of decision as a separate entity so as to have, at each stage, a problem we are capable of solving, it should not be forgotten that each stage will be followed by another stage and that we are dealing with a sequential process.

In my discussion of models I indicated that the choice of a model for a predicting system is a creative process. While this means that the selection of the model is more or less arbitrary, there is often a pattern—but not a rigid one—to the process. This pattern represents a compromise. The real world in which we live is a very complex affair but, for practical reasons, the models which we will use will have to be fairly simple. Hence, in choosing a model we compromise; we generally try to get by with the simplest model which will serve our purpose.

The principle of using the simplest effective model has been given various names such as the *principle of scientific economy* or the *principle of simplicity*. The ancestry of this principle goes back to the medieval theologists, such as William of Occam, who propounded the rule: "Never multiply entities without necessity."

The application of the above principle to the construction of a prediction system leads to the following general approach: We do not start our construction by trying to take into account every possible relevant factor. We start with the simplest model that none of the factors is relevant. If, in terms of significance tests, this hypothesis does not lead to adequate prediction, we grudgingly add what seems to be the most important factor to the model. If the model is still inadequate, we reluctantly introduce additional factors.

At each stage we have a model pitted against a more complex model, the simpler model being associated with the null hypothesis. If this hypothesis is rejected we go on to the next stage. Significance tests enable us to determine, in a relatively objective fashion, the degree of complexity which is necessary for the model. They therefore play an important role in guiding the sequential process of investigation to the choice of the model which will ultimately be used in the Decision-Maker.

Estimation

If the doctor demonstrates that there *is* a difference between the two therapies, he will want to go on to the next question: *How much* difference is there between the two treatments? If the new therapy is very expensive, and if the advantage is small, then the use of the new treatment may not be justified. The problem of "How much?" is called *estimation,* and this topic is the second major subdivision of statistical inference. There are a number of different approaches to this problem and I will describe only one, the method of *confidence intervals*.

A confidence interval is a rather cagey statement about a parameter. It does not give a single value as the estimate of the parameter; rather it gives an interval or range of values and says only that the actual value is somewhere in this range.

If I made repeated measurements on the length of a rod then the confidence interval statement that I might obtain would be of the form: This rod is between 72.3 and 72.6 inches long.

The procedure in setting up such a confidence interval is quite similar to the method for constructing a significance test. I first state certain specifications which I require of my rule for inference—perhaps that the statements made by using this rule for inference will be incorrect at most 5 per cent of the time. A second specification would be that the range, or length of the interval, would be as short as possible.

The actual construction of an appropriate rule for estimation proceeds more or less along the same lines that were described in connection with tests of significance. One major difficulty in the construction process (and this also applies to significance tests) occurs when a *nuisance parameter* is present. Nuisance parameters are the parameters of the mathematical model other than the particular one we want to estimate. We can usually obtain (by rather direct methods) upper and lower limits for an interval which will meet the 5 per cent specification but which, unfortunately, involve these other parameters. Since we do not know the numerical values of these nuisance parameters we cannot use limits of this type to set confidence intervals, but sometimes, by a little mathematical legerdemain, we can get rid of the unwanted symbols.

Once again it should be remembered that there is "nothing for nothing" in statistics and that confidence intervals are subject to definite limitations. If the risk of error is made very small, or if the observations are erratic, or if there is only a small amount of data, then the interval will tend to be a wide one. In fact, the interval may be so wide as to be useless for practical purposes. If I know that the length of a rod is between 2 inches and 200 inches. it does not help me to decide whether the rod can be used as a crossbrace in a chair.

I emphasize this point because there is a rather widespread misconception concerning what modern statistics has achieved in connection with what are called *small samples*. In the early days of statistics approximate tests of significance and estimates were developed which worked out well when very large samples were used. When these methods were applied to small samples (samples with between one and thirty observations) the techniques were no longer *valid*. In other words, if the specified risk of error was 5 per cent, these large sample techniques might have an actual risk of error of 6 per cent or even 10 per cent.

In the first quarter of this century new rules for inference which were *valid* even when used on very small samples were developed. These new techniques, the start of modern statistics, have been given a heavy emphasis by up-to-date teachers, but unfortunately some students managed to get the impression that the techniques of modern statistics had obviated the need to collect large amounts of data, and that small samples were just as useful as large samples.

This is not at all the case; statistical methods do not *add* information, they can only extract it. It is true that *valid* statements can now be made from both large and small samples, but validity is not all that is required of a rule for inference; the statements must also be *useful*. The utility of a statement about a parameter depends on the *length* of the confidence interval; a small sample may lead to a range which is so wide as to be, for all practical purposes, completely useless. In many practical situations the only way to get a useful statement is to take a large sample.

Tests of significance and estimation enable us to go from a sample to statements about the population from which the sample was drawn. This is a very important type of inference, but there are other types of inference. Another common purpose of inference is to classify individuals. The Great Detective, for instance, wants to classify one of the suspects as a murderer; he is not concerned with making statements about the population of murderers.

This phase of inference has been considered by statisticians under the heading of *discriminant functions*. In my opinion this topic has not yet received the attention that it deserves.[1]

Decision

The inferences of the Great Detective lead to action. If the Great Detective belongs to the grand old school he may wait until his risk of error is nearly zero; if he is a muscular modern he will operate with risks of error at 20 per cent or even 50 per cent and rely on his fists rather than his facts. In any event, the climax is reached when the Great Detective points his finger and proclaims: "That is the man who did the deed!"

The accusation is an action, and this choice of action leads to rather evident consequences. The individual so charged will be hung, electrocuted, or otherwise made to realize that "crime does not pay." Hanging an innocent individual is generally regarded as an unpleasant consequence not merely for the individual, but also for the Great Detective, who would surely be professionally embarrassed if this occurred.

In the inference of the doctor concerning the two therapies, or in any other nontrivial inference, there will be a consequent action and such action will have desirable or undesirable repercussions. This issue can be dodged temporarily by adopting a loss-control philosophy, by using a Simple Value System, and by using specified risks of error (such as the 5 per cent level). Ultimately, however, it will be necessary to judge a rule for inference by the consequences which follow from its use.

This point was raised in connection with the medical example in which, if the sample did not fall in the critical region, no real inference was attempted. But it was still necessary to take

---

[1] But the situation is improving! A good discussion appears in Rao, C. R., *Advanced Statistical Methods in Biometric Research,* John Wiley & Sons, Inc., New York, 1952.

some action—either to continue experimentation with the new therapy or to abandon it—so that although the problem could be dodged at the verbal level it could not be avoided at the practical level.

In pure academic work I suppose there is more damage to a person's reputation from making an erroneous positive statement than from failing to make a positive statement which could have been made. To this extent, the preoccupation with the first type of error (erroneously stating that there was a difference between treatments) would be justified. But for scientists who are not so pure it may be even more serious to fail to recommend a treatment which might save additional lives.

This problem is especially critical in medical research where it is often both difficult and expensive to do large experiments. A depressingly high proportion of actual experimentation is futile in this sense: If significance tests are used on a limited amount of data there is a very poor chance (perhaps less than 10 per cent) that appreciable advantages will be detected by the calculations. Most of the experiments of this type will lead to results from which no inference can be made.

There is no easy solution to this problem. One possibility is to do more extensive experiments or to try to arrange cooperative experiments in which data obtained by different investigators can be put together. Another possibility is to change the sacrosanct 5 per cent probability level to 10 per cent or even 20 per cent. The point I wish to make is this: I do not think that this type of problem can be handled within the framework of classical statistical theory. It is necessary to broaden the frame of reference, to introduce the concepts of Statistical Decision and, unpleasant as it may be, to face up to the problems of the Value System.

Summary

Statistical inference follows the same general principles as everyday inference. With the aid of probabilities, intuitive processes of inference can be converted into more objective rules for inference. The two main categories of statistical inference are *significance tests* and *estimation*. Examples of the theoretical and computational procedures for constructing significance tests are given. Some of the limitations of statistical inference are pointed out, and it is emphasized that a broader frame of reference, Statistical Decision, is needed in order to deal with the problem of inference.

CHAPTER 14

STATISTICAL TECHNIQUES

Tools of the Trade

A carpenter needs to know about the nature of his materials and the principles of construction, but to build an actual table he also needs hammers, saws, and other tools. In the same way, if we want to make an actual decision we will need specific statistical tools as well as general principles. While I do not intend to go into the technical side of Statistical Decision in this book, I would like to provide enough information about the statistical tools to allow an interested reader to pursue the subject further. Therefore in this chapter I will list the principal types of tools and indicate their uses. References to these tools will be found in the appendix.

In the last fifty years statistical methodologies have proliferated at a prodigious rate, and important new tools are continually being developed. There are, today, so many special tools, and these devices are so varied in character, that it is no easy matter to decide which, if any, of the existing methodologies are appropriate for a given problem. The concepts of Statistical Decision serve to integrate the various special techniques and therefore the decision point of view makes the choice of an appropriate tool somewhat easier.

Most practical decision problems will be much more complex than the little examples which I have presented; they will be decision chains with many links. Each link will be a distinct problem and consequently many different statistical techniques may be required to handle the practical problem (just as a carpenter would not expect to use only one tool in building a table).

I shall confine the discussion of tools to those devices used in the construction of the Prediction System of the Decision-Maker. As we have already noted, the fabrication of an advanced prediction system has two phases—model-making and data-gathering. Successful prediction usually requires an interplay between these two phases, but for purposes of exposition I will consider the two separately.

First, I will consider the techniques which deal with the evaluation of data. I have previously emphasized that it pays to scrutinize critically the procedures used in collecting the original data. The quality of the data which fuels the Decision-Maker often determines whether the mechanism is successful or not. The determination of the quality of the data will involve different techniques for classification data than for measurement data.

Classification

It may seem obvious to you that when classifications are used the very first step would be to see if the classifications are any good (i.e., unbiased, repeatable, and relevant). It may also be evident to you that if the classifications are inadequate it is rather futile to collect great quantities of this defective data. Yet strangely enough, there are many investigators who never try to check up on their methods of classification.

At the very least the individual who makes the classifications should be able to agree with *himself*. It often comes as a shock to investigators that, when this question of self-agreement is examined, the results indicate that the investigator does not even agree with himself. As an example of the use of statistical techniques to answer questions about self-agreement, I want to consider the following (rather common) situation in medical research. It is customary to use X-ray films to determine the severity of diseases such as tuberculosis. A doctor will examine a series of X-ray plates and classify them by degree of severity as (say) mild, moderate, or severe.

To check up on the classification system the doctor might read a series of plates and then, perhaps a month later when the original classifications were forgotten, read the same series of plates a second time. This little experiment can be presented as a *contingency table* (Figure 14.01). The name contingency

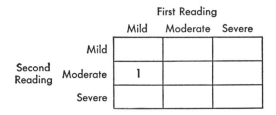

Fig. 14.01   Contingency Table for Examining Repeatability of Classifications

table arises because all possible contingencies or outcomes are given in the table.

The tally shown in Figure 14.01 would correspond to an X-ray plate which was read as mild the first time and as moderate the second time. Each plate in the series can be tallied in some cell of the table. If the doctor always agreed with himself, all the tallies would fall in the main diagonal of the table (i.e., mild-mild, moderate-moderate, etc.). Such perfect agreement is rarely encountered in actual experiments, however, and ordinarily there will be tallies in most of the cells of the table. Various statistical techniques have been developed for further analysis of contingency tables and in particular for measuring the degree of agreement. Often, however, a glance at the contingency table will suffice to indicate that the method of classification is in need of improvement.

Not only should the investigator agree with himself, but it is also desirable that he should agree with his fellow experts. The agreement between two doctors might be studied by having them read (independently) the same series of plates. A contingency table which would display the results of this further experiment could then be constructed.

Agreement as measured by the two previous experiments is closely associated with the concept of repeatability. But repeatability is not the only criterion for judging the quality of data. Suppose that the patients in the X-ray series are brought in for an intensive medical examination. Then these patients might be classified as mild, moderate, or severe on the basis of this further study and this second classification might be considered to be more reliable. If this examination classification is taken as the standard, it would be possible to compare the X-ray classification with this standard. It might be found that the X-ray readings were biased in the sense that the X-ray classifications were consistently more severe than the examination classification, or the bias might be in the other direction. It might also be possible that the X-ray classifications were irrelevant for the purposes of the investigation. The statistical techniques for testing relevance will be discussed later.

I do not want to give the impression that the contingency table is the only statistical technique for dealing with classifications, but it will serve as a point of entry to the literature.

Measurements

It has been emphasized in this book that *quantification,* the replacement of words by numbers, is a key step in science. The advantages to be derived from quantification are not inherent in the numbers *themselves.* The use of numbers and measurements does *not* automatically improve matters—the measurement must prove its worth by the standards which have already been applied to classifications.

This point deserves some emphasis because of an increasing tendency of some scientists to use numbers and statistical techniques as sheer window dressing, as a device for adding a tone of scientific respectability to trivial papers.

Numerical methods are a tool and, like any other tool, they

can be used frivolously. A buzz saw is also a fascinating tool, but the utility of a buzz saw is not intrinsic. A person can use a buzz saw to slice worth-while timber into waste ends and sawdust. The mere fact that a person is running a buzz saw does not mean that he is a good builder. The mere fact that an individual uses numerical analysis or statistical techniques does not make him a good scientist.

It will be necessary, when working with measurements, to study the quality of these measurements. The first step is to examine the repeatability of the measurements. If the measurements are approximately normally distributed (see Chapter 12), the variance (or standard deviation) of repeated observations can be used as a measure of repeatability.

Frequently a measurement is obtained by a series of operations. Measurements in chemistry, for example, are often obtained by an elaborate process involving pipetting, titrating, weighing, and other operations. We can think of the actual variation in the final measurement as composed of contributions from a number of different sources of variation. Some of the operations in the process may introduce large experimental errors, while the contributions of the other operations may be negligible. An improvement in the measurement process (i.e., a reduction in variation) may follow if the operations with large experimental errors can be improved. It is of interest, therefore, to determine which operations are major sources of variation.

The statistical techniques applicable to this problem fall under the heading of *components of variance* which is, in turn, a part of *analysis of variance*. With the aid of these methodologies, the contributions of the various sources of variation can be assessed numerically.

Questions concerning bias and relevance are also elucidated by the methods of analysis of variance. The information thus obtained may be used to improve and standardize measurement processes.

Recording and Storing of Data

Every field seems to present peculiar problems in the recording and storing of data. Most of the discussion of this topic will be found in the field of application rather than in the statistical literature. Lately, the development of the electronic brains has led to wider interest in problems of recording, storage, and recovery of information. Current research may lead to a systematic body of knowledge on these questions which will go beyond the "cut and try" procedures currently in use.

There is one device which deserves special mention in connection with recording and storing procedures. It is usually worthwhile to make a preliminary study ("dry run" or "pilot trial") as a test of procedures before any large scale collection of data is set into motion.

The collection of data may be divided into three categories—experimentation, surveys, and systematic observation. The distinction is somewhat arbitrary and experimentation is distinguished from other methods of collection mainly by the degree of *control* which is exercised.

Experimentation

There are a number of diverse statistical techniques which fall under the heading of *design of experiments.* These techniques are often simple extensions of common sense. Suppose, for example, that you were in the shoe business and that a new compound had been developed for making soles which was supposed to be far superior to materials currently used. You might want to test the new compound by making up a batch of shoes which differed only in the composition of the soles and then giving these shoes to various people with the understanding that after a fixed length of time the shoes would be brought back and rated as to amount of wear and other characteristics. Obviously different people will give different usage to the shoes. How can this factor be controlled?

A common-sense way of meeting this problem would be to

make up pairs of shoes, one of which had the old sole, while the other had the new sole. This pairing process would lead to a better comparison of the two materials. It would also be common sense to put the old sole on the right shoe half of the time and on the left shoe the other half of the time. This would control inequalities in wear which might occur between right and left shoes.

In the *design of experiments* the devices for control of sources of variability are extended to much more complex situations. For example, suppose that we wanted to test three or four new compositions to see which one made the best soles. If you like puzzles you might try to figure out a design for this new experiment which would control the variation due to the different amounts of wear for the different people.

The development of techniques for efficient and well-controlled schemes for collecting data is one of the most important contributions of modern statistics.

Sampling Surveys

In principle the collection of data by a survey, such as a public opinion survey, is closely allied to the collection of data in laboratory experimentation, but in practice the problems encountered are so dissimilar that it is convenient to treat the two procedures separately. Earlier I remarked on the care that must be taken in drawing the sample. The sampling problem is treated in detail under the heading *sampling survey techniques*.

Sampling is not the only problem in a survey, and sometimes it is a relatively minor problem. It may be more important to choose the questions in the survey with great care and to control the methods of asking these questions. There are a great many other problems associated with the survey method, but unfortunately in a good proportion of surveys these problems are either ignored or treated with disdain. As a consequence the survey method has a rather checkered record of performance.

I do not want to give the impression that a sampling survey

is not a useful instrument—I only want to emphasize that it is a tricky one. Surveys have been useful to the government (estimation of population and resources), to business (consumer reactions), and to science.

Summarization of Data

The traditional statistical techniques have been developed in connection with problems of summarization of data. From the standpoint of Statistical Decision, however, it is somewhat pointless to summarize data without taking into account the *use* which will be made of the summaries. There has been much wasted work in connection with summarization (particularly on the topic of *index numbers*) because of failure to realize that the *use* of summaries must be considered.

Elementary statistics texts tend to go into tedious detail concerning summarization and to spend much time on averages, medians, rates, ratios, indices, index numbers, and so on. This sort of text gives the reader the impression that statistics consists of endless and very dull repetitions of arithmetic processes.

In the early days of statistics there was little more to the subject than the details of summarization, but things have changed. There are much more important topics which deserve attention now.

Models

The first step in solving a decision problem is to try to set up some sort of model—a verbal model is better than nothing. This process of setting up a model is equivalent to formulating the problem in a clear-cut fashion.

When a mathematical model is used, the process of formulation may require not only mathematical methodologies but also techniques from the subject-matter field. In an engineering problem, for example, methodologies from physics and chemistry may be needed.

The *theory of probability* will be a basic instrument in the formulation of a model. *Frequency distributions* will also play a role. If probability event chains are involved, then the theory of *stochastic processes* may be useful. All of the above topics are branches of *mathematical statistics*.

In order to formulate a model for a prediction system we usually take three steps:

(1) Determination of the factors which are *relevant* for prediction.
(2) Determination of the actual *relationship* of the factors to the phenomena to be predicted.
(3) Construction of a prediction system based on this relationship.

The statistical techniques associated with relevance can be divided into three types. This division is based on the nature of the data. The factor which we wish to predict may be either a classification or a measurement, and the factor which we would like to use for prediction may also be either a classification or a measurement. The situations to be considered are:

(1) Class vs. class
(2) Class vs. measurement
(3) Measurement vs. measurement.

Class vs. Class

Much medico-sociological data will fall in this category and, in general, class vs. class data will be found in subject fields in which adequate measurements are still in the developmental stage.

Let us suppose that we are interested in a specific disease, and we think that there may be a relationship between housing conditions and this particular disease. We may, in the first stages of a study, choose a sample and classify every individual in the sample in two ways. First, the person may or may not have the disease under study. Second, the person may live in a house which is substandard or he may be adequately housed. After the information is collected it may be presented in what

is called a two-by-two contingency table such as the one in
Figure 14.02.

Number of Individuals in Categories

| Health Status | Housing | |
	Substandard	Adequate
Diseased	75	50
Not Diseased	1250	1790

Fig. 14.02

The numbers in this table (which I have manufactured) indicate that the proportion of diseased people is higher among
those who are living in substandard housing than among those
with adequate housing. But we must remember that we are
dealing with a sample. If, instead of considering housing, I had
divided the sample into two parts by flipping a coin for each
individual and assigning him to category A if the coin were
heads and to category B if the coin were tails, then I would not
expect the proportion of diseased people in category A to be
exactly equal to the proportion of diseased people in category B.
But it would obviously be silly to regard my flipping a coin as
relevant to the disease under study merely because there was
some difference between category A and category B.

In order to guard against meaningless association, we would
make a *chi-square test* (or use some related technique). First we
set up the simplest model: Housing is irrelevant insofar as the
risk of a given disease is concerned. The chi-square test allows us
to determine whether the simplest model can account for our
observations. To perform the significance test we would substitute the numbers in Figure 14.02 into the formula for chi-square.
We would then go to the chi-square tables which can be found in
almost all statistical textbooks. If our calculated number turns
out to be larger than the appropriate number in the table (and
if the sampling is unbiased, etc.), we reject the hypothesis that

housing is irrelevant. As I have emphasized previously, this type of statistical technique may lead us to assert erroneously that the disease under study is associated with housing, but mistakes of this nature should be infrequent.

The *chi-square test* can also be used in more complex contingency tables. There are also some alternative tests which can be used in special contingency tables. The other tests are necessary because if the numbers in the cells of a two-by-two table are very small there are some objections to the use of the chi-square test.

Class vs. Measurement

The commonest data of this type involve measurements made on individuals in various classes. In agriculture, for example, we may be interested in the yield (say in bushels per acre) of three different varieties of wheat. Ordinarily the varieties would be planted on a number of small plots, say ten plots for each variety, so that the experimental results would consist of thirty numbers. We would want to know whether the variety was relevant to the yield. The factor to be used for prediction would be the variety, a classification, and the factor to be predicted would be the yield, a measurement.

The reverse situation, in which the factor for prediction is a measurement and the factor predicted is a classification, is less common and the techniques applicable here go by various names. The statistical literature generally refers to such techniques as *discriminant functions*. In the fields of application there are different nomenclatures. In medicine, for example, the techniques go under the title of *diagnostic parameters*.

Now let us return to the problem of the three varieties of wheat. When the average yields for each of the varieties are calculated, they will not be exactly the same. We would not want, however, to jump to the conclusion that the true yields of the three varieties are different because there is always a possibility that our results are merely manifestations of experimental error.

As in the class vs. class example, we start by setting up a model which postulates that variety is irrelevant insofar as yield is concerned. We then apply *analysis of variance* to test this model. The test itself is called the *F-test* (in honor of R. A. Fisher). If this test is significant, we regard the variety of the wheat as relevant to the yield. As usual, we run a specified risk of erroneously concluding that variety is relevant.

Measurement vs. Measurement

A classic example of this situation is the study of the heights of parents and the heights of their children. The common method for presenting such data is a scatter diagram. In the scatter diagram the average height of the parents is plotted against the horizontal axis of a graph and the height of the child is plotted against the vertical axis. Each parent-child pair is represented by a point on this graph. Since the points are scattered over the graph, the name scatter diagram is quite appropriate.

If the height of the parents is irrelevant insofar as the height of the child is concerned, then it can be shown that a line parallel to the horizontal axis of the graph will fit the points as well as any other curve. The statistical techniques for testing the relevance of the height of the parents are *regression* or *correlation analysis*.

Relevance and Relation

The statistical techniques for testing relevance are designed to avoid wild goose chases. If a factor, Z, turns out to be relevant to the quantity we wish to predict, Y, then we proceed to investigate the matter further. We would try to discover the actual relationship between Z and Y. But we would not want to go on to this next step until we had some evidence that Z was relevant. If Z is irrelevant, the additional study would not be likely to advance us toward our goal of predicting Y.

The tests for relevance may tell us that it may be worthwhile to pursue our study of Z, but in order to use Z for actual prediction it will be necessary to find a workable relationship. This relationship may be expressed verbally, but it is usually more useful to try to describe the relationship in the symbolic language (i.e., as a mathematical relationship). In general, it is not an easy matter to discover a workable relationship, and it usually takes creative effort on the part of the investigator.

In the housing vs. disease example we might be satisfied with the *estimation* of the proportion diseased in both housing situations. This information might be used for prediction and action. It might tell us, if the disease happened to be tuberculosis, where we should send the mobile X-ray units in order to locate cases of T.B.

When the yields of the different varieties of wheat are estimated, this information may lead us to recommend a particular variety of wheat to the farmers in the adjacent area. On the other hand, we may feel that the experiment was too small and we might want more information before taking action. If relevance had been demonstrated it might then be worth while to go ahead with more comprehensive experimentation.

The determination of the relationship between parental height and child height would be the next step in the measurement vs. measurement example. We might see if a straight line (but not a horizontal line) provided a good fit to the points on the scatter diagram. In this particular case, and in other scientific work, we may not be interested in prediction per se; we may be interested in learning more about the phenomena without thinking in terms of immediate application.

Multiple Factors

In most practical situations the problem is more complex and involves not merely a predictor and a quantity to be predicted but many different factors. The contingency table approach, analysis of variance, and regression analysis can be extended to deal with these more complex situations. More advanced techniques, *multiple and partial regression,* and *multivariate analysis,* and others, may be pressed into service.

The consideration of several factors simultaneously may tell us much more than the separate consideration of each factor.

As an example of simultaneous consideration of factors, we might consider the work on intelligence quotients (IQ). The early work on the performance of Negroes and whites on IQ tests gave ammunition to the racists because of the poor showing of the Negroes. Many other factors besides race enter the picture, however. For example, there is a relationship between IQ and economic status. Since Negroes have a lower average economic status it would seem, at first glance, quite hopeless to try to disentangle racial and economic factors. Some progress in this direction can be made through the use of *partial regression,* however, and the results of this further study were highly disappointing to the racists.

The first studies indicated that, if the race of an individual were known, we could do a better job of predicting his IQ than if we did not have the information about race. What the further studies showed was that if we knew the race *and* the economic status of the individual our prediction would not be materially better than if we knew *only* the economic status. According to the racist model our predictions should be much improved by including information about skin color, so the results are hardly in accord with the racist model.

There are many "facts" which are widely accepted but which turn out to be fiction when investigated statistically. Statistical techniques furnish protection against prejudices and superstitions, and a wider understanding of the principles of Statistical Decision might lessen the influence that biases currently exert on choice of action.

Relationships Involving Time

There are various specialized relationships which have corresponding specialized statistical techniques. Time, for example, is often an important factor in the prediction of phenomena, and techniques appropriate to dynamic situations have been developed. Under the broad heading *time series* there are many methodologies. In the past, numerous attempts have been made to analyze time series into components such as trends, seasonal variations, cyclic variations, and so on. In engineering applications this type of analysis of time series has been an effective instrument, but the application of similar techniques to economic problems has led to improved forecasting only in isolated cases. Such devices as *correlograms* and *periodograms* have had some success, but this particular statistical pathway has to be posted with a sign: "Danger, proceed at your own risk."

Another type of problem in which time plays a major role is in the prediction of population growth. The particular population studied may be a human one, or it may be an animal or micro-organism population. There is an extensive literature on *growth curves*.

In industrial situations, time enters the problem of control of manufacturing processes. *Control charts* and *quality control* are statistical techniques which have been developed to meet industrial needs, but their application extends to other fields.

Other Techniques

It should be realized that I cannot give a complete listing of statistical techniques in a short chapter. There are many techniques which have been developed to meet rather special situations in the various fields of application. For example, *bioassay* is important in medical experimentation, and *factor analysis* has been used mainly in psychology. There are so many techniques nowadays that they crowd the three-year graduate course in statistics which leads to the Ph.D. degree. This does not mean, however, that there are statistical techniques which apply to all, or even most, decision problems. For many practical problems the statistical methodologies are rudimentary or nonexistent, and it is necessary to develop new methods for dealing with these decision problems. The job of developing statistical methodologies to fit practical problems is part of the function of a statistical consultant. It keeps him on his toes and makes his life interesting.

Summary

This chapter has essayed a quick survey of the more important statistical techniques. Mention is made of the position these methodologies occupy in Statistical Decision. It is emphasized that, although there is an extensive body of techniques, the field is rapidly growing, and in many practical decision problems new tools will have to be forged to meet the needs.

CHAPTER 15 /

DESIGN FOR DECISION

Speculations

Throughout this book I have been critical of armchair thinking, of people who sit back and produce beautiful thoughts with little or no data behind their cerebrations. In this, the last chapter, I intend to do just this sort of speculating. My excuse for this inconsistency? Well for one thing, although I try to be consistent in my professional remarks, it's a terrible strain on a human being to be consistent *always!* Furthermore, it has been hard work writing some portions of this book, and I am giving myself a little vacation in this chapter.

Some readers, I'm sure, have felt that the Decision-Maker is a cold-hearted—even grim—method of making decisions. These readers might be willing to admit that a machine may be all right for making the scientific decisions which I have largely emphasized in the text, or even for commercial decisions, but they may feel that Statistical Decision has no place in their own world, that it is meaningless insofar as personal, governmental, or international decisions are concerned.

I disagree with this view point. I think that Statistical Decision can play a useful role in a wider class of decisions and in particular in those decisions which have a direct influence on all of us.

I certainly do not consider Statistical Decision to be a panacea. It is one method among many methods of reaching decisions. It is not necessarily the best method; there are situations in which intuitive procedures lead to more effective decisions than any existing Decision-Maker. I have tried to mention the limitations of the techniques in the course of this presentation. In this chapter I want to discuss the potentialities of Statistical Decision, and, in particular, those possibilities which might affect the lives of ordinary citizens.

Personal Decisions

When I say that Statistical Decision can play a role in personal decisions I do not mean that everyone will have to take courses in higher mathematics before he can decide whether or not to go to the movies. Very few everyday decisions would have sufficiently wide differences in the consequences of the possible actions to make it worth while to expend the time and energy necessary to construct a formal Decision-Maker. However, I do think that the principles which underlie the Decision-Maker can also be used, informally, to arrive at effective choices of actions to be taken in everyday situations. In fact, I think that most people with common sense have already used many of the principles in making their decisions. All that the statisticians have done is to borrow these notions and dress them up in the symbolic language.

You may have felt that such concepts as mathematical expectation were new and unfamiliar. However, if you scrutinize the concept itself closely you will find antecedents in everyday experience. In the symbolic notation, mathematical expectation may look esoteric, but I'm sure that you can recall occasions when you have had to make decisions on the basis of expectations, when you have had to combine probabilities and desirabilities (though you probably did not use these names or make the combination in the same manner as a mathematical expectation).

Laplace once described probability as "common sense reduced to calculation" and I think this applies equally well to the whole of Statistical Decision.

In the process of reducing common sense to calculation, we are doing a job of translation. The mere *attempt* to make a translation into the symbolic language may be very useful. Even if the translation is only partially completed it may serve to bring into focus—or even resolve—problems which are almost insurmountable in the verbal language.

A large proportion of the controversies in science, and in everyday life, turn out to be basically *verbal* problems, and a symbolic translation following the pragmatic principle is often a good way to clear away the verbal underbrush and expose the path to decision. In this way we can avoid distracting verbal will-o'-the-wisps and concentrate on the essentials of the problem, the probabilities and desirabilities. I have found the concepts of Statistical Decision useful in this respect in the course of my consultations. You might try them.

As an example of a concept of Statistical Decision which deserves wider use in everyday decision, consider the notion that decision should be based on data. All the evidence that I have ever seen indicates that schemes for decision which are not based on experience are not effective. The astrologers, palmists, and others make a nice living when the public is not acquainted with the concept that data constitute the fuel for decision.

Far more dangerous than the phony prophets are the smooth-talking propagandists and public relations experts who have developed effective techniques for influencing our economic, political, and social decisions. These supersalesmen are well aware of the inadequacies of the decision-making equipment of the general public and exploit these deficiencies to the hilt. For a price these propagandists will peddle worthless medicines, partisan politics, group hatred, or any other product. These unscrupulous experts will successfully swindle the public as long as the Decision-Makers of many citizens are fueled by prejudices and emotions rather than by data.

I am optimistic enough to think that a reaction to the intrusions of the supersalesmen is setting in. However, this reaction has taken the form of complete disbelief in all information which comes through the media of mass communication. This is not, in my opinion, a happy solution to the problem. If we are to grow intellectually we must absorb information, and I do not feel it is wise to set up a mental block and refuse to believe anything.

What we need is a *filter*, not a plug.

We must develop in ourselves, and in our children, the capacity to sort out the incoming information, to determine what is incomplete, unreliable, biased, or irrelevant. The development of a critical mind is not a simple process, but the principles of Statistical Decision are helpful in this connection.

Administrative Decision

I earn my bread and butter by working on the statistical phases of medical research. As a result, my description of Statistical Decision has tended to emphasize the research applications at the expense of the administrative applications. However, there is a fertile field for the concepts of Statistical Decision in the broad area of administrative decision.

An administrator or executive needs many skills, but the making of decisions is surely one important part of his job. Most administrators face problems of *planning*, and the concepts which I have been discussing seem to me to be basic intellectual tools for planning. The notion of probability, for example, provides a balance between planning in terms of certainties (which lacks flexibility or adaptability) and planning on the basis of day-to-day expediency (which is so amorphous that it should hardly be called planning). The idea of Sequential Decision is also of prime importance in practical planning.

Many administrative problems associated with planning, it is true, necessitate prediction in situations in which relevant information is scarce or nonexistent. It is my impression, however, that the lack of data often arises because little advantage is taken of the data-collection processes which go on routinely in most organizations. With the expenditure of some ingenuity and a little additional money, it is often possible to utilize this routinely collected information.

In hospital administration, to take just one situation, the

day-to-day running of a hospital requires a tremendous number of records—case histories, accounting records, and so forth. Often this information is either thrown away or, what is much the same thing, stored in ways which make the recovery of information a difficult, expensive, and time-consuming process. A hospital administrator who is faced with an immediate decision may feel that he does not have the relevant data which he needs, even though somewhere in the stacks of files in the basement there may be a ton of relevant files. An appreciation of the principles which I discussed earlier would impel an administrator to take more advantage of his informational resources so as to avoid the necessity for blind decision.

While the administrator will not ordinarily be called upon to build his own Decision-Makers (such as the sampling inspection schemes), he may have supervisory responsibility for the technicians who will build the Decision-Makers or the personnel who will operate them. The administrator will require at least enough familiarity with the broad principles to realize that if the Decision-Maker is based on *random* samples it may break down if the operating personnel selects the samples in a haphazard manner.

Although the operating Decision-Maker requires only routine supervision, the administrator should know that a changing situation may require modification, or even scrapping, of the Decision-Maker. If a sampling inspection plan which returns bad shipments to the supplier is set up, the scheme may operate smoothly for some time. But if there is a change in the management or policy of the supplier, then the quality of shipments may become so poor that it is no longer efficient to reject the bad lots because of the interruption in plant schedules.

In this event the only appropriate action may be a change of supplier, and the executive may be warned of this by combining the inspection plan with a *control chart*. Such a procedure would allow the Decision-Maker to make the recommendations for action in usual situations, but when an unusual situation occurred, the machine would turn the task of making decisions back to the administrator (who has a wider range of possible actions than the machine).

When Statistical Decision is used for high-level executive decisions, the administrator may be called upon to play a more active role in the fabrication of the Decision-Maker. The technicians may not be capable of devising a realistic model for the Value System, and this responsibility may devolve onto the administrator. After all, the balancing of values is a fundamental part of the executive's task, and this will remain true even if a systematic procedure is substituted for intuitive judgment.

The executive, and possibly only the executive, is in a position from which he can see the operations of his organization as an entity. Not only does the administrator see the relationship between the various sections under his jurisdiction, but he also sees the functioning of the entire organization over time. Consequently, the administrator may be the only individual with the broad perspective of the Value System which will be necessary to construct a realistic model. Moreover, within the limits of the policies fixed by his superiors, the executive tends to set the Value System (i.e., the appropriate Value System is the executive's). In this circumstance the administrator has to play an important role in the formulation of the Value System. He may do this at a verbal level and let the technicians take over from there.

A few problems are so complex that the administrator may be directly concerned with the details of the Value System. If the administrator is a sanitary engineer in charge of a pollution-control program, he may have to try to measure how much it is worth to the residents of an area to be rid of the offensive sights and smells of a badly polluted stream. A suitable value scale may enable the engineer to set up his control program in such a way that the taxpayers will feel they are getting their money's worth.

Similarly, a health officer may have to tackle the difficult question of the desirability of good health in order to determine which of several possible disease-control programs might be initiated in his district. This example is one of a broad class of administrative problems which comes under the heading of "optimum allocation of resources." An extensive research program is currently underway on this problem, but most of this work is slanted toward military applications (since the armed services are financing it). Because of military secrecy it is not possible to say how far we have come toward an answer to the problem of allocating resources.

In any case it will probably be some years before Decision-Makers appropriate for these high-level administrative decisions will be available for civilian applications. The main utility of Statistical Decision in administrative problems will lie in the principles rather than in the technical parts.

Group Decision

In the interdependent society of today we recognize that the decisions of one individual will affect other individuals. In a democracy the individuals affected by a governmental decision have some opportunity to participate in the making of that decision. When a number of individuals must make decisions which will *interact,* a new problem arises. This problem has been partially explored for the case of *competitive* decisions (in which the individuals are out for themselves) and a little has been done for the case of cooperative decision (in which the individuals try to reach a single decision for the whole group). Research on this problem is called the *theory of games* or the *theory of organization.*

In my opinion, one of the great potentialities of Statistical Decision is that it can provide a mechanism for cooperative decision; that is, it may enable a group of individuals to reach, independently or by interaction, a single decision acceptable to the individuals. In many practical situations a single decision, or (as I will hereafter call it) a *group decision,* is prerequisite to effective action by the group.

In the scientific world the standard statistical techniques have

been an effective mechanism for group decision in the problem
of inference. Ten different scientists (with various predisposi-
tions and beliefs) can *independently* apply the standard analytical procedures to a given body of data and come out with essentially the same inferences. Without generally accepted and
objective rules for inference this same group of ten scientists
might reason intuitively from the same data and come out with
ten divergent inferences.

The success of statistical techniques in the scientific world
does not mean that there will be a corresponding success outside
of this realm. It should be remembered that before the introduction of statistical techniques the scientists managed to work
out procedures for inference which gave fairly good agreement.
Moreover, the scientists were *looking* for objective methods of
inference, and this was one of the main reasons why statistical
techniques appealed to scientists and were so readily accepted.
Outside of the scientific world there is a strong resistance to any
attempts to deal with problems in an objective manner. Many
people do not want (and would not accept) a rule for inference which *might* lead them to draw conclusions which
would be in opposition to cherished personal beliefs and
prejudices.

Although I anticipate no stampede to use Statistical Decision
as a mechanism for group decision outside of the world of
science and possibly business (where prejudices may interfere
with profit), I think that this aspect of the Decision-Maker
deserves serious consideration. In our civilization we have been
staggering from crisis to crisis because there is no adequate
mechanism for group decision when the "individuals" are nations. The same conflicts arise, on a smaller scale, within the
nation when the "individuals" who must make group decisions
are large organizations such as corporations and labor unions.

Even though the worth of Statistical Decision is unproved in
connection with group decisions outside the scientific world, it
represents a possible mechanism—and the need for an effective
mechanism is desperate. Very few mechanisms for uncoerced

group decision have been invented (although there are many mechanisms for *forced* group decision).

I know only two major devices for uncoerced group decision —voting procedures (such as majority rule) and verbal bargaining. A third device, turning the decision over to impartial experts acceptable to the various individuals in the group, might also be considered a mechanism for group decision.

The ballot box works well when decisions are relatively nontechnical and when the group loyalty is strong enough so that minority voters are willing to stay with the group and accept the majority decision. When the decision is complex and confused, the action of the voters tends to be based on irrelevant issues rather than upon the data relevant to the decision at hand. A Decision-Maker which is not fueled by relevant data cannot be expected to produce decisions which will lead to desirable consequences.

This point has been recognized and in America a multistage system is used wherein the electorate chooses representatives to make the governmental decisions. The elected representatives, Congress, presumably have the training and talent to deal with more complex issues, but even here the representatives tend to vote on policies and leave the technical decision questions to the administrators.

The method of verbal bargaining may, of course, operate in conjunction with the voting procedures (as in congressional debate). Presumably the relevant data for decision is introduced in verbal form and the rules for inference are those of logic. Verbal discussion represents a powerful mechanism for group decision, but it is subject to serious limitations. Many of these limitations arise from the weaknesses of language. It is possible to tie a verbal discussion into knots by haggling over words and the meanings of words. The deficiencies of language are often exploited deliberately to prevent agreement; even when there is a concerted effort by all parties to reach a group decision, these verbal snags often frustrate the attempt.

At the international level the verbal mechanism seems to

have broken down almost completely. This also occurs very frequently at lower levels of organization.

Let me emphasize again that I am not trying to sell Statistical Decision as a panacea for the problem of group decision. It has possibilities and it deserves a trial. Statistical Decision may be useful in breaking down a complex problem into a number of smaller problems concerning the Prediction and Value Systems. It may be easier to reach agreement on these smaller problems. In many situations there will be no model and little data available so that any attempt to substitute the symbolic language for words would be a fraud. At its present stage of development Statistical Decision is only a straw, but in view of the critical situation with respect to group decision we have to clutch at straws.

George

Whether or not statistical decision will be an effective mechanism for personal, administrative, or group decisions is a matter for speculation. But since I have come this far, let me go farther and try to look into the far future, to look ahead a few centuries rather than a few years. It is 2450 A.D., and at last a research team has designed, built, and debugged a super Decision-Maker which has been affectionately called George.

George has a prodigious memory. In his acres of memory tanks he stores most of the recorded past experience of the human race. His complex electronic and post-electronic circuits represent a translation into glass and metal of the principles of Statistical Decision (much advanced and improved). George is a psychologist as well; he can determine the value systems of his customers. In a blink of an eye, George can characterize the decision problems of these customers, calculate the probabilities and desirabilities, balance these quantities in a manner appropriate to the value systems of his customers, and arrive at a recommended course of action.

Whatever your problem, George can help. Is your difficulty technical? George is an expert on everything. Do you have a difficult and important personal decision? George will have your best interests at heart and will have a vast fund of passionless experience to draw upon. Is there a dispute which you and your adversary cannot settle? George is a truly impartial arbiter and very clever at finding a solution satisfactory to all parties concerned. Is it a matter of state? George knows history, politics, and economics—and he is a military expert as well.

George is a wise and trusted friend who will do his best for everyone. George is an incorruptible philosopher-king and Delphic oracle all rolled into one. George has no prejudices (apart from those which have been built into his circuits). In short, George is something of a paragon of virtue; he has human, even superhuman, abilities without the corresponding human weaknesses.

George is quite popular. Many people eagerly turn to George for advice. George betrays no confidences; moreover, he is never scornful or critical. Since he uses the customer's own value system, George is more understanding than a human advisor could be. What is more, his feelings will not be hurt if the customer does not take George's advice. George does not try to force anyone to follow any recommended course of action.

Yet curiously enough, George has what amounts to an ideal way of enforcing his decisions. The customer can take a different course of action, but he must do this with the realization that this different action is likely to turn out to his own disadvantage. If the customer disregards George's advice, he will have no one but himself to blame if things turn out badly. It will take remarkable personal confidence, even courage, to disagree with George. Most people will end up by doing what George says.

And this is why George poses a serious problem. George's evolutionary cousins (the steam engine, the mechanical ditch digger, the punched-card computers, the servo-mechanisms) have sometimes produced technological unemployment in various occupational groups in the human population. If, as I have maintained, man is a decision-making animal and this is man's main claim to distinction, then George (who can make better decisions than any man) threatens to produce technological unemployment on a grand scale. Quite painlessly no doubt (which makes matters worse), George can produce technological unemployment of the whole race of man.

FURTHER READING

Those of you who would like to know more about the various topics of Statistical Decision will have to come to grips with the technical side of the subject (which I have avoided). As of April, 1953 there is only one book, by A. Wald, which deals specifically with the topic of Statistical Decision. However, at least two additional books, one by D. Blackwell and M. Girshick and the other by L. J. Savage, are scheduled for publication in the near future.

Wald's pioneer book, *Statistical Decision Functions*,[1] * has already achieved the status of a classic but, unfortunately, unless you are a good mathematician, you will not get past the first paragraph. Shortly after Professor Wald completed his book he was killed in an aircraft accident in India. Consequently, progress in the development of Statistical Decision has been immeasurably slowed. Wald's book contains a bibliography of mathematical papers relating to Statistical Decision (up to 1950). A complete list of Wald's publications may be found in the memorial issue of *The Annals of Mathematical Statistics*, March, 1952.

Although the number of books devoted specifically to Statistical Decision is very limited, there are a great many books that deal with the various statistical topics that I have discussed. In fact, there are so many that a newcomer to the field is likely to be confused by the variety of offerings. Therefore I feel it worthwhile to single out a few of the books which in my opinion are especially suitable for those who may wish to go more deeply into the subject.

* See correspondingly numbered reference listed by topic, pages 269–272.

One approach to the subject is through the key concept of probability. For a very readable, though somewhat dated, account of the logic of probability I would recommend Lord Keynes' treatise.[4] The treatise takes the "degree of belief" point of view, so for balance you might read R. von Mises'[6] famous presentation of the "objective" position. In my opinion the work of the late Hans Reichenbach[5] comes closest to providing a sound philosophical foundation for the theory of probability. The mathematical side of probability theory is treated by William Feller[2] whose book virtually renders obsolete all previous texts.

If you would like to know more about the theory and practice of "classical" statistics, the appropriate reference will depend upon your mathematical and practical background. For the complete novice, the first few chapters of Croxton and Cowden[8] or Yule and Kendall[15] provide a fairly good introduction. For those of you who have had some practical experience with statistical problems, but whose mathematical background is somewhat hazy, the best book is still G. Snedecor's *Statistical Methods*.[14] This book has been the research worker's bible for many years. On the other hand if your mathematics runs through calculus, then Hoel[10] and Mood[12] are good introductions. If you are looking for a really comprehensive treatment at the calculus level (and can afford the price), then M. G. Kendall's book[11] is the best on the market. Those readers who like their mathematics straight (including some point set theory) will find H. Cramer's excellent text[7] both elegant and cogent.

Most of the current statistical methodology can be traced to the work of Sir Ronald A. Fisher. Much of this work is presented, but not demonstrated, in Fisher's classic, *Statistical Methods for Research Workers*.[9] The text is hard reading because it is incredibly concentrated. However Fisher's other book, *Design of Experiments*,[20] is relatively easy reading in the first few chapters (although it becomes more technical thereafter). Fisher's initial discussion of the principles of scientific experimentation in *The Design of Experiments* [20] is, to my notion, the best of its kind.

Another statistical pioneer, Jerzy Neyman, has written an elementary text [13] which discusses the basic concepts in statistics. Neyman early emphasized the concept of inductive behavior, which is the precursor of Statistical Decision.

In addition to the books which deal with statistical methods generally, there has recently been a large number of texts devoted to specialized methodologies. I shall not try to remark on these books individually. Rather I have listed one or two texts in each category. I have used the following numbers to give some idea of the nature of each book:

(1) Discussion of principles
(2) Presentation of methodologies
(3) Derivation of methodologies
(4) Derivation of underlying theory
(5) Related topics

and the following symbols to give some idea of the mathematical level:

Ar   Arithmetic
Al   Algebra
Ca   Calculus
PC   Post-calculus
NM   Non-mathematical
SL   Symbolic logic

Statistical Decision:
1. Wald, A., *Statistical Decision Functions*, John Wiley & Sons, Inc., New York, 1950.   (PC 4)

Probability:
2. Feller, W., *An Introduction to Probability Theory and Its Applications*, John Wiley & Sons, Inc., New York, 1950.   (Ca 4)
3. Fry, T. C., *Probability and Its Engineering Uses*, D. Van Nostrand Company, Inc., New York, 1928.   (Al 1,3)

4. Keynes, J. M., *A Treatise on Probability*, The Macmillan Company, Ltd., London, 1929.   (NM 1)
5. Reichenbach, H., *The Theory of Probability*, University of California Press, Berkeley, 1949.   (SL 1)
6. von Mises, R. E., *Probability, Statistics, and Truth*, The Macmillan Company, New York, 1939.   (NM 1)

General Texts:

7. Cramer, H., *Mathematical Methods of Statistics*, Princeton University Press, Princeton, 1951.   (PC 4)
8. Croxton, F., and Cowden, D., *Applied General Statistics*, Prentice-Hall, Inc., New York, 1939.   (Ar 2)
9. Fisher, R., *Statistical Methods for Research Workers*, Tenth Edition, Oliver and Boyd, London, 1946.   (Al 2)
10. Hoel, P., *Introduction to Mathematical Statistics*, John Wiley & Sons, Inc., New York, 1947.   (Ca 3)
11. Kendall, M., *The Advanced Theory of Statistics*, Third Edition, Vols. I and II, Hafner Publishing Company, New York, 1951. (Ca 2,3)
12. Mood, A., *Introduction to the Theory of Statistics*, McGraw-Hill Book Company, Inc., New York, 1950.   (Ca 3)
13. Neyman, J., *First Course in Probability and Statistics*, Henry Holt & Company, New York, 1950.   (Ca 1,3)
14. Snedecor, G., *Statistical Methods*, Fourth Edition, Iowa State College Press, Ames, 1946.   (Ar 2)
15. Yule, G., and Kendall, M., *An Introduction to the Theory of Statistics*, Fourteenth Edition, Hafner Publishing Company, New York, 1950.   (Ar 2)

Sampling:

16. Cochran, W., *Sampling Techniques*, John Wiley & Sons, Inc., New York, 1953.   (Al 2,3)
17. Payne, S., *The Art of Asking Questions*, Princeton University Press, Princeton, 1951.   (NM 5)
18. Yates, F., *Sampling Methods for Censuses and Surveys*, Hafner Publishing Company, New York, 1949.   (Ar 1,2)

Design of Experiments:

19. Cochran, W., and Cox, G., *Experimental Designs*, John Wiley & Sons, Inc., New York, 1950.   (Al 2)

20. Fisher, R., *The Design of Experiments,* Sixth Edit Hafner
    Publishing Company, New York, 1951.   (Al 1,2)
21. Kempthorne, O., *The Design and Analysis of Experime* John
    Wiley & Sons, Inc., New York, 1952.   (Ca 3)

Special Applications:

22. Hill, A. B., *Principles of Medical Statistics,* Fifth Edition, O d
    University Press, New York, 1952.   (Ar 1,2)
23. Mather, K., *Statistical Analysis in Biology,* Second Edition, Int r.
    science Publishers, Inc., New York, 1946.   (Al 2,3)
24. Mainland, D., *Elementary Medical Statistics,* W. B. Saunden
    Company, Philadelphia, 1952.   (Ar 1,2)
25. Rao, C. R., *Advanced Statistical Methods in Biometric Research,*
    John Wiley & Sons, Inc., New York, 1952.   (Ca 3)
26. Tippett, L., *Technological Applications of Statistics,* John Wiley
    & Sons, Inc., New York, 1950.   (Ar 2)
27. Youden, W., *Statistical Methods for Chemists,* John Wiley &
    Sons, Inc., New York, 1951.   (Ar 2)

Historical Landmarks:

28. Fisher, R., *Contributions to Mathematical Statistics,* John Wiley
    & Sons, Inc., New York, 1950.   (Ca 3,4)
29. Pearson, K., *Karl Pearson's Early Statistical Papers,* Cambridge
    University Press, Cambridge, 1948.   (Ca 3,4)
30. Pearson, E., and Wishart, J., *"Student's" Collected Papers,*
    Cambridge University Press, Cambridge, 1942.   (Ca 3)
31. Wald, A., *Sequential Analysis,* John Wiley & Sons, Inc., New
    York, 1947.   (PC 3)

Related Topics:

32. Arrow, K., *Social Choice and Individual Values,* John Wiley &
    Sons, Inc., New York, 1951.   (PC 5)
33. Dewey, J., *The Quest for Certainty,* G. P. Putnam's Sons, New
    York, 1939.   (NM 1)
34. McKinsey, J., *Introduction to the Theory of Games,* McGraw-
    Hill Book Company, Inc., New York, 1952.   (PC 3)
35. Morse, P., and Kimball, G., *Methods of Operations Research,*
    John Wiley & Sons, Inc., New York, 1951.   (Ca 5)

36. non, C., *Mathematical Theory of Communication,* University of Illinois Press, Urbana, 1949.   (PC 5)

37. Neumann, J., and Morgenstern, O., *Theory of Games and Economic Behavior,* Second Edition, Princeton University Press, Princeton, 1947.   (PC 4)

Wiener, N., *Cybernetics,* John Wiley & Sons, Inc., New York, 1948.   (NM 1)

INDEX